Comrades in Business

D1244698

Comrades in Business

Post-Liberation Politics in South Africa

Heribert Adam
Frederik Van Zyl Slabbert
Kogila Moodley

International Books

© The authors, 1998

First published by Tafelberg Publishers Limited, South Africa

Reprinted by International Books
A. Numankade 17, 3572 KP Utrecht, tel. +31-30-2731840
fax +31-30-2733614, e-mail: i-books@antenna.nl

Coverdesign: Marjo Starink

ISBN 90 5727 022 6

Acknowledgements

For three authors to collaborate in writing a coherent book would, under normal circumstances, be an improbable task. However, in our case, we have engaged each other on "the South African situation" over a period of more than thirty years. Although we still differ on some issues – which will no doubt be revealed in selective emphases in the text – we share a common passion for the subject and a spirit of intellectual tolerance. We also abhor dogmatic confidence and fashionable, unquestioned opinions.

Ours is a think-piece rather than original survey research. We interpret existing data out of a moral concern about the evolving new South Africa. What we hope will make it special are the conclusions drawn from everyday discourse.

Our reasoning owes gratitude to our many friends who have taken issue with us on so many topics. We bounced off our views on astute colleagues across the political spectrum over many years. These include many hours of challenging discussions with students at Wits and the University of Cape Town who also forced us to communicate in accessible style. Hopefully, this mixture of an academic and general, commonsense analysis pays back as a readable text what we learned from our students' questions. Our book is also meant to make ivory tower lectures accessible to a larger audience.

We owe a more concrete debt to people who have made this study what it is: To Kanya Adam, our thanks for the title from her forthcoming doctoral dissertation; to Jane Slabbert, a remarkable source of calm and uncontaminated mental hygiene; to Jenny Nothard, ever willing, competent and patient in typing and polishing the final manuscript. The two Canadian authors would not have been able to conduct their research without the generous hospitality of the University of Cape Town as an institutional base for three months each year and the continuous support of the Social Science and Humanities Research Council in Ottawa.

We can only hope that the confidence expressed and political discussions with so many friends is adequately reflected in this analysis. If it serves nothing more than to contribute to political literacy inside South Africa as well as undermine stereotypes about the country outside, the study has fulfilled its purpose.

Contents

Introduction

Moral, political and comparative perspectives

The greater the party, the greater the hangover, so the saying goes. This seems to be the mood amongst many observers of the "new South Africa". Even many effusive accounts of the "miracle" of South Africa's transition nowadays reflect on this painful sobriety. In contrast to these personalising journalistic reports, this analysis attempts to provide insights and arguments on the structure of South African society, the dynamics of its transition and the challenges facing it in the future. This should help to guard against easy optimism and so prevent disillusionment. Comparatively speaking, South Africa is doing remarkably well. Yet, for those caught up in the trauma of transition, it is like saying it is better being in a raging storm than in a hurricane. However, we argue while there is no room for easy optimism there is certainly no reason for abject despair either. The new South Africa, unlike the apartheid state, does not insult the intelligence, it challenges it. Overcoming obstacles to a prosperous democracy could not only be of enormous benefit to South Africa's inhabitants, but provide lessons to other countries in the world battling with similar difficulties.

Comrades in Business tells the story of how post-apartheid South Africa has transformed itself into a liberal democracy and a conventional consumerist society. Americanised consumerism has always lurked under the surface of racial restrictions. Yet a new elite of black South Africans has now embraced money-making and conspicuous consumption with a zeal that few older capitalist states have experienced, perhaps because private enrichment was denied them for so long. In this regard, a burgeoning black bourgeoisie does not behave differently from its counterparts in China or the former Soviet Union where ideology also prohibited private capital accumulation for long decades. Moreover, blacks in South Africa only emulate whites who had enriched themselves with their poli-

1

tical monopoly at the expense of an 85 per cent majority of second-class fellow citizens.

There is nothing morally wrong with an individual or a collective inclination to become wealthy and utilise new opportunities. On the contrary, if a nation elects to stay poor because its citizens lack the capacity or drive to improve themselves, they deserve their misery. In short, we do not associate affluence with immorality. However, what is at issue is how an elite becomes wealthy, what it does with its capital and how it rationalises inequality in the light of its own historical struggle for a more equitable, just order.

A major paradigm shift towards neo-liberal market policies has taken place in the ANC that once flirted with much more socialist state intervention. South Africa had to take global realities into account. The ideological reversal does not imply betrayal. It cannot be a "sellout" if no alternatives exist for a government that may be in office but does not necessarily hold power. After all, post-apartheid South Africa's successful transition contrasts sharply with many failed multi-ethnic states.

We explore comparatively the reasons for the globally admired but little understood "miracle". With insights from a rich literature on ethnic conflicts around the world, we draw lessons from what went right or wrong, and probe the reasons. We review the directions taken by new ANC rulers and assess the future of the fragile post-apartheid democracy. However, ours is not only an area study. We use the South African case to illuminate broader theories of transition, transformation and liberation in ethno-nationalist conflicts.

South Africa represents a compromise. Moreover, the extent to which the sovereignty of all small states has been undermined by economic globalisation or international capital, with national states still exercising important control, is an empirical question and very much contested. In many ways globalisation is still managed by nation-states. They are all subject to the same forces but respond to them differently according to their own historical traditions and economic priorities. The compulsion of market forces does not entirely eliminate choice, although choices have become limited. Not everything is dictated by necessity. What is to be questioned, however, is making a virtue out of necessity.

The spectrum between choice and necessity can be illustrated with the example of union investment companies. From the ANC to

COSATU, SANCO and even the SACP, former socialists have now quietly set up investment arms in order to make capitalism work for themselves. If the general secretary of the ANC can move from being the leader of the mineworkers' union to heading a powerful corporate conglomerate, lesser figures can follow his example. The "unions' asset managers", as they call themselves, have fully adopted the capitalist logic of ruthless exploitation of all opportunities.

Not for them ethical funds and other corporate sobs of the guilt-ridden liberal shareholders and fund managers in North America. Johnny Copelyn, once a dedicated workerist, later an MP and now president of Hosken Consolidated Investments, asserts that you cannot be "moralistic in business". Traditional union values such as solidarity, internal democracy and transparency are quickly shed when they pose obstacles to business opportunities. "You cannot run a business in a capitalist society on a comradely basis," Kgalema Motlanthe, the general secretary of the National Union of Mine-workers, comments realistically. While an old left still romanticises the working class as the progressive motor of history, the new union capitalists shrewdly trade with union credentials in order to reap benefits for their members. In the process they quietly incorporate a last outpost of militant socialism into the new world order without much dissent.

Mark Gevisser has dubbed this ideological shift "the quietest and most profound revolution of our time".[1] Whether the independent South African unions eventually end up as equivalents of the Israeli Histatrud, tied to a supportive state, or split into official and unofficial militant unions as in Mexico, or whether union enterprises collapse in corruption, scandals and bankruptcy along the lines of German precedents, remains to be seen.

South Africa has one of the highest gini-coefficients (0.62) in the world, a measurement of the gap between rich and poor in a society. It is ultimately a moral and political judgement as to how much effort should be made to bridge the gulf between the haves and have-nots, which still overlaps largely with race in South Africa. The struggle to abolish apartheid pales in comparison with the task to address apartheid's material and psychological legacies.

3

Share of income going to:

	Poorest 20%	Second 20%	Third 20%	Fourth 20%	Richest 20%
South Africa	3	6	10	18	63
South Korea	7	12	16	22	42
Thailand	6	9	14	22	50
Singapore	5	10	15	22	49
Malaysia	5	8	13	20	53
Indonesia	9	12	16	21	42

Source: World Bank, World Development Report 1995, Government Gazette, Vol. 373, No. 17303, Pretoria 1 July 1996

Yet our book consciously avoids specific policy prescriptions. Devoid of a master narrative that guides dogmatic followers to utopia according to a predetermined doctrine, be they socialists, free marketeers or ethnic nationalists, we negotiate our way through many contradictions between theory and reality. We are puzzled by paradoxes and unintended consequences. We aim at demystifying ideologies of any kind without falling into the trap of post-modernist relativism. We do hold certain values to be universally true and applicable but probe their continuing validity open-mindedly. We pay attention to the historical conditioning of all intellectual traditions, including the potential bias of our own Eurocentric viewpoints. We recognise and respect different concerns and political stances deriving from different life experiences. However, we also claim that all perspectives can and must be analysed critically. It is up to the reader to judge who presents the better argument.

Much of the previous literature on South Africa constitutes accusatory protests, based on moral outrage. Uncritical praise-singers of Mandela and the ANC have followed suit. These authors often merely preach to the converted and stridently state the obvious. During the apartheid days much wishful thinking flowed from those moral accounts that always falsely assumed that a racist regime is necessarily also an obstinate one, incapable of liberalisation from within and only to be changed from without. A scrupulous realism therefore has to be injected into the study of immoral regimes even if the conclusions go against one's own moral preferences. An analytical approach – which is interested in what is likely to happen rather than what ought to happen – cannot afford moralising and pathologising. Yet a critical social science analysis that deserves its name can also not afford to ignore the moral implications of the subject under study.

Of course a moral discourse on the recent history of South Africa, as well as its current transition, is necessary, if only to remind us of the values that have been undermined and the need to reaffirm them for the future: values such as tolerance, respect for life, objectivity, freedom, responsibility, accountability and transparency. Not only do they have to be reaffirmed, but constantly analysed and probed as to their relevance and applicability to the problems of transition South Africa is encountering.

However, there is nothing sacrosanct about a moral discourse as such. The fact that it is conducted in highly judgmental and normative terms cannot place its basic assumptions beyond criticism: a fundamentalist theocratic state and an extremist dogmatic government ideology create a political culture in which moral principles are presented as immutable laws of nature. An atmosphere of uncritical conformity and personal apprehension predominates. Such a climate does not bode well for a country's capacity to deal with the problems of modernity and economic globalisation.

South Africa has begun a transition that for many is seen, or experienced, as a triumph over evil. Moral hyperbole and repugnance pervade analyses of the past, and justifiably so in many instances. However, there is a danger as well. When moral principles are presented as sociological generalisations it is not difficult to end up in a position of sanctimonious paralysis, of believing that the future guarantees one a good deal because the past has given one a bad one and to approach the complex problems of transition with an attitude of moral entitlement.

A large number of the difficulties experienced by the Truth and Reconciliation Commission arise from a confusion between moral discourse and sociopolitical analysis. Nobody suggests that to discover the truth about something is "bad", or that reconciliation is "not a good thing". But it is naive and dangerous to predict that the one (truth) will necessarily lead to the other (reconciliation); or that amnesty will necessarily have "a healing effect". There are perhaps more factual case studies that demonstrate that truth, such as it is presented, leads to bitterness, anger, revenge and disillusionment and that amnesty can lead to a pervasive sense of injustice and aggrievement. On the balance of probability that this is so, the Commission could end up achieving exactly the opposite of what it set out to do. Not to anticipate such an eventuality is to abdicate an important responsibility for managing a difficult aspect of South Africa's transition.

In short, the Truth and Reconciliation Commission is faced with the contradiction that the more the gory truth is being revealed, the stronger the clamour for justice and revenge. Previous supporters of apartheid, on the other hand, feel even more alienated as the entire Afrikaner nationalist community is being put under the cloud of collective guilt and responsibility. Hence, reconciliation is undermined by truth.

On the other hand, forgetting the past without the exorcising process of grappling with national inhumanity, as happened in Zimbabwe and Mozambique, short-changes the victims.[2] Amnesia also undermines the moral foundations of the new order. Amnesty upon full disclosure proved a feasible compromise when faced with the impossibility of bringing an undefeated opponent to justice, à la Nuremberg.

The prospects of reconciliation, therefore, hinge heavily on the perception of the commission as impartial. Unlike its Latin American predecessors by whom the South African sixteen-member commission was inspired, it is heavily loaded with ANC sympathisers, particularly among its staff which numbers 300. The eight-member Chilean commission, in contrast, was comprised of four known supporters of the old and four of the new regime and reported without revealing the identity of the perpetrators, thus preventing private revenge.

An even more complex question than how to deal with torturers is posed by the many beneficiaries of the apartheid laws. Mahmood Mamdani has pointed to the difference between Rwanda where there are many perpetrators but few beneficiaries of genocide, and apartheid South Africa with few perpetrators and many beneficiaries.[3] The focus of the Truth Commission on "gross human rights violations" obliterates the systemic discrimination and its beneficiaries. Individualising the process ignores the many other victims of apartheid: the millions imprisoned under the Pass Laws, the tens of thousands displaced from their homes by the Group Areas Act and ultimately all disenfranchised whose life chances and dignity were damaged. Should the beneficiaries of these practices pay compensation? Can victims and beneficiaries be defined in racial terms – as there were also black beneficiaries and white victims? Can there be reconciliation without economic justice?

At the outset of our analysis of South Africa's transition, we wish to state unequivocally that we believe it is unhelpful and dangerous to substitute moral discourse for social, political and economic analysis. At the same time, we wish to be equally unambiguous by saying that an analysis of this kind is not devoid of values or moral commitment. The values that guide intellectual inquiry have been distilled through ages of rigorous debate: objectivity, openness to contradictory evidence and critical scrutiny of assumptions. We also do not pretend that other moral values may not impinge on our analysis, such as preference for a certain kind of democratic state or economic system; a preference for the rule of law, a sense of transparency and accountability. But we ask that where such impingement does take place, it be pointed out and that the manner in which it distorts analysis be identified.

To illustrate our approach, we thought it appropriate to investigate the relationship, often implicitly and explicitly alluded to, between Nazism and apartheid, where words like "genocide", "moral depravity", "racism" and "ethnic cleansing" are used interchangeably to describe both systems. The nature of apartheid can be clarified by a detailed comparison with German fascism. Is it true that people who hate Jews are most likely to hate blacks? Did the same forces that destroyed Nazism also destroy apartheid? Were the instruments of repression against Jews the same as those used against blacks? If not, what are the differences? And if there are differences of importance, what is the usefulness in insisting that apartheid is Nazism?

We conclude that despite the ideological affinities between some Afrikaner and German nationalists, the two systems differ in their ultimate goals of exploitation and elimination. Anti-Semitism scapegoats an imagined conspiracy to cope with the anxieties of modernity. Its extreme irrationality contrasts with the comparatively "rational" exclusion of the majority population in order to maintain the privileges of a minority. Anti-Semitism fulfils psychological needs while anti-black racism in settler colonies is guided and constrained by economic interdependence.

The chapter on anti-Semitism and anti-black racism not only demonstrates the usefulness of distinctions between different forms of racism, but the insights of a comparative approach in general. We therefore employ a comparative method throughout our analysis. The uniqueness of a political culture can only be understood in comparison with similar situations elsewhere. Our comparative approach is qualitative and interpretative. We do not aim at comparative country studies that list variables quantitatively. Such studies of societies in transition in the American political science tradition often raise interesting questions but they also often compare the incomparable mechanically and at a rather superficial level. Penetrating the unique particular culture and historical tradition of a society hermeneutically with other situations in mind yields superior insights that comparative transition studies from Latin America, Southern and Eastern Europe miss. The sensitivity for South African specificity does not mean that a South African exceptionalism is advocated.

The chapter on South Africa as a deeply divided society is meant to demonstrate such claims. Drawing together illustrations from the Soviet Union, Central Europe, Asia, Canada and Australia, we try to bring some coherence into a confused debate about racism, nationalism and multiculturalism. Concepts such as ethnicity, identity and nationality are clarified in the political and historical contexts in which they are used. Three types of divided societies are distinguished: (1) indigenous minorities, (2) immigration societies and (3) competing nationalities. In each of these settings different priorities and solutions for intergroup harmony have emerged. Subsequent chapters on negotiations, the founding elections and the new constitution explain the "miracle" that turned out to be different from Bosnia or Rwanda or Sri Lanka, although most observers predicted racial war.

The central chapter on nation-building in South Africa not only questions whether a nation-state can be moulded out of the different ethnic traditions but whether such a project should be attempted in the first place. The historical ANC-Inkatha rivalry is reviewed and the potential for an Afrikaner nationalist secessionist resurgence is reassessed in this context.

8

The last part of the book then takes up the crucial issue of economic justice and reconciliation. It probes capital-labour-state relations. Corporatism has emerged as both a promise and a problem in solving the necessary adjustments of economic globalisation. The emergence of a black bourgeoisie is traced and the black empowerment lobby is assessed. Whether an embourgeoisement of the ANC has taken place or not, whether the new elite engages in self-enrichment or is finally empowering an entire community of formally disadvantaged, is fiercely contested. The tensions between an underclass of outsiders and a liberation aristocracy of relatively privileged insiders would be a normal feature of all democratic societies were it not for the deepening cleavage between rich and poor and the sheer size of the impoverished unemployed. Unlike China or the Soviet Union, South Africa has always accommodated a wealthy capitalist First World with a communally orientated Third World living side by side. Whether the deracialisation of privilege is sufficient to ease tensions between the haves and have-nots shapes the future stability of the country as well as the electoral fortunes of the ANC. The ruling party has to deliver, and not only to an elite, if a liberal democracy is to be consolidated in South Africa.

Many parts of our story have been told by others, some aspects in great detail. For example Patti Waldmeir's *Anatomy of a Miracle*, and Allister Sparks's *Tomorrow is Another Country*, provide fascinating tales of negotiation intrigues and trade-offs. These journalistic accounts excel in personalising complex deal-making, based on verbatim interviews with rich characters. Our book, in contrast, represents a much more abstract, analytical account where the persons fade into the background as illustrators of socio-economic tendencies. Therefore, we do not dwell on anecdotal revelations but hopefully highlight and synthesise underrated or ignored trends. We aim at teasing out theoretical and comparative lessons from a range of disparate material.

Our research is based on personal interviews with policy makers, attendance at numerous conferences, participant observation and focus group discussions during many years of lecturing, consulting and active political involvement in the South African drama. Impressionistic and speculative as many of the insights may appear to a sceptic used to statistical or documentary evidence, much of what goes on behind the public scene is only accessible in the informal sphere. There is always a publicly revealed as well as a hidden reality. Our concern is to make sense of the sentiments behind the surveys and headlines, although we follow the public discourse closely.

Some of the chapters have been presented at conferences or other public lectures, which explains an occasional overlap or repetition of a point. When three authors work and rework the same book it is also inevitable that each wishes to state his/her reasoning in his/her own words. We hope that the book represents more than a collection of disparate essays and that it is a comprehensive, although eclectic, assessment of South Africa's sociopolitical future with an emphasis on some novel or neglected aspects. We see our study as a controversial attempt to review the first period of the first post-apartheid government by giving credit to achievements as well as pointing out even more salient shortcomings.

Chapter One

Comparing ethno-nationalism: Identity, racism and multiculturalism in a global context

The disintegration of the former Soviet Union and the events in Eastern Europe have again confirmed the rallying power of suppressed nationalism despite seventy years of sustained efforts to create a new "Soviet citizen". Through official compulsion the dominant ideology said: "You are all the same, there are no differences between you." When this ideology collapsed, the response seems to be: "We are all different, we have nothing in common." In South Africa the opposite seems to be happening. For decades the official ideology, also through brutal compulsion, seemed to say: "We are all different, we have nothing in common." When that collapsed, the response seems to be: "We have more in common than divides us." Why do South Africa and Bosnia seem to occupy opposite ends of a continuum of divided societies? In South Africa, with official nonracialism as the new core state ideology, the country seems to run counter to re-ethnicisation everywhere else. Why?

The collapse of the last colonial empire, the Soviet Union, has left the problem of substantial numbers of Russian settlers in the newly independent states who frequently assert their nationhood. In the process they practise reverse discrimination against Russian minorities. As in South Africa, the previously dominating minority has become the politically powerless minority. In the shrunken Russian heartland, only the Chechnyan region insists on partition and total sovereignty in the face of continued Russian occupation. In the former Soviet Union, military nationalism has collapsed with the end of the cold war. During the Afghan war and later in Chechnya, the glorious Russian army was exposed as vastly overrated. Economic nationalism now filled the ideological vacuum left after the demise of the Communist centre. It is fuelled by protectionist interests against Western penetration of the Russian market, be it by United States chickens or evangelistic preachers. During the 1996 presidential campaign, all candidates played on the same variant of Russian nationalism: populist nationalism (Yeltsin), ethnic nationalism with concern for Russian minorities abroad (Lebed), chauvinist nationalism of the imperialist kind (Zhirinovsky), and communist nationalism (Zyuganov). Observers noted: "Even the Communists have transformed themselves into Bible-quoting, icon-waving Russian orthodox warriors," whose campaign rallies echoed with religious singing against a background of church banners.[1]

How does one make sense of this almost international revival of ethno-nationalism? For decades, one of the supreme articles of faith of modernists, of both the capitalist and communist/socialist variety, denied the power of ethno-nationalism. With the advance of industrialisation and affluence, race, ethnicity and nationalism would weaken and disappear as factors of social and political mobilisation. After seventy years of sustained egalitarian indoctrination in Central/ Eastern Europe and the former Soviet Union, the collapse has revealed societies almost more deeply divided than they were before it all started. Yet, before the collapse in 1989, South Africa was held up as the supreme example of a deeply divided society heading for a revolutionary racial conflagration which strained the limits of the imagination. Commentators outbid one another in anticipating the inevitable bloodshed of a South African apocalypse. Many of the same analysts now grope for superlatives in breathless gratitude at the "miracle" of a conciliatory South African transition. Where lies the difference? What are the lessons for liberal-nationalist competition in the same country? What after all is a deeply divided society and to what extent is South Africa one?

Before we answer these questions, it is necessary to draw some conceptual distinction and clarify terms like *race, racialism, ethnicity, minority, nations* and *nationalism.*

The conventional racial labelling of people as Caucasians, Orientals and Africans/Blacks must be questioned. Race constitutes an arbitrary classification with no scientific base. Sociologists call this "figments of the pigment", a social construction. Race is an invented category to ascribe alleged behavioural or genetic characteristics to racial groups. However, the human species has been mixed through migration and intermarriage throughout our history. A pure race, therefore, does not exist anywhere. Yet racial labelling persists because it enables people to be denigrated on the basis of skin colour for exclusion or for the justification of conquest and privilege. Such racist ideologies legitimised European colonialism with "a civilising mission" of superior people.

Racism can be defined as the pseudo-scientific ideology of inferiority or superiority whether based on biological or cultural stereotypes of group differences. *Racialism* is the implementation and practice of racism in discriminatory behaviour. There can be racism (ideology) without racialism (practice) and vice versa. For example, a prejudiced individual may be racist but does not show his or her attitude for fear of sanctions. Therefore, anti-racist legislation is useful to suppress discriminatory behaviour although we cannot legislate how people think. It is also possible that people discriminate without being racist on the basis of cultural, religious or linguistic grounds without necessarily regarding "others" as inferior. "Separate development" or apartheid justified its legal domination of a disenfranchised majority by a privileged white minority on grounds that people prefer to be among their own kind.

The desire to be among your own is not in itself racist, particularly in the private sphere. Even in the public realm, for instance, groups with the same language or religion can make a legitimate claim to be educated in separate schools where their particular tradition is cherished and affirmed. However, when such segregation is sought on grounds unrelated to the purpose of an institution or with the intent to exclude others for the purpose of privilege maintenance or exploitation, it is racist in its effects. In short, there can be objective racialism without subjective intent. Apartheid (keeping people apart) in South Africa was such a design to preserve the privileges of a racial group by denying access to equality in every sphere of life. The US Supreme Court in a landmark decision in the 1960s confirmed that the nice-sounding phrase "separate but equal" always implies inequality as long as it is imposed on those who seek equal access. However, if discriminated people voluntarily isolate themselves to strengthen their own worth and shield themselves from the psychological damage of majority domination, such self-protection cannot be called racist.

In short, racialism is always linked to *power*. Racialism needs power to be implemented. Its victims are minorities whom sociologists define as powerless groups, regardless of numbers. Therefore, numerical majorities, such as women or Africans in apartheid South Africa constitute minorities in a sociological sense. Racism is not practised exclusively by whites, although only European colonisers legitimised conquest and slavery with an elaborate social-Darwinist ideology of superiority. When blacks exercise power over others, they can also practise racially motivated genocide, as happened in Rwanda, Liberia and the Sudan. In Japan, Koreans are targeted as inferior people. The Hindu caste system represents a religiously sanctioned form of division of labour with accompanying hierarchies of stigmatisation that still survives despite being outlawed in India.

Most societies harbour various degrees of ethnocentrism. Ethnocentrism can be defined as the uncritical glorification of one's own group. Members of the "in" group despise or inferiorise members of "out" groups. They are also called chauvinists. Accusations of racism, chauvinism and oppression should not be made flippantly. If everything is racism or chauvinism, then nothing is racism and the label becomes meaningless. Most people constitute a bundle of contradictions so that even the most ardent anti-racist could be shown to be prejudiced to some degree. Prejudgements in the form of cherished stereotypes are made by everyone, although most people reject the idea that they are biased.

It has so far been argued that racism is real – race is not. Should we, therefore, not forget about racial classifications altogether and strive for colour blindness? That was the ideal of the US civil rights leader, Martin Luther King, who dreamt of a world where people are judged on merit and not on the basis of their skin colour. Nelson Mandela practises a similar colour-blind nonracialism. His ANC party preaches reconciliation with his former white oppressors rather than a reversal of power relations. Nonracialism differs from multiracialism which still recognises race but aims at integration. However, is it realistic to dream about a colour-blind society when such a long history of racialism still has to be overcome? Therefore, programmes of anti-racism target the in-built, intrinsic racial bias of Western institutions by transforming curriculums and power-holders through deliberate racial representativeness. Affirmative action programmes often imply racial quotas and thereby reinforce racial perceptions as long as advantage or disadvantage is connected to racial group membership. Its advocates emphasise that such

14

racial preference policies are necessary to deal with discrimination until greater equity is achieved. Opponents argue that such well-intentioned policies are short-sighted and counterproductive by perpetuating racial stereotypes and inadvertently lowering the self-esteem and outside perception of affirmative action appointees, because it can always be doubted whether they hold their position on the basis of merit or irrelevant considerations of race.

The American philosopher Naomi Zac, herself of Jewish, African and Native American origin, has summarised her book *Race and Mixed Race*: "I have been arguing through this work that in a context where a race is devalued, such as in the United States, racial designations are as racist, i.e. as cruel, as racist devaluations. Such racial designations limit individuals in their subjectiveness, even when they take up the designations themselves, about themselves."[2]

Difference is frequently considered the cause of discrimination. However, a stronger case can be made for the opposite, namely that discrimination produces different identities. Exclusion or designation reinforces historical identities that would otherwise have faded away. On the other hand, some physical or cultural difference facilitates the task of the ethnic mobilisers. They can, as Joan Scott notes, "naturalise identity, making it a matter of biology or history or culture, an inescapable trait that can matter more or less, but is inherently a part of one's being".[3]

Once such an essentialist perception of the other becomes accepted, discrimination can be justified because "they" are already different. Therefore, eliminating perceptions of difference as a long-term goal counters the agitator who dwells on the "we" and "them".

Equality in the treatment of difference as well as equal respect for differences remain the obvious starting points. Both the equality of opportunities and the symbolic recognition of difference go hand in hand. If there is only theoretical equal acceptance without eliminating historically entrenched racist inequality, minorities will reject multiculturalism as a hypocritical sop. Likewise, no well-intentioned equity policies will prove successful without respectful recognition of difference. Such equality does not mean sameness. For example, in a multi-ethnic society the holy days of all major religions need to be publicly recognised. The state could approve a list of recognised holidays (Christmas, Eid, Divali, Hannukah, Purim, Chinese New Year) from which individuals could choose according to their own preferences. Such recognition should not be granted as the right of a group, but it should be allotted to individuals who can express their fluid ethno-cultural identity flexibly without being forced into group membership in order to exercise their choice.

From race we must distinguish ethnicity. Race is concerned with alleged biological differences – ethnicity denotes different cultural practices. A good case can be made that racial consciousness should be eliminated; an equally good case can be made for the retention of ethnic heritage by those who wish to do so. Multiculturalism expresses the desire to recognise different cultural traditions on an equal footing and at the same time pay loyalty to an overarching state.

One can usefully distinguish between three types of ethnically divided societies. These three types derive from specific historical beginnings; different kinds of problems for state policies and distinct forms of resistance and conflict resolution. They are:
a) indigenous minorities
b) immigration societies, and
c) nationalities in competition.

All three types can be found in the same state boundary as in Canada and South Africa. They represent fault lines of societal division and overlap and change through time. It is possible for indigenous minorities or immigrant groups who are victims of discrimination to evolve into fully fledged nationalities with their own separate institutions and politicised awareness. On the other hand, previous distinct nationalities may lose their sense of separate awareness and merge with the mainstream or revert to simply being an ethnic group, satisfied with cultural recognition. Religious minorities without any political ambitions can be seen as a variation of an ethnic group that withdraws from the customs of mainstream society to pursue their own ideals of a good life in communal settings (Hutterites, Doukhobors, Hasidic Jews). In short, there is nothing essentialist or immutable about ethnicity. It is a concept social scientists have invented to describe a sense of belonging to a group. This ethnic identity can manifest itself in a variety of ways in different social, economic and political circumstances. These ethnic variations can combine in different ways to create different kinds of ethnically divided societies. They in turn can vary in the intensity of

16

their occurrence and change their composition over time due to a variety of circumstances.

For purposes of analysis it is important to draw a distinction between *ethnicity, nationality* and *state*. It seems that the idea of a nation can have three distinct references which may or may not overlap in reality: there is a geographic reference as in the idea of a territorially based nation-state with the concept of citizenship and political sovereignty; there is a culturally defined reference to nationality without a state, e.g. Welsh, Kurdish, Flemish; and a religious reference, e.g. Islam. In all three cases it refers to a community of people with a shared sense of belonging and common history who aspire to be politically self-determining and to a certain extent seek to establish their own political institutions.

The idea of a nation-state with loyalties of all residents based on common citizenship is a fairly recent one, not older than 200 years. As nation-state boundaries became established through conquest or convention, there was no snugness of fit between state boundaries and religious and/or cultural nations. This was particularly so in the colonised worlds of Africa, Latin America, India, Central and Eastern Europe. Multi-nation states evolved where geographic boundaries that coincided with religious and/or cultural nations were redrawn and incorporated into newly formed independent states.

Thus today, a modern nation need not be ethnically homogenous as the European vision of a *Kulturnation* in a *Volkstaat* aspired to be. Indeed, more often they are not. For example, Canada and the (misnamed) United States are both nations and states, but each is best characterised as a multi-nation state. The former Soviet Union formally recognised its constituent nationalities by inscribing passports with the different nationalities of Soviet citizens. A common citizenship bound these multi-ethnic or multi-nation states. How far people derive their primary political identity from national subgroups or the common state is an empirical question, i.e. a matter of practical analysis that differs in each context. It is possible for individuals to frequently adopt multiple political identities simultaneously, or they emphasise their citizenship while travelling abroad, but their subgroup membership at home.

In the above sense, nationalism is nothing else but politicised ethnicity. As we have seen, there can be different kinds of nationalism that politicises ethnicity in different ways. A divided society is one which grapples with the problem of competing politicised ethnicities; usually a multi-nation state which attempts to create a transcending nationalism based on common citizenship that overrides the centrifugal pull of subsidiary ethnic nationalisms. It is invariably also a multi-ethnic state. Some such states are more successful in creating transcending nationalisms than others. Those that consistently seem to fail are seen as deeply divided societies, e.g. Israel, Northern Ireland, Rwanda-Burundi. South Africa has conventionally been regarded as one, but now, increasingly, no longer. Why?

A few more observations are in order before we attempt an answer to this question in subsequent chapters. There are two important aspects to the issue of ethnic identity – one is the subjective identification of the person with his/her group; the other is the ascribed characteristics which others give to persons whom they think belong to the group. These two aspects interact with one another in the sense that how mainstream society defines people as members of a group helps to shape their own "self"-definition. If, for example, group members are defined as "different" in a pejorative sense, and they identify with this "difference", this could constitute internalised domination. If there is a strong rejection of such imposed categories (such as enforced racialisation by apartheid South Africa), the labelling leads to active resistance. Whether there is identification or rejection of such definition, state policy very often sets the scene for such responses.

It is very important to understand that ethnic differences do not stem from "natural" differences, but are always socially constructed. Such constructions may even try to "naturalise" the differences. Thus, contrary to a primordialist or essentialist view that considers all members of a group as "essentially" the same "by nature", there are often as vast differences *among* ethnically defined members as there are *between* different ethnic groups.

The study of the dynamics of ethnic relations in society is a highly controversial and intellectually contested field. The conceptual clarifications and disclaimers we have pointed out are necessary in order to take a closer look at three types of divided societies mentioned earlier on, namely: (a) indigenous minorities; (b) immigration societies, and (c) competing nationalities.

Indigenous minorities, such as the San speakers (Bushmen) in

Namibia and Botswana, the 3 per cent aboriginal people in North America and Australia and the 11 per cent Maoris in New Zealand perceive themselves as the conquered owners of the original land. Although they claim title to large parts of state land and resources, they lack the voting strength or economic clout to achieve their aims, and usually appeal through the legal system to the self-definition of liberal democracies. This symbolic power as "First Nations" or, in some cases, based on treaties with the colonial power, can embarrass liberal states or even lead to mini-revolts by severely aggrieved people.

Even when indigenous people represent sizeable minorities, as in Mexico and other Latin American states, and in some regions in India, modern states often suppress the protests of "tribal" people, if necessary by renewed genocide. In more liberal democracies, state policies towards the legitimate grievances of subjugated minorities have wavered between forced assimilation in residential areas and schools, legal suppression of cultural traditions, conversion by missionaries, benign neglect, or a welfare colonialism in Canada and Australia. Aborigines were treated as immature wards under state tutelage. More recently, limited autonomy and self-rule in education and policing on reservations were granted. This corresponds with a cultural revivalism and ethno-exclusivism stressed by once nearly extinct but now growing and politically conscious aboriginal minorities, who do not consider themselves bound by the laws of the state of which they are "forced citizens".

Above all, indigenous minorities all over the world demand recognition of their special status as aboriginal people, with claims to the land as original owners dispossessed by conquest. In liberal democracies courts decide about the entitlement of indigenous minorities. In some cases court decisions and lengthy negotiations with state representatives have led to the recognition of substantial land claims with compensation flowing from such newly confirmed ownership. Native title remains a controversial issue wherever democratic regimes followed conquest. For example, a 1992 High Court ruling in Australia allowed aboriginal people to claim native title to vacant state-owned land. A few years later, this judgement was extended to the effect that traditional ownership of land could co-exist with pastoral leases. However, pastoral leases cover about 40 per cent of Australia's land area and are held by farmers for grazing. Far-flung gold and other metal deposits are also on pastoral leases. While under previous rulings pastoral leases extinguished native title, the new law restored at least the right of aboriginal people to hunt and hold tribal ceremonies on leased land, provided they could prove a traditional connection to the land. Although such jurisdictional disputes will change little in the actual use of land, co-ownership could also entitle indigenous people to royalties from the mineral or tourist exploitation of the land.

Immigration societies can be divided into those that soon grant recognition to newcomers as equal citizens (the US, Canada, Australia) and those which treat foreign migrants as sojourners or "guest workers" (Germany, Switzerland). The Central European countries do not perceive of themselves as immigration societies. Normally they do not allow double citizenship even to those second or third generation migrants born in the country. Only after stringent criteria of cultural assimilation are met do a small minority receive passports of their country of residence. Xenophobia (fear of strangers) and anxiety about *Überfremdung* (cultural alienation) characterise some European countries which house up to 25 per cent official foreigners. In contrast, Canada and Australia grant citizenship quickly and easily. They have adopted an official policy of multiculturalism, celebrating diversity as a source of enrichment and national unity. A common patriotism based on loyalty to the constitution and the ideology of upward mobility serves as a binding glue for the newcomers in traditional immigration societies. In the United States, the immigrants are supposed to melt into an American society that is perceived as a mixture of people with different origins. This melting-pot ideology has not prevented the continued survival of ethnic identities. In contrast, ethno-nationalism derived from ancestry excludes those not of the same mythical descent in Europe.

In Germany and France moves are afoot to facilitate the integration of immigrants by making the acquisition of citizenship easier and faster. The policy changes are motivated more by attracting new voters as well as pre-empting growing right-wing parties than by empathy with people in legal limbo. It is also still cultural assimilation rather than multicultural co-existence that concerns European politicians. A French cabinet minister (Jean-Claude Gaudin) for example declares: "We reject racism, but we also reject the voluntary existence of self-enclosed communities." This antagonism is directed primarily against Muslims whose mind-set and lifestyles are perceived as clashing with the values of secular French society. Turkey's admission into the European Union is postponed because the country is a Muslim society and therefore seen as incompatible with the Euro-Christian character of the rest of the continent. Why should religious differences prevent people from being granted equal citizenship in a secular community, unless the religious minority adheres to the dictates of the majority?

It is important to note that immigrants everywhere primarily strive for individual integration and enrichment and not autonomy or special treatment as in the case of indigenous minorities. Immigrants do not aim at establishing a new state but strive to fit into the new homeland and exploit its better opportunities. However, where coerced immigration took place through slavery as in the case of African-Americans, separateness is often adopted as a self-defence and political strategy in the face of continuing discrimination. The same applies to so-called middlemen minorities (Gypsies/Romanies in Europe; Indians in East and South Africa; Chinese in East Asia; Palestinians in Arab states; Jews across the world), derived from indentured labour or trading opportunities in hostile host societies. Therefore, it is useful to distinguish, as Jean La Ponce does, between "minorities by choice" and "minorities by force". "Minorities by force" under the current impact and fashion of cultural revivalism and exclusivism also tend to adopt some of the strategies of indigenous minorities as "forced citizens" in a state not of their own making.

The most problematic of the three categories is that of divided societies with competing nationalities bound to a geo-historical territory in which they strive collectively for dominance, or equal treatment, or even secession. Nationalist mobilisation of a distinct group of people trying to maintain their own institutions based on different cultural, linguistic, religious or ethno-racial mythologies can lead to severe strife, unless federalism or power sharing (negotiated consociationalism) satisfies the elites (leadership cadres) on all sides to adhere to agreed-upon political rules. Self-reliant competing nationalities in multi-ethnic states have the capacity to change the balance of political power or even destroy the state, which is not possible in the first two cases discussed. In the case of indigenous minorities and immigrant communities, ethnic conflicts can be solved through reforms of the political and legal system while in the case of competing nationalities revolutionary violence looms and the stakes are much higher for all antagonists.

The boundaries of most former colonies were drawn for the administrative convenience of the colonial powers with scant regard to the ethnic composition of the population. Consequently, almost all of the new states comprise several distinct nationalities. An initial program of nation-building (more accurately state- or institution-building) was supposed to create loyalty to the new state, but in many cases achieved the opposite. Entire regions or ethnicities were totally alienated from the centre, which had been captured by one ethnic group that suppressed others in the name of combating tribal divisiveness. Kleptocracies of urban elites excluded and exploited others in the name of Islam (Sudan), or Buddhism (Sri Lanka) or clan membership (Somalia) or ethnicity (Rwanda/Burundi) to name just a few so-called "failed" states. More stable pseudo-democracies, such as Turkey, deny the very existence of the separate ethnic identity of its 20 per cent Kurdish population, who are not allowed cultural expressions of distinctiveness. Other countries, such as Israel, openly define themselves as "ethnic states", a sanctuary only for the Jews of the world. Jews receive instant citizenship under a law of return, while Palestinian refugees and their descendants born in pre-Israel territory are barred. Although the 15 per cent Arabs possess the formal equality of Israeli citizenship, they are clearly second-class citizens in an ethnic state. The politicised ethnicity that develops in the competition for scarce resources allows the dominant group to monopolise the state and extend patronage to its members only.

Especially with rapid urbanisation, dislocated peasants are predisposed to fall back on ethnic support networks in a threatening environment. As Robert Kaplan has aptly observed, "fundamentalist extremism is the psychological defence of urban peasants whose values are under attack".[4] The Hindu nationalists of the BJP who tore down a mosque in Ayodhya, the Hamas supporters in overcrowded Gaza and the Jewish settlers on the West Bank are part of an urban proletariat that displays fanatical intolerance primarily in order to establish a recognised identity in an ideological vacuum. Insecure collectivities strive for moral security. Competing nationalities threaten even the more affluent liberal democratic states, as evidenced in the resurgence of Quebec and Scottish and Catalan nationalism. A high degree of federalism, particularly complete cultural autonomy for distinct regions, provides only a partial answer because regional elites have successfully utilised myths of past conquest or hurt pride that aims for total sovereignty. Quebec separatists for example, peddle the idea of a colonised people, "the white niggers" of North America, whose defeat by competing imperialist forces 200 years earlier can only be extinguished through separatist liberation from the ongoing "political terrorism" of Ottawa. Almost half of Quebec residents and 61 per cent of French-speakers in Quebec endorse the delusion of being better off alone both psychologically and materially, as two referenda on secession have shown.

Some analysts distinguish between state-sponsored and state-seeking nationalism. This is a modification of Lenin's distinction between "reactionary" (colonial) and "progressive" (anti-colonial) nationalist mobilisation for independence or self-determination. State-sponsored nationalism is usually associated with ethnic self-glorification (ethnocentricism), the exclusion of minorities at home and imperialist ambition or aggression abroad. State-seeking nationalism, on the other hand, is frequently presented as "liberation", the self-fulfilment of people's dream of freedom from alien domination. The distinction is however, problematic. In the first instance, some nationalisms fall into both categories. Quebec separatists, for example, control most of the coercive powers of a state (the province of Quebec). The Separatist Parti Québecois in power marginalises non-Francophones and denies indigenous nations (Cree) the right of self-determination which it claims for itself. Yet Quebec separatists simultaneously portray themselves as victims of Canadian federalism from which they seek to escape through full sovereignty.

In the second instance, state-seeking nationalities can behave as despotically as their state-sponsored dominators. Tamil nationalists in Sri Lanka terrorise their opponents as ruthlessly as their Sinhalese government enemies. IRA activists are far ahead of Ulster unionists in intimidatory violence. The main Kurdish nationalist group in Turkey matches the state, if not in resources, certainly in ruthlessness. Palestinian officials on the West Bank learned quickly from Israel how to suppress their own human rights dissidents.

In the third instance, in those ethno-nationalist confrontations the state-seeking minority not only mirrors the terror methods of its more powerful state opponents, but also uses those methods unceasingly against internal dissidents within its own group. A progressively restrictive definition of the "in" group seems to accompany ethno-nationalist polarisation. Sri Lankan Tamil separatists now exclude Tamil-speaking Muslims and Christians and have narrowed the boundaries of a true Tamil to a Hindu-Tamil. The conflict started with a linguistic controversy about the official language and the resulting differential access to bureaucratic jobs and academic credentials. A similar restriction of the "in" group has taken place in Quebec. Initially all residents of the province were considered Québecois. Subsequently, only French-speaking residents qualified and now Francophones with a different ancestry and colour (Haitians and Lebanese) are informally excluded in the racist popular perception of a *pure laine* (the original settlers of French descent).

The really controversial question in all peaceful secessions is: Who decides the process? Quebec separatists argue that they alone decide, exercising an inviolable right of self-determination of a people on the basis of 50 per cent + 1 voter support in the territory. Their federal opponents argue that the rest of Canada would be severely affected by the exit of a substantial part, and therefore it must have a say. Secession, Ottawa insists, must adhere to the laws of Canada. Some suggest a national referendum, others at least that federal approval of the secession question to be tested in Quebec must be given. This is also the position of the final South African Constitution which explicitly does not preclude the right of self-determination of any community – such as a Volkstaat – within a territorial entity in the Republic. However, this recognition is subject to national legislation to which the process of seeking self-determination must apply. In practice, this means that a hostile majority through national legislation can set conditions that no separatist minority is ever able to fulfil. Therefore, the conditional constitutional recognition of the right to self-determination proves meaningless, as it did in the former Soviet constitution. It is also worth noting that the latest peaceful partition in Czechoslovakia took place without a referendum, and on the basis of elite negotiations that ignored the majority support in the Czech part for a united country.

Secessionist movements can originate in the more affluent parts of the state or in poorer regions. This demonstrates the secondary nature of material interests compared with the primary motive of escaping perceived ethnic domination. Partition can happen despite the high material sacrifice of secession. Quebec and Slovakia are examples of state contraction initiated by the elites of poorer segments and against the majority opinion of the rest of the state. On the other hand, the more modernised and affluent sections of the population started the unravelling of Yugoslavia (Slovenia and Croatia), the disintegration of the Soviet Union (Baltic States) and motivated a growing separatist party in Northern Italy. Economic globalisation has weakened the traditional nation-state by subjecting it to the forces of ever larger markets, currency movements, cultural dictates (CNN, Sky) or terms of trade. At the same time, global outsiders have penetrated the most remote regions in trying to homogenise the world. This has led to a recovery of distinctiveness and regional identity, as a protest against alien domination.

The construction of naturalised distinctiveness against unwelcome outsiders ("othering") is independent of cultural tradition and should not only be attributed to Eurocentric racism. Ethnocentrism is particularly evident in relatively closed societies with only a small ratio of "foreigners". For example, a senior Japanese cabinet minis ter, Isutomu Hata, fended off pressures for imports of foreign beef in the late 1980s by arguing that Japanese intestines were too long to digest it. Similarly, some European skis were initially barred from Japan because the bureaucrat in charge said that they would not slide on Japan's "unique snow". Koreans who have lived in Japan for generations, let alone the indigenous Burakunin, can testify how racially conscious and exclusive Japanese society is to this day. Other Asian countries do not lag far behind. Malaysian prime minister Mahather's political tract *The Malay Dilemma* comprises a collection of the worst essentialist stereotypes. Amongst them: "The Jews are not merely hook-nosed, but understand money instinctively." Malays are described as "easy-going and tolerant", Chinese "not just almond-eyed people, but also inherently good businessmen". While Malaysia's affirmative action policy in favour of the 60 per cent "sons of the soil" (Bumiputras) clearly discriminates against the 30 per cent citizens of Chinese and 8 per cent of Indian origin, it also eased racial tensions. An expanding economy allowed all groups a growing share of the national pie with the Chinese educational and economic head start hardly being affected. For this reason, many South African whites hold up Malaysia as a model to emulate. In China traditional theories of Han superiority have been somewhat diluted by the incorporation of 55 official minorities, including colonised Tibetans. Foreigners are perceived more from pride in a 5 000 year old culture rather than from a position of racial superiority. Shame about the backward state of the country and its defeat by Western and Japanese colonialism also dampens Chinese ethnocentrism.

There are, of course, abundant examples of romantic ethnocentrism from Africa as well. "Ubuntu" has been ascribed as almost a generic predisposition of blacks (Allister Sparks)[5] despite dramatic instances of cruelty and indifference. Afrikaners are eulogised as simple rustic people despite having been more than 80 per cent urbanised for the last forty years. Adedeji Adebayo, economic adviser to the OAU, blandly states: "Africans are past masters in consultation, consensus and consent. Our traditions abhor exclusivism."[6] This whilst genocide raged in Rwanda and Burundi and ethnic conflicts remain unresolved in Ethiopia and the Sudan and warlords kill each other in Somalia and Liberia. Former UDF activist and author Chris van Wyk has caricatured the Ubuntu philosophy by contrasting its humanitarian idealism with the daily reality of crime in South Africa: "Does the rapist possess this wonderful African humanism everybody talks about? The student who toyi-toyi's on other students' desks when he cannot get his way? The community worker who steals the bread and milk money meant for hundreds of poor kids? Or is Ubuntu a gadget whose batteries go flat when you decide it is about time you shoot a doctor in a Jo'burg street and take his car?"[7]

Comparative conceptual distinctions, observations and insights help to come to grips with the question: Is South Africa a deeply divided society? Well, is it? It certainly was, is less so now, and still has the potential to become so again. Whether it will is locked up in the current dynamics of its transition to democracy. Part of these dynamics is the manipulation of the myths of race and ethnicity and how this will interact with problems of class stratification, religion, traditionalism, modernity and the quest for political power.

The rest of our book investigates different aspects of these dynamics of transition. Our analysis attempts to evaluate the concrete working of the new South African sociopolitical system in comparison with other communal conflicts around the world. It takes issue with some of the literature on transition that constructs abstract models of democracy and negotiations and determines which cases fit or fail the test. Each chapter is guided by a central question related to particular aspects of South Africa as a divided society. In answering these questions, we try to avoid the Scylla of excessive voluntarism where "everything is possible and nothing is necessary", and the Charybdis of excessive determinism where "everything is necessary and nothing is possible". Instead, we analyse structures and trends, locate actors who shape the sociopolitical trends and are in turn constrained by their local and global conditions. We speculate why they exercise the options that they do and others that they might. In doing so, we hope to illuminate a spectrum of so-called divided societies in a comparative analysis where the "good surprise" of South Africa can shed light on wider theoretical controversies around the nature of ethno-nationalist mobilisation.

Chapter Two

Anti-Semitism and anti-black racism: Nazi Germany and South Africa

Conventional wisdom holds that antipathy towards one minority is usually combined with prejudice toward other "outsiders". Disdain for Jews goes along with contempt for blacks. Various scapegoats are manufactured interchangeably. Often they are blamed simultaneously. Even if "Bolsheviks" and "capitalist exploiters" share nothing, the conspiratorial mind lumps them together as causes of misery, without bothering with the contradiction. Yet racism shows many faces. Where several targets and potential "enemies" can be manufactured into threats to national survival, some are more, others less, discriminated against. The cultural characteristics or the behaviour of the minority hardly influence such selective stigmatisation. Ethnicity is never the cause of antagonism, only its vehicle and demarcation. Specific discrimination depends on political circumstances. State responses to ethno-cultural diversity and fluctuating elite interest account for stereotyping and ethnic mobilisation.

Such revisions of conventional wisdom can be concluded from Milton Shain's intriguing book,[1] which corrects a common misconception that the early apartheid state was free of anti-Semitism because it was preoccupied with anti-black racism. On the contrary, Shain documents comprehensively how anti-Semitic ideas "provided such a useful means of political mobilisation for the Afrikaner right-wing", particularly in the 1930s and 1940s.[2] This nuanced history of Afrikaner perceptions of Jews traces the evolving stereotypes: from welcome peddlers of wares in the Transvaal hinterland to the exploiting plutocrat and indulging parvenu (Hoggenheimer) in city luxury. Nationalist mobilisation easily reconciled such imagery with the later label of Jews as subversives, in league with Bolshevik-inspired strikes and anti-apartheid activism at the height of Afrikaner domination. Yet Shain also points out how anti-Semitic ideology was tempered by Jews as part of the white ruling class in

South Africa. Despite negative stereotyping, "they faced little formal exclusion and ostracism",[3] in contrast to South African Indians. While Indian competitors of white traders were disdained and progressively restricted, Shain diagnoses even "a grudging respect"[4] for the Jewish fortune-seeker in a frontier society that "put a premium on rugged individualism". Political expediency in collaborating with Israel further facilitated the incorporation of the Jew as "one of us" compared with the non-white Indian alien.

Who is included or excluded from an arbitrary pigmentocracy may have also been influenced by two other factors to which Shain pays little attention: (1) The religiously inspired notion of a "chosen people" at odds with a hostile environment predisposed Afrikaner Calvinists to look at Jews as compatriots. (2) Unlike the much less developed coloured and Indian mercantile capital, alleged Jewish economic control of major conglomerates at home and abroad made a rising Afrikaner bourgeoisie appreciate the value of collaboration for common benefits. In short, Pretoria could hardly afford to alienate such powerful forces with official anti-Semitism when a sanction-battered state needed allies. Such political-economic exigencies, more than the psychological explanation of blacks serving "as the lightning rod for racism" would seem to account for "the virtual absence of white anti-Semitism"[5] in the later periods of apartheid South Africa.

Shain's insightful study on the changing sociopolitical circumstances that shape stereotyping suggests a much wider comparison between different forms of racism. Instead of viewing apartheid as madness or moral pathology, could it not be understood better as rational racism, in contrast to the irrational anti-Semitic fascism? A comparison between the two most horrendous systems of racism, namely Nazi Germany and apartheid South Africa, can reveal significantly different intentions and modes of domination that the popular "fascist apartheid" analogy misses.

The old controversy about the comparison between apartheid and Nazism has been refuelled with the publication of a book by Kader Asmal, Louise Asmal and Ronald Suresh Roberts[6] – a book which should not be dismissed as mere propaganda simply because Kader Asmal is a well-known cabinet minister. Precisely because the ANC's chief ethics commissioner and widely respected legal expert and human rights advocate articulates controversial opinions forthrightly, his account has to be taken seriously.

The authors' powerful polemic seeks to remind South Africans of the atrocities committed by a "criminal regime"; it records the well-known racial laws and exhorts apartheid's beneficiaries to take collective responsibility. It denies that defenders and resisters can be placed "on an equivalent legal footing". Asmal seems to side with those in the ANC who incited Tutu's ire when they argued that because they fought "a just war" they therefore did not need to appear before his Truth Commission. Asmal et al. admit to "comparatively few" or "scattered human rights infringements" on the part of the ANC. They are called mere "lapses" of an "under-resourced" organisation under stress, "never condoned" but "actually forbidden". If that is the case, why the initial leading ANC members' reluctance to appear before the Commission? In their eagerness to establish that resisters and defenders of apartheid inhabit "fundamentally incompatible, moral universes", the authors ignore the classical philosophical distinction between a "just war" and "justice in war". No one doubts that the anti-apartheid movement fought a just cause. The complementary principle of "justice in war" insists that, even in such cases, conventions of justice have to be followed and the just party must be held accountable if it does not do so (for instance, killing prisoners of war or unnecessarily harming civilians) regardless of the moral evil of the opponent. The oppressed are also bound by the rules. Tutu, to his eternal credit, brought this principle home.

The Asmal indictment becomes more problematic in its constant references to the Nazis of Africa in order to justify classifying apartheid as a "form of genocide". The Nazi analogies are supposed to sweep the reader into outrage. South Africa resembles an open-house concentration camp. Indeed, it is generally known that many leading apartheid ideologues sympathised with the Nazis in the 1940s. But that was mainly because they were opposed to fighting on the side of the British. It is unclear in Asmal's account whether they adopted this attitude because of racist and anti-Semitic beliefs, or because of anti-British sentiment.

The 1948 victory of the National Party is usually portrayed as the triumph of racist apartheid ideology. However, in the perspective of Afrikaner nationalists at the time it was much more a victory over the British than a racial mandate to suppress blacks. Ethnic concerns competed with and often predominated over racial anxieties. This is best demonstrated by the change in immigration policy of the new government, which ended the previous Smuts regime's drive to encourage white immigration, particularly from Commonwealth countries. English-speaking white immigrants and Catholic southern Europeans did not fit into the emerging Afrikaner nation and therefore were discouraged. A gain of 29 111 immigrants in 1948 dropped to losses in subsequent years. In terms of strengthening whites over blacks the policy did not make sense and was counterproductive. It can only be understood as a priority of asserting Afrikaner political dominance over their British rival during the first years of official apartheid. Therefore, South Africa missed the emigration boom from post-war Europe and only from 1962 did immigration increase again with a peak of a total gain of 40 200 in 1975.

Afrikaner nationalism had always been influenced by British parliamentary traditions. Malan's early National Party strongly opposed the semi-fascist Ossewa Brandwag and the rival Greyshirts who wanted to overthrow the state. Malan advocated gaining power by democratic means and honouring the constitution. The same cleavage emerged sixty years later when Eugene Terre'Blanche's AWB clamoured for "bullets not ballots", rejecting parliament as a "British-Jewish" invention. This minority among the Afrikaner right wing was marginalised by Constand Viljoen's Freedom Front that brought the majority of the right-wingers into the rules of parliamentary democracy in 1994. The German Fascist model had also been discredited on account of its anti-religious stance among deeply religious Afrikaners. Secularisation in South Africa was slow in coming and still makes its Calvinist section, in particular, less susceptible to a worldly dictatorship replacing divine authority with a Hitler-type philosophy. Nowhere in the book is it mentioned that a leading Nazi such as Prime Minister Vorster later visited Jerusalem's Holocaust memorial, and that Israel, more than any other independent state, collaborated with the South African "Nazis". While Israel also collaborated with other unsavoury regimes, the real Nazis would not have been able to collaborate with Jews (and vice versa) even out of necessity or expediency.

Sloganeering about "Verwoerd's ideological klansman Adolf Hitler", frequent comparisons between the Nuremberg Laws against Jews and apartheid laws miss the different context behind the anti-black and anti-Semitic racism. For example, to claim that apartheid "was a principle around which large numbers of people actively rallied, as they rallied around anti-Semitism in Nazi Germany"[7] suggests similar reasons for the support when in fact the reasons for Afrikaner and German nationalism differed substantially. The comparison ignores the fact that apartheid tolerated an outspoken white opposition, in contrast to Hitler's totalitarian control of the population. That made support for apartheid actually worse in the presence of clear alternatives. Asmal et al. write, "In analogy with Heydrich's Nazi reliance on the watchful eyes of Germans to oppress Jews, section II enabled neighbours to object to the classification of any fellow-resident as a white person."[8] No German had any veto against the classification of neighbours as Jews. Nor did the Nazis rely on "watchful eyes" but on ancestral records, because Jewishness was not visible but had to be made so by a mandatory wearing of the yellow star. Other false analogies abound, such as: "The Broederbond was remodelled on the lines of Hitler's Nazi Party with secret cells and a secret membership."[9] In fact, the Nazi Party (NSDAP) was an open mass party, hardly comparable with the 15 000 carefully selected members of the Broederbond. The Broederbond initially formed an employment agency for Afrikaner professionals and later served more as a political think-tank. As an elite organisation, it could at most be compared to the SS without uniforms and military functions.

Asmal et al. rightly point to the seemingly forgotten collaboration of many business tycoons with apartheid, just as Krupp, I.G. Farben and other beneficiaries of the German war machine went along quietly with Nazi policy. In seeming contradiction, however, the authors also assert: "Thus, for apartheid's functionaries, as for the Nazis, international capital and its most bitter opponents (Communists) were one and the same."[10] This simplistic conclusion from the well-known stereotyping of "Jewish financiers as agents of communism" overlooks the fact that apartheid advocates extended great efforts and resources to woo international capital. In contrast, the German Nazis despised international capital as controlled by Jews. Apartheid always presented itself as a bastion against communism which needed the help of the West to fend off sanctions and secure South Africa for free enterprise. Ironically, the abolition of apartheid achieved this goal far more successfully than its worried advocates could have dreamed of.

In South Africa, a minority regime fought "by all means possible" the seizure of power by the majority. In doing so, it tortured, killed, and disregarded human rights conventions as it pleased. In Nazi Germany, a sectarian elite set out to eliminate systematically designated minorities who had no political ambitions and were therefore no threat to the ruling group except in the fantasy of rulers who constructed them as the major enemy. Unlike the fictitious conflict between Germans and Jews, in South Africa a real civil war took place with self-declared opponents on each side. In Nazi Germany, a struggle existed only in the imagination of the anti-Semite. No Jew ever dreamt of overthrowing a German government before the pogroms started. Even then, many Jews foolishly did not realise the impending threat and believed in the false security of real assimilation. This different constellation does not absolve the apartheid executioners of their crimes. However, it locates their deeds differently, requiring more nuanced explanations to comprehend their motives.

Most of Asmal et al.'s text utilises UN resolutions to substantiate their claim that apartheid was genocide. While the UN played a strategic role in giving international prominence to injustices under apartheid, the language used is not very useful in gaining an understanding of the phenomenon. The quest for the elimination of racial inequality calls for nothing less than a scrupulously honest deconstruction of the underpinnings of racial ideologies and the personal motivations of its beneficiaries. Neither of these aims is met through the uncritical use of hyperbolic description, though it may have had its strategic value at certain historic junctures. Nor is a distinction between types of oppression intended to trivialise the experiences of victims of each kind of racialised situation or to give moral support to the former oppressors, as Asmal hints his critics do when they try "to preserve a semblance of morality" underneath apartheid. The authors call this "our own brand of holocaust denial". Steven Friedman[11] has drawn attention to another danger of this partisan denouncement of all critics as willing or unwilling allies of apartheid: those who fought the moral evil of apartheid in the ANC place themselves beyond reproach. With their moral credentials, they now claim "a licence for them to govern in whichever way they please", because they need not be judged by the same standards. If all criticism of liberation politics is automatically tainted by the suspicion of apartheid support, the new rulers have successfully delegitimised all opposition and given themselves a free hand. To rely solely on UN resolutions to discern the nature of a regime can be misleading. One only has to be reminded of the ill-considered "Zionism is racism" verdict, later rescinded. The so-called international community – in the form of national government representatives with their own agendas – functions as a poor forum for reliable moral judgements. Yet taking its rationale from a UN sub-committee, Asmal and his co-authors insist that apartheid as genocide is not hyperbole but "an understatement".[12]

It is always a macabre undertaking to compare degrees of oppression. One dissenter harassed is too many. It is also a futile exercise to argue, as has been done in the South African press, whether apartheid constitutes a crime against humanity or something either more or less offensive. The fact that the notion of a crime against humanity has been pushed by states allied with the Soviet Union in a Cold War climate and resisted by Western democracies is equally irrelevant for the correctness of the verdict. If words have any meaning, apartheid did not amount to genocide – even if the term is stretched to include any harm done to the life chances of ethnic or racial collectivities. Profound legal discrimination and genocide remain two distinct events. Apartheid robbed the South African majority of dignity and countless opportunities. It deprived the disenfranchised of land, jobs and equal pay, of the right to family life and equality of education, and tried to make them foreigners in the land of their birth. It terrorised those who resisted and, in the process, maimed and killed some of the best and the bravest. But genocide it was not. Otherwise, the number of blacks, both in absolute terms and relative to the ruling group, would not have increased steadily, notwithstanding higher child mortality and lower life expectancy of Africans. Ironically, the authors themselves unwittingly confirm this when they compare the thousandfold more people killed in the mines than by police torturers: "throughout the entire apartheid period 68 political prisoners died in police detention". This could be an average figure of Jews killed in a month in a small Ukrainian town by the German occupiers and the auxiliaries.

In short, if anything and everything amounts to fascism and genocide, then nothing is fascism and genocide. The propagandistic inflation of serious accusations cheapens the fate of the real victims of fascism. By being blind to nuances and necessary differentiation by ahistorical labelling and false analogies, well-intended polemicists may be able to incite passion, even combat dangerous historical amnesia, but hardly contribute to political literacy.

If Daniel Goldhagen's central thesis is correct, far more ordinary German soldiers and prison guards voluntarily participated in the Nazi atrocities than is generally believed. They were keen to act out their own deficiencies on dehumanised objects. Under apartheid, however, a different constellation prevailed. The vastly outnumbered ruling group could not seek to eliminate but only control the majority. This required the active participation of willing members of those who were discriminated against. At the height of apartheid, during the 1970s and 1980s, about two-thirds of the South African police were already black. Far from being reluctant co-optees in their own subjugation, the black police personnel, on the whole, had fully internalised the official doctrine of fighting terrorism. They frequently outperformed their white masters. They, in turn, prided themselves on fighting a common enemy together. No Nazi official would have accepted Jews within their ranks. This dependence of the apartheid regime on their "others" – not only in assuring security but at all levels of life, from economic survival to administrative capacity – also required a general perception of the subordinates that differed from the Nazis' generalised demonisation of the Jews. Apartheid advocates could only afford selective reprisals against suspected activists, not the indiscriminate terror of the Nazis against all members of the "out" group, regardless of their political outlook. At the same time, comprehensive legal control in South Africa discouraged private unofficial violence. Ku Klux Klan vigilante activity was relatively rare. The phenomenon of a "Third Force" of policemen killing on their own volition with the tacit or explicit approval of politicians escalated only when the regime was already losing control. However, even during this transitional era, the apartheid government had to pretend that policemen complied with "the law" which was supposed to apply equally to white and black, master and servant. In contrast, Nazi Germany explicitly placed Jews outside the law and thereby legitimised arbitrary terrorism. Had apartheid Pretoria pursued a similar strategy, it would have incited massive upheavals. The appearance of legality and impartial justice was a necessary instrument of minority domination to the extent that the government sometimes paid compensation to victims of police torture and always cultivated the image of independent courts. Unlike Hitler's followers, apartheid's "willing executioners" were always constrained by legal authority. In the German case, the will of the leader reigned supreme. In the colonial setting, far more complex factors intervened to make it both easier and more difficult to combat oppression.

The struggle against apartheid suffered from the manipulation of the opposition, from co-optation to sophisticated concessions alternating with outright repression. In Hitler's case, only repression prevailed as a matter of principle. The anti-apartheid struggle, however, was also facilitated by circumstances that were not allowed to surface in Germany: the victims in South Africa could expect to find influential allies within the ruling group. Any expression of empathy or support for Jews in Nazi Germany was considered an act of treason that threatened heavy penalties. While some heroic whites from Bram Fischer to Neil Aggett paid this price in South Africa as well, many sympathised actively or passively with the black cause in a variety of ways and for a multitude of reasons. Whether out of self-interest or moral qualms, by openly appealing to the better sense of the rulers the apartheid opposition strengthened itself immensely.

It was the split in the ruling group, the cleavage between "softliners" and "hardliners" (*verligtes* and *verkramptes*), that ultimately allowed for the negotiated revolution when the more far-sighted Afrikaner majority backed De Klerk's strategy of compromise. In the absence of such a public discourse about a group's self-concept, the Hitler opposition could not function in a totalitarian environment that silenced all dissent. By contrast, in the authoritarian South African state, despite censorship and emergency laws, projections of alternative orders exposed the bankruptcy of apartheid, undermined the moral certainty of its upholders, and ultimately forged a new hegemony of negotiated co-existence. Thus an old lesson is again confirmed by the dialectic of repression: in order to succeed it has to be self-sufficient, total and ruthless. Any concession bears the seeds of an accelerating collapse.

Stereotypes help organise a complex world. They provide instant meaning by making it unnecessary to judge every situation according to its own merit. These core judgements are inevitable guideposts and no one can function without them. The interpretative repertoire of every individual is a complex mix – there is no simple, pure racist. Nor is the opposite possible. Most people hold ambivalent attitudes. Stereotypes themselves include typically contradictory images. For example, Jews are accused of being clannish, aloof and distant. When they forego ethnic specificity in favour of assimilation, as in late nineteenth century Western Europe, the anti-Semite sniffs a cunning ploy to sneak in.[13] In nineteenth century European medical literature, the alleged greater frequency of mental illness of Jews was ascribed to inbreeding and even incest. At the same time, images of "black Jews" or Jews as "white Negroes" were attributed to racial mixing in the Diaspora.[14]

It is doubtful whether any easy association of Jewishness and blackness still applies. The myth of blacks may still lend itself to bear similar projections but in quite different ways. Thus, in the realm of secularity, Jews are nowadays considered perverse rather than, like blacks, sexually aggressive and unrestrained. They are both associated with sexual excess. Yet, the supposed Jewish orgies of Hollywood's affluent media moguls or wheeler-dealers in New York contrast sharply with the perceived promiscuous behaviour of juvenile drug-peddling ghetto-dwellers or the customary polygamy of blacks in the colonies or under Islamic license. At any rate, losing sight of the class difference between Jews and blacks in Western societies or the power of Israel compared with the relative powerlessness of black states in global politics misses important aspects.

According to Shain, anti-Semitic stereotypes were the "barometer and facilitator of prejudice."[15] They prepared "the way for the growth and dissemination of anti-Semitism". Thus, given the monstrous consequences of both anti-Semitism and racism, the analysis of stereotypes is politically relevant. In order to combat racism, it is essential to grasp its constantly changing nature. For example, the new racism that utilises culture instead of "race" inferiorises through a more subtle "othering". When Brian Bunting, Kader Asmal and other polemicists in the anti-apartheid camp equate Nazism with apartheid by laboriously diagnosing the same essentialist racism in *Mein Kampf* and Verwoerd's writings, they are not only wrong but they harm their own cause. Fascist racism could only be overthrown from without, while apartheid racism could reform itself from within when it became too costly.[16] It is inconceivable that a Nazi Gorbachev could have come to power if National Socialism had survived a bit longer – certainly not as long as Hitler and his henchmen had been alive. While that also applies to Bolshevism under Stalin, the rationality of both mobilising ideologies differed so fundamentally that Nazism could not have faded away without being physically defeated. The category "race" is subject to enormous variation in different times and places.[17] What can a comparison between the two most vicious and widespread forms of exclusion and denigration – Nazi anti-Semitism and South African racism – yield?

Anti-Semitic stereotypes spring from different needs than anti-black images. In the colonial context, anti-black discrimination has an instrumental function: to exploit, subjugate or dispossess the colonised and legitimate the process with a racist ideology of a biological or cultural inferiority. Dominant attitudes are primarily paternalistic. They always distinguish between a majority of "good" and a minority of "bad" blacks. Only those who step out of their assigned place are targets of terror, while the majority are treated like unruly children in need of a stern father. Modern anti-Semitism, on the other hand, fulfils primarily psychosocial needs. The utter irrationality of an imagined Jewish threat contrasts sharply with the more rational behaviour of colonists to secure power and privilege through exclusion. Jews are not merely excluded, but exterminated. Jews do not face paternalistic selected terror, but indiscriminate persecution against all, regardless of their status or behaviour. In short, the roots of modern anti-Semitism must be sought in the psychosocial realm of ego-weak characters who construct their identity by denigrating others. They need scapegoats to externalise what cannot be sublimated. Anti-Semitism constitutes externalised repression. This does not mean that anti-Semitism cannot also be analysed in terms of its "rational" functions. As far as Nazis were concerned, having an imagined Jewish enemy inside the nation moulded a strife-ridden, heterogeneous Nazi movement into a more unified force. Anti-Semitism provided an esprit de corps. Yet it was an already existing psychological predisposition that made large sections of the European population so susceptible to fascist agitators.

In the colonial context, blacks were treated as part of an exotic fauna; the naturalised ingredients of a game park could amuse but not threaten. As faceless objects, they existed outside a "civilised society" of which Jews were very much an integral part. Jews represented the city, the dangerous cosmopolitan melting pot, the future threat to a glorified past. In racist imagery, blacks represent the opposite: the primitive countryside, potentially violent if not controlled, but in principle good-natured. Unchecked, both Jews and blacks, however, constitute an imagined threat to European values. The stress on ordered life during unsettling wars and economic depressions explains the subjective vigour with which the racist stereotypes were and still are pursued.

In all Western countries, attitudes toward minorities, immigrants and the poor have also hardened, particularly in regard to spending money on them or creating equal opportunities. For instance, in a July 1994 US survey, a majority of whites (51 per cent) believed that equal rights for racial minorities had been pushed too far, up from 42 per cent two years earlier.[18] Eighty-two per cent of US residents believed that people moving to the US to live should be subjected to more restrictions and controls. An economically motivated intolerance seemed to have replaced traditional bigotry because the same respondents displayed greater approval of post-modern lifestyles. A record 65 per cent of US whites approved of cross-racial dating – up from 47 per cent in 1987. Sixty per cent denied school boards the right to fire teachers who were known homosexuals, up from 42 per cent in 1987. As long as altruism does not threaten jobs or wallets, respondents are less interested in enforcing a traditional moral order against outsiders.

Anti-Semites consider Jews as cancerous parasites. In its extreme form, these outcasts become so dehumanised in the perception of prosecutors that emotional attitudes of hate or fear hardly apply. The other is a dangerous object to be eliminated rather than hated. In the case of colonial racism, the European supremacists *despise* their subordinates. Their dominant attitude is one of tolerant dismissiveness, bordering on contempt mixed with pity and, occasionally, even guilt. At all times, master and servant engage each other emotionally. With this emotional investment, the Afrikaner farmer can be extremely kind to his faceless labourers and brutalise them at the same time. They are bound in a relationship that does not exist between the anti-Semite and his victims. Jews are considered so alien, so far beyond the bonds of common humanity, that the Treblinka guards merely did their job when herding naked women and children into the gas showers. Like a surgeon who cold-bloodedly excises a sore, the SS guards "cleansed" the body politic of unwanted "material". Rare non-police killings of blacks by pathological whites in South Africa always involved an emotional act. One of the AWB bombers broke down and cried when confronted with his carnage. Very few SS officers asked for a transfer from their morbid duties.[19]

It would be wrong, however, to consider the average SS guards as sadists, as Hollywood always portrays them. Sadism implies enjoyment of cruelty. Eichmann was neither sadistic nor even pathologically anti-Semitic. Only his obsession to impress authority figures by his efficient work marks him as a deviant. The banality that Hannah Arendt diagnosed in Eichmann's mentality also characterised his underlings: normal human beings with the average range of feelings. It was the coldly planned industrialised genocide that distinguished the Holocaust from other types of extermination. All other historical genocides occurred in the context of wars, colonial conquests or disputes over land and resources.

Enrichment was more of a side effect rather than the prime purpose of the Nazis' obsession with Jews. It was a purposeless, irrational killing. This distinguished the Holocaust from medieval pogroms. Then, killing Jews was frequently instigated by the desire to get rid of debtors. The 0,3 per cent of Jews in the German population of 1933 hardly possessed sufficient wealth or other resources to make their acquisition a prime motive for the killings – individual NS looters notwithstanding. On the contrary, rounding up Jews all over Nazi-occupied Europe diverted considerable resources from the German war effort, particularly in Eastern Europe. Here, the advancing and retreating *Wehrmacht* was engaged more frequently in shooting poor *Ostjuden* than engaging Stalin's army. Therefore, materialist explanations of the Holocaust miss its ideological dimension.

Equally problematic is the insistence that the Holocaust was part of a series of unfortunate genocides and oppressions which took place throughout history. Concentration camps were not primarily a form of "industrialised slavery" as Pierre van den Berghe states. Since 1941, in the aftermath of the Wannsee conference, 90 per cent of the human freight to Auschwitz landed immediately in the gas chambers, not in the adjoining I.G. Farben compounds. Unlike in the case of slavery, the main thrust of Nazi persecution was extermination, not exploitation. In conclusion, the Nazis fought a war against a generalised "international Jewry". Blacks, on the other hand, merely had to be kept at bay in order to preserve the purity of the race. In the Nazi perception, Jews had already polluted the spirit and finance of the Aryan world. They had to be eradicated and prevented from causing further damage to a threatened nation.[20] This *imagined* threat, out of all proportion to the real importance of Jews in the lives of nations, has never applied to anti-black racism. At most, blacks have to be prevented through "Mixed Marriage Acts" and "Immorality Laws" from contaminating the nation. In the racist view, blacks may lust after white women (and vice versa) but are not credited with the ability to engage in a conspiracy to rule the world. Where entire indigenous communities were wiped out in colonial conquests, they were not killed for religious reasons. Perhaps they were not even considered worthy of a legitimising ideology to rationalise their conquest.

German historians have argued that the genocide of the Hereros by the German colonial army in then South West Africa foreshadowed the Holocaust forty years later. Nonetheless, colonial genocide as a dry run for the Jewish killings in the Nazi period seems problematic because it lacked ideologically driven irrationality. While a brutalised military may already have acted out a German national character, similar atrocities were perpetrated by other colonial armies (e.g. the massacre of Amritsar).[21] The unique aspects of the Holocaust lie in (a) its targeting of a minority that constituted no real threat, and (b) genocide outside the context of civil war or conquest.

Various forms of anti-Semitism should be distinguished. The classical religious anti-Judaism of orthodox Catholicism differs from Nazi anti-Semitism, which in turn was not typical of other forms of fascism. Mussolini and Franco did not share Hitler's obsession with Jews.[22] The "anti-Christ" image of Jews as infidels and betrayers of Jesus was undoubtedly fed into the indifference and ambivalence of the general population towards Jews. "They brought it upon themselves", as the stereotype goes. Perhaps the more a united world of Christendom was faced with heretics and non-believers during the Renaissance and the Reformation, the more the Jews served as evidence of the living truth of the Christian faith. As Ettinger put it: "Their degradation and oppression would convey the point that external punishment is suffered by those who dare to reject the revealed redeemer."[23] To medieval Christians, Judas Iscariot was the wicked betrayer of principles, the Jew incarnate. In medieval stereotypes, Jews had rejected Christ and aligned themselves with Satan. They practised witchcraft. Therefore, they represented the forces of darkness and evil. In contrast, blacks engaged in witchcraft out of ignorance. Their pagan souls begged to be saved by dedicated missionaries. Once saddled with the label "others" and "different" anti-Semitic mobilisers found a fertile ground to set up Jews as targets for exclusion. Given the long history of anti-Semitism in the West, the Nazis carried a long tradition to its extreme.

The Jewish cultural heritage of Christianity obviously played a crucial part in perpetuating the stereotypical image of the minority, even in countries and periods where there were no Jews. Religiously inspired hate, however, should have declined with secularisation. Instead, anti-Semitism has increased with the Enlightenment. Indeed, Jews are blamed for all of modernity's ills. Hatred of Jews goes beyond being an invention of Christianity. It merely provided the pretext for stigmatising a minority. In principle, however, Jews as a target remain interchangeable. Homophobia, for example, fulfils the same psychic functions. Jews and gays represent imagined threats to an established moral order.

Anti-Semitism is an age-old part of an entire Western tradition, not a German aberration. The indifference of the Allies toward refugees from Nazi-occupied Europe – from the UK to liberal Canada – constitutes a well-known part of the ingrained anti-Semitic strain. Thus, "none is too many", was the slogan with which Canadian politicians rejected pleas for admission from European Jewish asylum seekers. Nobody will know how many lives in the extermination camps could have been saved had the Allied airforce bombed the railways on which the freight cars shuttled their victims to Poland. The failure to come to the rescue of a racially defined section of humanity – although technically feasible and only explicable as lack of political will – constitutes a lasting indictment of Western liberalism.[24] Nazi anti-Semitism merely perfected an ingrained disposition in Western societies (conservatives, liberals and socialists alike) similar to the way in which the Afrikaner state enshrined a long tradition of English informal racial discrimination into formal apartheid. However, social conditions and historical circumstances differ vastly. While the latent potential for racial mobilisation and exclusion persists almost everywhere, a variety of factors determine whether the population is susceptible to the tunes of agitators.

The magic difference between anti-Semitic and anti-black racism lies in its greater socio-psychological functions in the former and the heavier economic and political constraints on anti-black racism in the colonies. Having to work with a numerically larger indigenous population on whose labour the colonial economy depends forces pragmatic limitations on racial ruthlessness. Those structural exigencies also translated into internalised attitudes over time. In short, while the anti-Semite could afford to annihilate the other, the colonist was bound to his subordinates. Not only did their numerical strength and resistance prevent genocide, but the conquered were indispensable to the conquerors while Jews were not. The latter were an expendable minority, irrespective of their behaviour, similar to other marginalised outgroups such as gypsies, homosexuals or mentally disabled persons. Where colonial racism did not depend on the co-operation and labour of indigenous people, such as in the case of hunting and gathering societies, they were also decimated. Tasmania and Newfoundland were ethnically cleansed long before the concept became fashionable. The indigenous populations of North America and Australia almost suffered the same fate through both physical and cultural extermination. In the African colonies, however, such genocidal colonialism towards formidable peasant societies proved unfeasible and counterproductive.

As archetypical subversives, Jews could easily be associated with Communism. As Marx was Jewish and some Jews had played a role in overthrowing the Czar, and as many Jewish intellectuals were prominent on the left, the association of Jews with Bolshevism personified the anxiety about a changing world order. Particularly in countries such as South Africa, where most immigrants from Eastern Europe were Jewish, suspicion and antipathy were fuelled by this labelling. As Shain points out, for the fledgling Afrikaner Nationalists in the 1930s, the Jew "symbolised all that was foreign and oppressive".[25] Here was an alien group that could be singled out as the unassailable enemy of the national aspirations of a downtrodden people despite the friendly attitudes toward Jewish traders visiting farms. This happened in almost all Western nationalist movements, from Czech to Quebec separatism. More than the anti-Christian imagery or even the ideological affinity of the 1930s nationalism around the world with Nazism, it was the contradictory stereotype of the Jewish exploiter that made anti-Semitism so appealing. The anti-Semite could easily reconcile the imagery of Bolshevism and capitalism in the common denominator of a political enemy to the emerging nationalist identity. Whether Jews were portrayed as super-capitalist exploiters ("Hoggenheimers"), deceitful traders and creditors with a questionable commercial morality, on the one hand, or as union organisers for the socialist cause, on the other, their activity combined to undermine the nationalist cause. Jews served an allegedly cosmopolitan cause – whether global capitalism or socialism.

While Jews were painted as alien exploiters, in the colonies blacks were perceived as inferior competitors by the European working class. In the vision of Afrikaner nationalists, blacks had to be protected from English-Jewish machinations designed to thwart Afrikaner goals. Blacks were considered too weak or too naive to withstand being used. Without legislation ensuring appropriate labour relations, Afrikaner nationalists correctly argued, the mining houses would prefer cheaper black labour over more troublesome Afrikaner workers. Hence, job reservation and "civilised labour policies" had to be imposed on "English-Jewish capitalists", in the interest of protecting white standards from falling to native levels. At the same time, it was also deemed necessary to protect the impressionable African psyche from foreign influences, be it the missionary education of liberals and Jewish communists or English-language universities. Hence, "bush colleges" were established from the mid-1960s where most of the teaching staff came from the Afrikaner civil service. There blacks were supposed to develop their own culture in hermetic isolation from the outside world. Little did the initiators of the tribal universities envisage the backlash in the form of the Black Consciousness Movement that aimed at psychological liberation from liberal and Afrikaner dominance alike. Jews were conceived as the embodiment of decadent Western liberalism. In this role they already dominated the English universities. "Noble savages" were to be immunised against this contamination by being made proud of their own culture.

In the "terrorist ANC" before 1990, Jewish communism and African nationalism had already merged in the "total onslaught". If they could only be separated, apartheid South Africa could be saved. Without the Slovos, Kasrils and Sachs (all Jewish) as mentors and instigators, the average white South African thought, blacks would be quite content with their assigned place. Moreover, they would be incapable of really threatening Pretoria were it not for foreign assistance aided by the moral exhortation of an Oppenheimer-controlled press and Jewish do-gooders such as Helen Suzman. Thus it is ironic that in post-apartheid South Africa white anti-Semitism has been replaced by occasional black stereotyping of Jews. Cosatu shop stewards' frequent attacks against "Jewish bosses" compete with Islamic solidarity with Palestinians in denouncing the 80 000 South African Jews as loyal to foreign rather than native interest. "Kill the Jews" and "Death to America" were the slogans as a crowd of Muslims moved on the Israeli embassy in Cape Town to burn the Star of David in March 1995. While some progressive Muslims disassociated themselves from such intolerance, no official condemnation was issued by the ANC government or other opinion-leaders.

A second irony lies in the fact that South Africa's peaceful transformation was saved in the end by the moderation of Slovo's SACP that allegedly sought to destroy the last bastion of Christian civilisation. Indeed, without the SACP's ingrained nonracialism, together with its push for reconciliation, power sharing and economic accommodation, African nationalism may well have dominated within the ANC. The great surprise for South African racists was the ANC's policy of reconciliation. The threatening Mandela changed into a saviour before incredulous eyes. More democratic and nonracial than its apartheid oppressors, the ANC suddenly turned all stereotypes about blacks on their heads. Asked about recent developments, the almost unanimous answer of South African whites reveals the bewilderment: "So far, it has gone far better than we ever expected." Only the metaphor of a miracle can "explain" what was not expected to happen in the first place: that the "semi-animals" (Herbert Vilakazi) do not seek revenge for being incarcerated and abused for so long.

Michael Ignatieff has observed that nationalism is at its most ferocious "where the group you are defining yourself against most closely resembles you".[26] Atrocities among neighbours baffle rational explanations. Indeed, Serbs and Croats speak the same language. Bosnian Serbs consider Bosnian Muslims as forcibly converted Serbs in disguise. The difference between an Irish Republican and an Ulster Protestant is only visible to the insider. Sephardic Jews and Palestinians are both Orientals in customs and lifestyle and cannot be distinguished from each other at first sight, yet many in each group consider their counterparts mortal enemies. The correlation between violence and likeness also seems to be confirmed by the contrasting South African case. Here the conflict *within* black and *within* white factions is far more intense than the relatively minor racial violence between blacks and whites. Despite apartheid oppression, counter-racism on the part of the victims of white racism always remained surprisingly weak: blacks and whites do not seem to hate each other. Race relations in South Africa are far better than in other divided societies.

An explanation of this paradox must go beyond the popular psychology that hate among kin exceeds contempt for strangers because "hatred is a form of love turned against itself".[27] Psychoanalysis views rejection of others as resulting from projection of one's own dangerous impulses onto outsiders. This mechanism succeeds best when the other resembles oneself. Visible racial differences usually make for great social distance but hardly generate the nationalist fervour that views the other as the cause of one's downfall. Colonial racism is based more on social distance than on fear or hate. In the colonial situation, the racist sees himself as superior. This superiority does not lend itself to envy which is a powerful motivation in nationalist mobilisation and anti-Semitism.

Likeness also sheds light on the difference between Nazi anti-Semitism and anti-black racism. Supremacists the world over want to put blacks in their place but seek to stop Jews from living altogether. People of colour are despised as incompetent and lazy, but Jews are considered to be too clever, engaged in a grand conspiracy to control the world. Supremacists feel threatened by a tiny minority of Jews but not by a majority of blacks. It was because European Jews were so well integrated in their host society – as "German" as their tormentors – that the invisibles were made visible as scapegoats. Along with other minorities, Jews are denounced as clannish, aloof and distant, but at the same time they are also accused of sneaking about in disguise to hide subversive activities. A cheat is portrayed as being both weak and strong. This contradiction is best communicated with the metaphor of a parasitic vermin. The dehumanised other is dangerous to the body politic if not watched, yet the virus can be stamped out with vigilance and ideological protection. Mobilised against a poisonous cancer, every right-minded citizen has a duty to be as watchful as in the protection of individual health.

There are elements of a manufactured threat also in the perception of blacks by whites. For example, Africans are frequently equated with snakes that can bite, unexpectedly, the hand that feeds them. Therefore, segregation and social distance should be adopted as precautions. Overwhelmingly, however, the colonial mind denigrates the conquered other as "semi-animal" in the evolutionary hierarchy. Primitive, wild, sexually permissive and uncontrollable in their breeding, the semi-animal has to be tamed. An early apartheid edict defined Bantu education as an attempt to stop blacks from wanting "to graze" in white areas. To this day, mine management characterises its migrant worker informally as "raw natives". A strong hand and authoritarian rule can easily achieve this task, unlike the much more complex measures necessary toward smart Jews, who are out to control the world through money and Hollywood manipulation. Black male bodies are portrayed as physically strong, unspoiled examples of natural beauty. To this day, South African tourist advertisements display bare-breasted Zulu maidens in the same ways Lenni Riefenstahl – the superb creator of fascist aesthetics – in her later period glorified perfect Nubian bodies. Jewish bodies, on the other hand, are always caricatured as shrunken, bent, hook-nosed examples of degenerate brains.

The anti-Semite supremacist sees his moral order undermined from within; the anti-black racist condescendingly stands on guard against "the return of the bush" from without. Therefore, the neocolonial attitude toward Africa borders on pity and charity. So-called underdeveloped and inherently violent people are encouraged to adopt civilised rules. According to anti-Semites, Jews are overdeveloped and their wings have to be clipped. The dichotomy between superior Jews and inferior blacks as two sides of the racist coin can be illustrated with the treatment of artistic representations ascribed to the two outcasts. The Nazis distinguished between "healthy" (German) art and degenerate (Jewish/alien) art. No clear criteria existed for this arbitrary distinction, emanating from the whims of leaders and the expectations of a philistine public. In this judgement, the degenerate art bordered on the insane. It contradicted *gesunde volksempfinden* (healthy popular sentiment) nowadays called nebulously "community standards".

While Jews were depicted as cultivating an overdeveloped, mad imagination, blacks were perceived as possessing an underdeveloped, primitive art. Allegedly, Bushman paintings and Michelangelo frescos could not be compared. For the extreme racist, blacks were incapable of artistic performance altogether, save drumming, dancing and singing as part of their natural character. The Nazis even considered the complex jazz of African Americans a primitive import, in contrast with the classical symphonies of European composers. Where were the great black painters, writers or architects that a rich European tradition had produced? If slavery and colonialism had destroyed indigenous culture, where was the evidence of art from pre-colonial times? Such Eurocentric questioning not only displayed ignorance about the survival conditions of hunting and gathering societies and the material technology and social arrangements in subsistence economies, but disregarded a rich oral tradition. For example, it insisted on a Zulu Tolstoi as a precondition for taking Zulu culture seriously. Nowadays the frantic search for township painters in South Africa or the successful marketing of indigenous airport art the world over merely represents the other side of the same coin. Political correctness now demands ethnicising fashions and home furnishing as displays of nonracial relativism – regardless of quality.

The reactions of the targets of anti-Semitic and anti-black racism also differed widely. Much has been written about the Jewish "lack of prescience as to their dismal future".[28] As Max Horkheimer has remarked, so integrated and assimilated were German Jews that the worst anti-Semitism occurred in the society that was the least anti-Semitic. German citizens of Jewish origin who had fought patriotically in World War I had long before converted to Christianity or abandoned Judaism for a secular agnosticism. They simply could not anticipate that they would be singled out on the basis of ancestry for having had one Jewish grandparent. The relative lack of resistance that haunts survivors and descendants in Israel alike has not characterised the victims of anti-black racism. The physical difference, the segregation and social distance that accompanied even the most paternalistic colonial racism always sustained a consciousness of difference. While blacks have internalised the definitions of their oppressors to various degrees at various times, a colonial hegemony has not been achieved anywhere. In the US, the uprooted slaves obviously found it more difficult to establish a separate cultural identity in an all-pervasive consumer culture than people subjugated in their own territory and in possession of their own language and ethnic traditions as in South Africa. Covert resistance against unfair treatment characterised racial contact from the days of the early Cape Colony.

A consciousness of watchful scepticism toward the designs of the superordinate always marked the subordinates' attitudes in the colonial context. Distrust of promises of liberation shaped political activists' minds, quite apart from the fact that the option of assimilation was not available to non-whites. Thus the apartheid system allowed South African Jews full integration as white, while slightly darker middlemen groups who were similarly stereotyped, such as South African Indians, were increasingly segregated. When scapegoat minorities come to occupy specialised economic positions, they serve as ready targets for the less fortunate majority population. Like the Jews, the Asians in East and South Africa, the Armenians in Turkey, the Chinese in Malaysia and Vietnam and the Lebanese in West Africa form so-called middlemen minorities on the basis of their dominant role in distinct economic activities. Without the political power and the network of social connections of the culturally different majority, these trading minorities find themselves in a tenuous position, despite common citizenship and attempts at political identification with the majority. Their insecurity also leads to frequent alternative life planning (children's education abroad, foreign accounts, bribery), which in turn gives rise to accusations of disloyalty from the dominant group. It is the weakness of middlemen minorities that has led to the worst state atrocities against these tenuously placed ethnic outsiders, of which Jews are the classical example.

In light of this structural ambiguity, scapegoat/middlemen minorities have tended to cultivate cultural narcissism when faced with hostility. Exclusivism, endogamy, self-help, and cultural revivalism

49

become the armour that permits them to survive in a hostile environment. These communities have acquired few psychological scars. They have immunised themselves, so to speak, from the outside stigmatisation by withdrawing into their own psychological and material world. The success stories of Indians in South Africa, of Palestinians in the Gulf States, and of Chinese migrants in South Asia, bear testimony to a remarkable adaptation despite racism and intense discrimination. In short, it is not so much the cultural tradition of a group as the social environment, epitomised in state policies, that activates or lays to rest cultural heritage. In summary, like Jews in the Diaspora, scapegoated middlemen minorities have, through their cultural strength, partially succeeded in overcoming discrimination, despite a hostile social environment.

In post-apartheid South African cities, urbanised blacks also display little of the deference toward whites, the fawning over and obsequiousness that guided widespread slave survival in paternalistic race relations in the US south. Nor are South African blacks inspired by an obsessive search for identity, conversion to a liberating Islam or pilgrimages to African roots that make the headlines among an atomised black population in the US. Africans in South Africa know their roots – they never lost them – and therefore they need not partake in the reiteration of black values and the lament about loss and neglect. Above all, black self-respect is reinforced by majority status and political power that their US counterparts lack. A most intriguing question, therefore, concerns the behaviour of anti-black racists when power relations are reversed. No Nazi would ever have served under a Jewish president. Nazi-Jewish power sharing would have been inconceivable, even under the most trying circumstances. Nazi ideology could not liberalise itself as other totalitarian and authoritarian systems successfully did when pressed. While Nazism was an irrational ideology which at its core bore the seeds of its own destruction, colonial racism, even in its elaborated apartheid application, adapted to new realities.

Chapter Three

How did South Africa talk itself through a revolution?

There are not many cases where a privileged ethnic minority has negotiated itself out of power. Even more rare seem situations where a dominant ethnic minority loses power *peacefully* to a different ethnic majority with whom it now has to co-exist in the same state, despite a legacy of past discrimination and accumulated bitterness. The few examples that come to mind include the English in Québec, the Russians in the Baltic Republics and the Chinese in Malaysia. However, in all these cases, the option of relocation or support and protection of fellow ethnic minorities by neighbouring ethnic mother states facilitated the transfer. Only in the Afrikaner case does the new ethnic minority stand entirely on its own.

How did this extraordinary case of dramatic, peaceful capitulation come about? Contrary to almost every available stereotype about the modal personality type of the Afrikaner, when the chips were down, Afrikaner negotiators meekly handed over power without even seriously attempting to bargain any special group privileges. Pre-transitional analyses abound, describing the Afrikaner's obduracy, brutality and almost suicidal instinct for self-preservation and collective survival. A variety of strategies, apart from bloody revolution, were concocted to ease a minority out of power: sham consociationalism, confederation, partial partition. None seriously considered the possibility that Afrikaners would enthusiastically, through consensus-seeking negotiations, help to construct a process of dislodging themselves from power and into a liberal democratic constitution. They even agreed that political decision making should be based on unqualified majority rule, knowing full well that this would be exercised by black South Africans whom they had subjected to systematic apartheid domination for decades. Why?

One could go through a list of external predisposing structural conditions: the collapse of communism, increasing international isolation, the settlements in Angola and Namibia and increasing global pressure for negotiated conflict resolution. Similarly, on the internal situation the same can be done: accelerating economic decline, increasing polarisation, industrial action and violent opposition leading to escalating costs of servicing domination. One could argue rationally that the very absence of relocation – "nowhere to go" – must be seen as a main reason for compromise. The risk of destroying a country in civil war is more readily entertained if resettlement in a former homeland remains an alternative. This clearly happened in the Algerian and Rhodesian cases. The risks of civil war are much higher, however, if you have to live with the consequences. Thus the argument goes that, faced with a racial war, South African whites opted for negotiations precisely because there existed no other way out of an existential predicament. Settlers who had become indigenous finally realised that they had to co-exist on equal terms with the disenfranchised, even if this meant losing political power, but falling short of a destructive war that neither side could win.

It could also be pointed out that the dispersal of the white minority throughout South Africa facilitated the "no choice but negotiate" option. Unlike minorities attached to a historical territory, the option of partition, except in the most sacrificial symbolic sense, did not exist for the ruling minority. Creating a separate ethno-racial entity of sufficient size and scope through internal migration would have involved the relocation of great numbers of people, an alternative that most advocates of a "Boerestaat" or "Volkstaat" themselves were unwilling to pursue voluntarily.

No doubt all of the above factors, and others, were relevant to creating a climate conducive for negotiations. But they had been known and used in analyses for decades before actual negotiations started. What made 1990 special?

There is very little doubt that if P.W. Botha or Magnus Malan or Gerrit Viljoen had been president in 1990, the National Party would still be in power today and we would still be treated to anecdotes of Afrikaner obduracy and will to self-determination. No doubt, new, innovative and unworkable strategies would have been devised to create the illusion of sharing power without losing any, which was the hallmark of the co-optive domination of the Tri-Cameral Parliament instituted in 1984. There is very little doubt that the Afrikaner minority as represented by the National Party could have dominated into the 21st century if it had so wished. Undoubtedly at considerable cost to the country and the region. Why did they not?

The answer must surely be found in the autocratic style of leadership of the National Party and in the personality of De Klerk. The National Party as a political machine governed through its caucus in Parliament and the caucus in turn was governed by the Cabinet, which in turn was governed by the leadership, at the apex of which was the President or Leader. It was a profoundly undemocratic organisation when it came to policy shifts and dispensing patronage. Certainly the election of the Leader by the caucus took place democratically and was preceded by intense lobbying, but once elected, he (a female leader would have been out of the question in the patriarchal Afrikaner culture) had extraordinary discretion and those who had not voted for him knew that their political careers had come to an end for the time being.

Most important, some major policy shifts in the National Party were never properly caucused or subjected to provincial or rank and file approval. Verwoerd almost unilaterally announced the homeland policy in a three-hour speech in Parliament, Botha's conditional offer of release to Mandela visibly caught the Nat Caucus members by surprise and the shift to a Tri-Cameral Constitution was certainly not understood or properly debated within Nationalist Party ranks. The referendum outcome in the 1983 vote was more "for a step in the right direction" than for the nonexistent merits of the Tri-Cameral Constitution. In short, a determined and small leadership cadre could move in policy directions which were, if not in direct contradiction to the party line, certainly way beyond what was ever contemplated by the rank and file supporters of the party.

There is ample and comprehensive evidence that De Klerk's speech on 2 February 1990, announcing the unconditional release of Mandela, the unbanning of the ANC, the scrapping of key apartheid laws and the onset of open-ended negotiations, was a sellout of everything the National Party had held near and dear since 1948. Certainly, if those options had been put to a popular vote amongst whites generally and rank and file Nationalist Party members in particular, there was not the slightest possibility that they would have been carried.[1] Election after election since 1948 provided ample evidence for this. The subsequent referendum which De Klerk won with a two-thirds majority was again not about the substance of some negotiated constitution but that the whites should express themselves in favour of continued negotiations. "Negotiations Yes, Surrender No" read the NP referendum posters. But by then transitional politics had developed its own compelling logic and would have been impossible to reverse.

The autocratic culture of National Party decision making provided the backdrop within which the Leader, De Klerk, exercised a choice. He may have consulted with a few trusted colleagues, but it is extremely doubtful whether he canvassed widely within the various structures of the party. It was more a case of De Klerk precipitating the process of capitulation and his supporters then following him in a process that developed a kind of telescopic ineluctable logic where each step narrowed down the options of the next step.

Why did he do it? Was it the action of a political visionary or a case of serious miscalculation? De Klerk was one of apartheid's most eloquent, intelligent and articulate defenders right up to his own election as Leader of the National Party. Party colleagues cite many instances where he opposed even some of the limited reforms attempted by his predecessors. By his own confession, he underwent a "spiritual leap" (*geestelike sprong*) once he became Leader. This moral shift was accompanied by a sense of shrewd political expediency. Sensing that, because of the collapse of Communism, the ANC had lost a very important resource base and patronage, he thought that he could bring them into negotiations in a much weaker state. He certainly developed a vision once he had made the speech on 2 February, but he seriously miscalculated his own and his government's capacity to control the pursuit of this vision. He and his government never dreamt at the outset that everything would be over by 27 April 1994. One of his colleagues told us in confidence that they thought they could keep the ANC negotiating for at least five years whilst the National Party government governed the ANC support base away from them. However, once the Nationalists had agreed to Slovo's proposal of an election date *before* having settled most contentious issues, they had handed the initiative to their opponents and had to go along with their proposals.

This miscalculation was compounded by the manner in which De Klerk chopped and changed his key negotiators. He started off with tough conservative persons like Gerrit Viljoen and Tertius Delport but eventually they were replaced by Leon Wessels and Roelf Meyer who were much more amenable and susceptible to the rhetoric and assumptions of liberal democracy. They were soundly outmanoeuvred by their ANC counterparts Cyril Ramaphosa, Valli Moosa and Joe Slovo. De Klerk kept at arm's length from the negotiations and was often confronted with concessions made that were extremely difficult to reverse.

In short, given all the external and internal factors conducive to negotiations, what made the critical difference from the dominant Afrikaner minority's side in the transition was an autocratic leadership style within the National Party, the personality of De Klerk that combined a newly experienced moral shift with political expediency and a strategic miscalculation as well as susceptible negotiators who were outmanoeuvred in terms of the logic and assumptions of majoritarian democracy.

But, it could legitimately be asked, why did Afrikaners in particular and the white minority in general not revolt against this political abdication? Given all the dire predictions which accompanied white racial elections for decades about the dangers of black domination and swamping, even the threat of physical survival, it would have been reasonable to expect some form of resistance or even rebellion. For a brief moment before the April 1994 elections, it seemed as if the far right would unite behind Constand Viljoen of the Freedom Front, but after the traumatic debacle of Mmabatho the right split terminally. Constand Viljoen even participated in the elections and became leader and member of a parliamentary party. To better understand this development, it is useful to refer to some of our theoretical insights discussed earlier.

South Africa represents a multi-ethnic society where elements of indigenous people, immigrants and competing nationalities co-exist in the same state. Africans, whether white, coloured, Asian or black perceive of themselves as indigenous to various degrees. South Africa also attracts a large number of (illegal) immigrants with which it deals by deportation rather than integration. Above all, competing ethno-racial nationalities (Afrikaner, Zulu) with their own distinct institutions and traditions co-exist side by side in an interdependent economy and now, in an evolving fragile democracy.

Afrikaner Nationalists' closest equivalents elsewhere are not Israeli or Ulster Unionists, as they are frequently portrayed, but Quebec separatists. The ancestors of both Afrikaners and Québecois settled on foreign shores more than 300 years ago and therefore their descendants lost all links to the homeland. Both were defeated by British forces and threatened with cultural assimilation. They felt colonised and developed a strong national identity in response to subjugation and pressure for Anglicisation. As poor "cousins of the Empire" (Dan O'Meara)[2] and in the thrall of an almighty church, both agrarian peoples joined the industrial revolution late. In "a quiet revolution", they successfully liberated themselves psychologically, educationally and economically by using the state to get ahead. However, while Quebec separatists are only in control of provincial power so far, and constrained by the Federal State, Afrikaner nationalists had achieved their goal of exclusive state power by 1948. Yet as a minority of less than 10 per cent of the state's population (as opposed to 25 per cent Québecois in Canada), Afrikaners in 1994 finally relinquished state power. The first thing to grasp however is that they had it and they used it.

In the second place, one has to understand the position of a disempowered privileged minority. The entire literature on minority rights focuses on relatively powerless minorities that were previously discriminated against and who strove for greater equality. An academic discourse on the legitimate rights of privileged minorities has yet to be established. All seventeen articles in "The Rights of Minority Cultures" in the Kymlicka[3] collection either deal with ethnic minorities in the abstract-legal sense or assume that minorities are always powerless by definition. Most analyses fail to take the socio-economic position of a minority and its history into account. If a privileged minority situation results from past conquest or administrative confiscation of land, for example, does a constitutional protection of all property relations not freeze unjust acquisition? Likewise, all international guidelines for minority protection recommend the right of mother-tongue instruction and religious education. However, if tests of religious affinity or language competency are used to bar other students and preserve privilege for own group members, can an absolute right of mother-tongue instruction be claimed? Alternatively, has a new ethno-cultural segment the right to insist on its own language preference, thereby changing the institution's traditional character so cherished by the previously dominant group? These are not hypothetical questions but were two of three core issues of bargaining during the final South African constitutional negotiations between the National Party and the ANC in May 1996.

The relevance of the theoretical distinction of the position of a previously dominant privileged minority refers to the Afrikaners' exclusive control of the state in 1948 which was used to vastly improve their socio-economic position vis-à-vis other groups in South Africa. Afrikaners came to power poor, and abdicated it vastly more affluent. However, not all Afrikaners were equally wealthy. Much research shows that the intensity of ethnic identification correlates strongly with socio-economic position. In other words, the poorer one is, the easier it is to sense an ethnic threat from economic competitors. It was not the Afrikaner working class but a self-confident bourgeoisie that had captured control of the party and the key positions of state. To put it bluntly, the affluent Afrikaners sold out the poorer Afrikaners because they felt more confident about their ability to either survive in, or leave "the new South Africa". The poorer Afrikaners, politically represented by the Freedom Front (Viljoen), the Conservative Party (Hartzenberg) and the AWB (Terre'-Blanche), would have liked to prevent the abdication, but they lacked the very instruments that the affluent Afrikaners were negotiating away. Even if they wished to, there was very little they could have achieved in the light of overwhelming state power. Some of them placed a few bombs on election day, were arrested and sentenced to long terms of imprisonment. The rest were reduced to bargaining some kind of cultural, territorial or communal enclave before the constitution became finalised. Unlike in Northern Ireland, where the Protestant working class substantially shapes Ulster politics and thereby prevents the Protestant bourgeoisie from making a deal with Irish nationalists and Britain, a reverse relationship was in place in South Africa. For self-confident senior civil servants, professionals, academics and Afrikaner business executives, ethnic ideologies had faded. A wide variety of individualistic identities had taken the place of collective security which had become an albatross in light of the new legitimacy that a reconciled South Africa promised to bestow on cosmopolitan minds. This section of the Afrikaner elite was liberated by its own success in ethnic mobilisation and could hardly see itself as a victim of self-initiated negotiations with a weak ANC.

In short, affluent Afrikaners increasingly became indistinguishable from other affluent whites. Almost all whites already lived among their fellow white South Africans in affluent suburbs, city centres and small towns due to the previous legal ethno-racial cleansing under the Group Areas Act. Further irredentism, the gathering of all people with the same ethnic outlook in the same territory, appeared superfluous. As long as capital was locked in, emigration proved an option only for a minority of younger, highly educated professionals. Thus the newly disempowered minority in South Africa still commands vast material and cultural capital that had been accumulated during its previous dominance. The key political question for the future will undoubtedly be: how is the impoverished majority ever to achieve a semblance of equality if the historical discrepancies remain sacrosanct in the name of minority rights? The affluent Afrikaners, led by De Klerk and his negotiators, peacefully negotiated away their position of ethnic dominance on the gamble that these historical discrepancies would be a long time in disappearing and would, in any case, be protected by the rights culture of a liberal democracy. Given the global predominance of a competitive market economy as the preferred mechanism to generate wealth and the political predominance of liberal democracy, this was not an unreasonable gamble. However, it meant that the poorer Afrikaners were left to fend for themselves in a vastly more hostile and competitive environment. They will be the obvious victims of affirmative action taken by the new rulers of the state. Whatever kind of ethno-racial mobilisation will take place in the future will come from this section of the Afrikaner community. But then, they will be no different from other deprived and powerless minorities which have been the real focus of the literature, except that the poor Afrikaners have lost the support of the better-off group members who normally lead an ethno-nationalist mobilisation.

This accounts for how the Afrikaner minority helped to talk South Africa through a revolution. But what about the other side? It could not have happened unilaterally. Stereotypes about Afrikaner intransigence were matched by similar views of the ANC as a liberation movement that would "never compromise" ("victory had to be final and complete", "a negotiation table is no substitute for the battlefield", "colonial humiliation demands the defeat of the coloniser in order to establish the dignity of the oppressed"). Convincing evidence is available that the leadership of the ANC, particularly in exile, became increasingly militant in their convictions on how transition away from racial domination would and should take place. The conference in Kabwe in Zambia in 1985 adopted a four-pronged strategy for the "National Democratic Revolution" consisting of armed struggle, international isolation, underground operations and mass mobilisation.

Armed struggle was eulogised as the vanguard of the strategy. At the same time, the general ideological position became far more uncompromising: the political system would be a "people's democracy" based on the principles of democratic centralism and the "commanding heights" of the economy would be "seized" and transformed into a socialist economy where the state and the workers would own and control the means of production.

Eventually, the ANC ended up working for a negotiated rather than a revolutionary transfer of power, a liberal democratic constitution and a competitive market economy with privatisation of state assets as official economic policy instead of nationalisation and redistribution. How did this come about?

Again, the predisposing structural conditions mentioned earlier, both external and internal, have to be taken into account. However, one of them on the external side needs to be singled out as far as the ANC is concerned. There is no doubt that the strategic options for "the struggle" were intimately tied to the fortunes of East European Communism and the Soviet Union and the ANC-in-exile's relationship with specific countries in this group. The rapprochement between Reagan and Gorbachev in 1985 led to their agreeing not to allow what they perceived to be "regional conflicts" to lead to confrontation between themselves. This had a profound impact on the settlement in Afghanistan, Angola and Namibia. By the end of the 80s exporting revolution (i.e. "armed struggle") was out and negotiated settlements were in. This was certainly not lost on the ANC leadership in exile who were strategically divided between the pragmatists who wished to explore the possibilities of negotiation and the hardliners who insisted on "transition through attrition".

It is still difficult to adequately analyse the impact of the October

1989 collapse of the Berlin Wall on the ANC at the time. One thing is certain: internationally it was heralded as the ideological and political collapse of organised communism, and there was a spirit of (premature) triumphalism and the vindication of capitalism. If nothing else, this must have created dismay and confusion amongst the SACP who were, in the words of Mandela, "highly valued and staunch allies of the ANC" during the long years of struggle.

However, what was not in dispute and was even in ideological ascendance, perhaps because of the foregoing developments, was the ANC's commitment to nonracialism. Undoubtedly the Communists within the alliance must get the lion's share of the credit for this. Within the non-communist ranks of the ANC this philosophy was accepted with varying degrees of enthusiasm, but was never seriously in doubt as far as the ANC leadership was concerned. It was this characteristic more than anything else which facilitated and engendered enormous international support across national interests and ideological predispositions as far as democracy and the economy were concerned. Communists and capitalists, liberals and socialists, united behind the essentially nonracial struggle for liberation of the ANC. It was in this atmosphere of intense international support for a negotiated settlement and a nonracial outcome, as well as the ideological retreat and confusion of Communism internationally and within the ANC, that Mandela was unconditionally released.

As in the case of De Klerk, the person and leadership of Mandela had a profound impact on the outcome of negotiations. But unlike De Klerk, Mandela could and did exploit the prevailing mood like a master technician. His personal legitimacy, born out of his prolonged incarceration and increased by his personal style of magnanimity and lack of bitterness and sense of retribution, exploded exponentially after his visit to the USA (his first, significantly, after his release) and all the other visits, amongst others when he received the Nobel Peace Prize with De Klerk. It is the "Mandela factor" which De Klerk, understandably, had miscalculated as well. As a national and international figure, De Klerk was simply not in the same league.

Very soon after Mandela's release, the armed struggle and international isolation were sacrificed on the new altar of negotiated transition. But, again unlike De Klerk, Mandela appointed an uninterrupted team of negotiators in Ramaphosa, Moosa and Slovo. Backed by the strategic expertise of Mbeki these were pragmatists and shrewd analysts of the unfolding transition. Slovo in particular played a crucial role after the breakdown of CODESA 2. He saw quite clearly that De Klerk was heading for capitulation and that the transfer of power could be peacefully negotiated. Thus, he proposed power sharing for five years and a re-opening of negotiations at a multi-party forum. Internally, the ANC negotiators could depend on the leadership keeping the militants and ideologues in check. In a sense Mandela and his negotiators sold out the "National Democratic Revolution", whereas De Klerk and his negotiators sold out Afrikaner minority domination. The one sacrificed ideological purity and correctness, the other political power. The negotiated outcome was a liberal democratic constitution which neither had ever seriously believed in or was quite sure it wanted.

Stripped of all the rhetorical extravagance, what comes out in compelling simplicity in Patti Waldmeir's effusive account, is how an elite conspiracy emerged between both sides, quite willingly, to keep their respective constituents in the dark about how they were bargaining away fundamental policy positions that they had promised were completely non-negotiable. This was as true for the ANC as for the NP, but much more so for the latter. As Cyril Ramaphosa put it, "sufficient consensus means, if we and the NP agree, everyone else can get stuffed" (p. 41) (including the bulk of their supporters). The negotiators on both sides had indoctrinated, manipulated and coerced their followers to accept "the line", i.e. the resolvability of the conflict *on their own terms*. When the elite or leadership on both sides agreed that this could not be done because of a commonly accepted stalemate, they were progressively forced to deceive the expectations of their constituents through negotiations.

Out of such mundane and ignoble origins, democracy is born. Not out of some grand inclusive democratic process. Put simply, the process leading up to democracy does not have to be, in fact more often is not, democratic in order to produce democracy. This was so in Chile, Poland, Russia and elsewhere. However, if one took at face value in the South African case what each side was promising to deliver to their respective constituents, then what actually happened must seem a bit like a miracle. But then reality often is stranger than fiction, especially if the fiction is ideologically inspired.

South Africa was fortunate that it had the political leaders who were prepared to compromise away the dogmatic convictions of their followers and open the way to a democratic outcome. Mandela provided extraordinary moral and political leadership in this regard. He never wavered for one moment in what he wanted – a simple majority rule democracy. For that he would compromise on economic policy, the civil service and transitional arrangements. His negotiating team was never in any doubt as to what they had to do – they may sometimes have doubted whether they would achieve it, but never what they had to achieve.

De Klerk on the other hand, lost it early on. Even in a largely homogenous society like Chile, Pinochet extracted far tougher concessions from the civilian political leadership – the so-called "authoritarian enclaves". It became increasingly difficult to understand what De Klerk thought he could pull off. Right to the end he refused to recognise the inevitability of majority rule, as Waldmeir puts it: "to this day" (p. 149). And yet, his chief negotiator, Roelf Meyer, "once morality and ambition had set him on the road to majority rule, pursued it with a vigour and commitment not shared by anyone else in the National Party" (p. 209). To a large extent the other key facilitators/negotiators, S.S. van der Merwe and Leon Wessels, did the same. What Waldmeir shows clearly was how De Klerk's negotiators were really part of Mandela's team in facilitating the transition to majority rule. In the end it was a push-over. Through it all De Klerk was convinced he could unleash and manage a process with which he refused to come to terms.

It would be a serious omission in trying to give an account of how South Africa talked itself through a revolution if the role of the Freedom Front under the leadership of General Constand Viljoen and the Inkatha Freedom Party under the leadership of Mangosuthu Buthelezi were not considered. Both represented the clearest cases of politicised ethnicity, i.e. nationalism in the South African context, and both certainly had the capacity to wreck, if not the negotiations, then certainly the subsequent elections. No doubt, without their participation in those elections the outcome would have been seriously questioned internationally as well as domestically.

Both boycotted the negotiation process. Viljoen, former head of the South African Defence Force, was and still is, a reluctant politician, and only became one when he saw what he called "the inevitable sellout" of the Afrikaner. His initial response was to prepare for civil war and with the formation of the Transitional Executive Council he had trained men under arms with arms caches stashed all over the country at strategic points. When the TEC confronted Mangope with his inevitable demise in Bophuthatswana, Viljoen rushed to his aid to provide him military support. However, the banditry and recklessness of Terre'Blanche leading the AWB on the same mission so disillusioned Viljoen that he broke away from that strategic option and decided to explore negotiated ways to achieve his objectives. Mandela from the outset had a shrewd and deep appreciation of the threat that Viljoen and the Freedom Front posed, and pulled him into whatever bilateral discussions he could. Even today, should Viljoen get out of politics altogether, it would be short-sighted to overlook the disruptive potential of the Afrikaners who follow him.

Since 1979, as a result of a crucial meeting between Tambo and Buthelezi in London, the ways of the ANC and the IFP developed in an adversarial direction. Buthelezi was formally promoting the IFP as a national nonracial inclusive political movement, but practically his support base remains predominantly confined to KwaZulu-Natal and is largely dependent on the traditional, more ethnically exclusive Zulus. From the outset Buthelezi has transferred the threat that the ANC's National Democratic Revolution seemed to constitute for him personally as well as his traditional support base to the way in which the ANC conducted negotiations. In particular, Buthelezi was deeply suspicious that once in power the ANC would abuse the provisions of a liberal democratic constitution to entrench themselves in power and suppress minorities like himself. This was the precise reason why Buthelezi withdrew Inkatha from negotiations.

Throughout the negotiations, his absence was felt and consistently analysed. Would his lack of concurrence be translated into violent disruption and opposition? It was when he threatened not to participate in the elections that the possibility of disruptive violence became accepted as almost inevitable. No one is quite sure how and why Buthelezi decided to participate, but the fact that he did was crucial for the peaceful nature of the elections and for the general acceptability of the outcome.

So in short, how did South Africa talk itself through a revolution? As we have tried to indicate, apart from the structurally conducive factors which predisposed parties toward negotiations, there were a number of key factors without which it would not have been possible. They were:

1. The autocratic leadership style of the National Party in power;
2. The personality of De Klerk, his moral shift and vision, his political expediency and his strategic miscalculations;
3. The quality of the negotiators that De Klerk appointed and how they were outmanoeuvred by their opponents;
4. The fall of communism and the international revulsion against terror and armed struggle;
5. The person of Mandela, his extraordinary qualities of leadership;
6. The quality of the negotiators he appointed and how they out-manoeuvred their opponents;
7. Viljoen refraining from violence and ethnic mobilisation and Buthelezi participating in the election at the last minute.

These are the factors that, at the end of the day, really made the difference.

Academic analysts of democratisation and compromise in South Africa can be crudely classified as pessimists or optimists. The pessimists point to the absence of social requisites for the consolidation of a liberal democracy: sufficient broad-based economic development and national homogeneity. They stress the communal nature of the power struggle and the deep ethno-racial divisions hidden behind a facade of nonracialism. The ANC's project of building a common South African nation is distrusted as a Jacobean design to subjugate the Afrikaans- and Zulu-speaking minorities by imposing English-medium education instead of allowing true federalism and genuine multiculturalism. Politically South Africa is said to be heading toward a one-party dominant system along Mexican lines with a weak opposition and high levels of corruption. In the absence of a floating vote, due to a high degree of ethnic voting, South Africa, the pessimists assert, lacks the democratic precondition of alternating parties in power. For all these reasons, Hermann Giliomee, for example, maintains that "the evolution of a liberal democracy is most unlikely and tensions within and between ethnic groups will be managed with great difficulty by a single dominant party".

The optimists doubt the significance of deep ethno-racial divisions. They stress common bonds in an interdependent economy. Ethnic voting for example, they argue, derives from perceptions of common material and symbolic interests rather than the assertion of racial identity. The optimists give the ANC far more credit for achieving a multi-party democracy with progressive civil rights and a vibrant civil society despite the legacy of apartheid. Class divisions and labour relations are managed with a new innovative system of negotiated co-determination whose success or failure shapes the prospects of South African democracy far more decisively than anxieties over cultural identity.

In answering the question. how did South Africa talk itself through a revolution?, there is enough to feed the preferences and convictions of both pessimists and optimists. What has become clear, however, is that whichever you are, the dogmatists have invariably been wrong.

Chapter Four

The first elections in South Africa:
What miracle?

It is easily forgotten that two elections, both national in scope and organisation, took place in South Africa between 1994 and 1996. The first involved elections for national and provincial governments, the second for local or municipal governments. The second set of elections may yet prove to be more profound in their impact for successful transition than the first. A more technical analysis of the difference between the two will highlight this. In fact, if the over-used word "miracle" has any relevance, then it is that both elections took place in the technically organised sense at all. Certainly there was nothing highly astonishing or unpredictable in voting patterns and voter turnout in either of the elections.

In a sense, it is understandable that the 1994 elections provided fertile soil for hyperbole and breathless adjectival extravagance. They received unprecedented media coverage. Hagiographies of Mandela alternated with images of racial reconciliation in the streets and all South Africans embracing each other and Western liberal democracy. The entire world appeared to have projected its own deep-seated stereotypes and anxieties onto the country. The interpretation of the live drama by various observers revealed much about the global state of mind, the supposed role of race and ethnicity, the merits of reform versus revolution and the possibilities of peace, economic improvement and ultimately, human solidarity in a divided world. For a brief moment, the world basked in the unanticipated benign consequences of a paradigmatic melt-down.

Among the more sensitive foreign observers envy prevailed. Some wished to be South African during these elections. In this vein, Canadian columnist Michael Valpy mourned: "There was, there is, no struggle in my own sullen little country, and hence no collective purpose, no struggle to build a better society, or protect the society we have. To talk about Canadian culture invites mostly sneers and hostility."

The most common foreign reaction to South Africa's successful 1994 electoral transition also revealed much about the prejudicial mind-set of the observers. Instead of the expected bloodbath, a peaceful election. Instead of an unravelling state as in Yugoslavia, South Africa engaged in nation-building. Africa was not supposed to change through rules of democratic liberalism. In the Western racist mind, "civilised" Bosnia should be a haven of peace, whilst "primitive" Africa revels in tribal warfare.

Such mind-sets were not confined to foreign observers. One of South Africa's own perceptive journalists, a celebrated Afrikaans author, stated as an empirical fact: "We are Africans, riddled with ethnic and tribal sentiment. We do not trust each other. We have no great vision to unite us, no shared myths to light our way. We can barely communicate because we have no languages in common." Rian Malan, the author of the riveting *My Traitor's Heart*, also expects the liberal constitution to fail, because it makes no provision for ethnicity (*Style*, May 1994).

As befits a "miracle", many South Africans explained the peaceful elections by citing divine intervention. They would probably agree with the editor of *The Sowetan*: "The factors that influence Mangosuthu Buthelezi and changed his mind, do not make rational sense. No, it needed an act of God, and it was." Of course, it could be argued in far more secular terms that Buthelezi had to choose between the political wilderness and participation; that the Zulu Royal House had indicated its willingness to accept the ANC offer and the land deal signed by the De Klerk government; that some influential Inkatha Central Committee members were keen to get elected rather than face political oblivion under an ANC-controlled central government and, finally, that Inkatha in control of KwaZulu-Natal through an election deal seemed preferable to a divided civil service in Ulundi, and were sceptical of labouring under a more remote and alien paymaster in Pretoria.

However, the underlying religious sentiment in South Africa, bolstered through decades of redemptive political rhetoric from different political persuasions expecting different forms of eschatological liberation, could also partially explain the mass appeal of Mandela as a saviour. Crucified for a large part of his life, he nevertheless emerged triumphantly in a political resurrection. Like Jesus, he sacrificed his life for his people who now felt obliged to reward him with their devotion. This made the 1994 elections more a celebration of liberation than a judgement on competing political virtues. Unlike Arafat who became exposed as fallible during his reign as a voice of his people, the long imprisoned silence of Mandela only increased his mystique. Most analysts expected Mandela's appeal to evaporate during the four-year long negotiations. Horse trading normally does not elicit admiration. Yet Mandela achieved a surprising increase in his popular support during an unpopular sale of a compromise.

Part of Mandela's strength derives from this state of charismatic absolution and uncritical reverence. He can utter simple contradictions without losing credibility. After repeatedly calling De Klerk "a man of integrity", he snubbed him and at the Nobel Peace Prize ceremony referred to him as a "political criminal", only to contradict this by calling him "one of the greatest sons of Africa" at Mandela's own inauguration ceremony. The ambiguity of the Mandela-De Klerk relationship gives the lie to the myth that here were two great statesmen with hearts beating as one, acting harmoniously together to bring about a democratic transformation. Without diminishing the historical role of the duo, their major function was to market a "grand historical compromise". As agents of their respective constituencies and underlying interests, they certainly facilitated reconciliation, but they did not invent it. Mediated by their persuasive articulation, they embodied and translated the contradictions of the process into a credible vision.

As we pointed out in the previous chapter, it was and still is a process generously stocked with powerful and contradictory forces, where competing options confront strategically located and powerful personalities caught up in the ineluctable logic of negotiation politics. One of the culminating points of these negotiations was the management and holding of elections at national, provincial and local levels. The holding of elections was an integral part of the negotiating process.

Two key technocrats, one from the ANC and one from the De Klerk Government, were critical in structuring and overseeing the process. From the ANC it was Mac Maharaj (soon to become Minister of Transport), from the De Klerk government it was S.S. (Fanie) van der Merwe (former Director General of Constitutional Affairs) who then became Constitutional Adviser to the Department during negotiations. The latter summed up the chronological stages of the transformation process as follows:

"We went through the following stages: * Bilateral and multi-lateral talks about talks (Groote Schuur, Pretoria. D.F. Malan Minutes and Agreements on the Steering Group, the TBVC states and the self-governing territories.) – * The Peace convention – * Preparatory Conference – * Convention for a Democratic South Africa (CODESA) – * After the failure of CODESA, we went through a phase of getting back to the table from which emerged the Record of Understanding and COSAG – * Multi-party Negotiating Process (MPNP) – the happening that never got a name because we could not agree on one – * The Transitional Executive Council (TEC) with the Independent Electoral Commission (IEC), the Independent Media Commission (IMC) and Independent Broadcast Authority (IBA) – * Elections – * Government of National Unity and Constitutional Assembly .[1]

Maharaj states that two issues were critical for the ANC in the beginning stages of negotiations: the issue of majority rule and the creation of a temporary transitional mechanism that could take sovereignty away from the old regime and gradually transfer it to the incoming one. Of the former he states: "The liberation movement had to make uncomfortable compromises. At times I had to ask myself whether the compromises were not going too far. However, there was one real test: whether the compromises would open the road to majority rule. Any compromise became tolerable if it did not block majority rule."

As for the latter, he argued: "Even more critical than the two stage process, (i.e. interim elected government and then final constitution and elections) was crafting the Transitional Executive Council (TEC). The former government saw this as a process where we sought to rob it of all its powers. In return, we thought the regime would remain effectively in power. Mr van der Merwe and I were able to work out a common framework in which we tackled all problems. We avoided all prejudices and reported on the basis of what we saw. The TEC began to acquire power." [2]

Four critical legal instruments were negotiated which guided the 1994 elections: the Transitional Executive Council Act (TEC) which effectively took over government in that critical stage just before the elections; the Electoral Act which determined what kind of elections would take place, i.e. national and provincial elections on a pro-portional vote basis with party lists; the Independent Electoral Commission Act which set up the Electoral Commission that had executive authority not only to see that elections took place fairly and freely but to certify them as such afterwards, and the Interim Constitution Act which effectively determined how an interim elected government should govern and how the Constitution should be finalised.

The 1994 elections, like the 1995-96 local government elections, introduced the third and final transitional phase of an interim elected government which, by common agreement, would last until 1999 when the first elections under a final constitution would take place. The first phase was a negotiation phase in which parties sorted out the kind of structures that would govern during the next phase, which could be termed the appointed phase, in which non-elected jointly appointed structures effectively governed the tran-sition until the final phase which was the interim elected phase. This led at national level to the Government of National Unity (GNU), at provincial level the provincial governments, and at local level the locally elected governments.

However, the elections which heralded the interim elected phase at national and provincial level on the one hand, and at the local level at the other, were substantially different from one another. Some of the more salient formal differences were:

NATIONAL/PROVINCIAL 1994   LOCAL ELECTIONS 1996

1. An independent Executive Authority to oversee and sign off on the fairness and freeness of elections

1. An Electoral Task Group with no executive authority, but which had to co-ordinate, standardise and advise on 80 local elections with central and provincial governments

2. An election budget over which the IEC had sole discretion

2. No election budget, but a budgetary system which was effectively controlled by

	the Treasury, the Department of Finance and the Department of Constitutional Affairs
3. An open voters' roll based on IEC approved ID documents	3. A voters' roll based on voter registration for bona fide South African citizens
4. Voting solely on the basis of proportional representation of voters on a Party list system	4. A combination of proportional representation and constituency representation in which ratepayers associations and independent candidates could stand for election
5. Outside observers were invited to monitor the elections, e.g. Commonwealth and European Observer Groups, and they had to assess the fairness and freeness of the elections	5. No outside observers were invited or given a formal role. "Fairness and freeness" was judged by how parties responded to the election management and outcome at the local level. In short, if no formal complaint, the elections were accepted as free and fair
6. Massive state and NGO directed efforts at voter education	6. Little voter education and low participation

The elections for national and provincial governments were held on 27 April 1994. They were preceded by weeks of great anxiety and anticipation and when they went off without any significant disruption or violence, the relief was so great that the leaders of all the major parties pronounced them "substantially fair and free" even before the IEC did. The IEC subsequently did the same, but none of the foreign observer groups did. There were serious irregularities,

71

but as one IEC member said, "The irregularities were not so significant as to affect the outcome."

Independent analysts conceded the negotiated election result in KwaZulu-Natal. The 250 000 votes collected in "pirate" polling stations were justifiably disallowed, as should have been similar suspect cases of exclusively ANC-controlled ballot boxes. However, most outside observers would also agree with Tom Lodge[3] that "Inkatha's margin of victory, over 600 000 votes, was so large that it is likely that it would have won even if the elections had been conducted with complete propriety". In addition, the ANC admitted to having bused voters from the Eastern Cape into southern Natal, so that the accusation of Inkatha ruling Natal on the basis of fraud needs to be put into perspective. How free and fair elections can be held in areas in which the dominant party denies its opponents access even on polling day remains to be seen.

Just over two years later, the bulk of the local government elections took place on 1 November 1995. The provinces of KwaZulu-Natal and the Western Cape postponed theirs until May the following year and KwaZulu-Natal postponed its election again until July 1996 because of organisational problems and difficulties with ongoing violence in the province. Both the November 1995 and the postponed elections went off without any serious violence or disruption. However, as with the 1994 elections, there were even more serious flaws and irregularities.

Technically and organisationally speaking, if one considers the following factors, it was "a miracle" that the elections happened at all:

☐ In both the first and second set of elections, there was no reliable estimate of the number of voters eligible to vote. In fact, many people who voted in the national and provincial elections were not bona fide South African citizens. This came out quite clearly in the local elections when foreign migrants complained that they could vote in 1994 but could not in 1995 and 1996 because they could not register.

☐ Both elections were subjected to impossible timeframes for their completion. Politicians decided on dates for both without bothering in the slightest whether this was feasible or not and then appointed bodies to fulfil them. Consequently, serious logistical problems developed about the location and operation of polling booths and transporting ballot papers to and from them.

☐ The Local Government Transition Act (LGTA) which prescribed in detail how local elections had to take place, initially made no provision for rural voters, who constituted at least a third of potential voters. Planning for local elections was already well under way when ad hoc and incomplete arrangements were made for rural structures and voters. This, more than anything else, led to KwaZulu-Natal and the Western Cape postponing the 1 November polling date in 1995.

☐ In most provinces, but particularly in the Northern Province and Eastern Cape and KwaZulu-Natal, rural voters had great difficulty in coming to terms with election regulations and preparations. In KwaZulu-Natal "no-go areas" were accepted as part of the deal and no multi-party competition could take place at all.

Yet, despite these factors and many other lesser technical/organisational problems, there was an almost palpable haste to get elections at whatever level over and done with. Why?

In the first instance, these were founding elections concerned with establishing legitimacy. The crisis of legitimacy was pervasive and created an atmosphere of uncertainty and anxiety.

In the second instance, one must not underestimate the impact that the proliferation of negotiation structures had on the average South African. It was calculated that more than two hundred negotiation structures were in operation in some capacity or other before the 1994 elections. There were forums negotiating electricity supply, housing, health, local government, the economy, labour, agriculture, traditional authority and policing among others. Certainly the preparations for local elections, by law, created 680 negotiating forums that had to decide who the appointed bodies were that had to govern until interim bodies could be elected. The climate of negotiations had thoroughly prepared South Africans for compromise and electoral transition.

Finally, a mood had been cultivated and sustained that to postpone establishing legitimacy was to delay delivery, and that delivery of promises and socio-economic benefits was after all the real *raison d'être* of transition. Elections were instrumental, not an end in themselves. The fact that they fundamentally shifted power and might, particularly at the local level, have created structures incapable of efficient delivery was ignored in favour of getting them over and done with. Resolving the crises of legitimacy was a necessary and for some sufficient step to address the crises of delivery.

It is in the crisis of delivery where the really significant difference between the national/provincial elections and local elections come to the fore. Houses, schools, hospitals, parks, cemeteries, libraries, electricity, refuse removal, and water are services delivered at the local level. These are seen to be the primary responsibility of local government. There are basically three categories of local government:

1. Metropolitan structures with substructures. (Of these, there are six in South Africa: four in Gauteng, one in Cape Town and one in Durban);
2. stand-alone towns, and finally
3. structures of rural local government.

They differ widely in capacity, experience and skills. All of them suffer from the same fundamental dilemma: a more or less static revenue base is to be exposed to almost three to four times the number of people who were previously dependent on it for services. In addition, the poor (i.e. blacks) who were largely excluded from the benefits of service delivery had embarked on a campaign of boycotting payment for the provision of segregated and inadequate services and now could hardly be persuaded to break the culture of boycott under the new circumstances. The Masakhane campaign ("Let's Build Together") was set up to rectify the boycott culture but has not been particularly successful. Cash-strapped local authorities increased rates and taxes substantially and white ratepayers in the wealthier suburbs began to boycott payment because blacks were not paying. These are all preliminary signs of a deepening crisis of delivery which will be particularly acute at the local level.

To sum up: What is miraculous about the South African elections? Not that voters voted the way they did; nor that there was a general atmosphere of tolerance and absence of violence. The "miracle" is that elections were in some way technically and organisationally possible. The 1994 elections were "prepared" in two months, effectively from February to April 1994. The local elections had less than a year, from January to November 1995, to be organised. The fact that they happened shows how ready South African voters were to vote and exercise their cherished rights. However, these were founding elections, full of flaws and short-comings. Similar problems will most certainly not be tolerated in the second electoral test of the fragile democracy in 1999. The magic of founding elections will not be available to facilitate the process of democratic mobilisation. It is comforting to conclude that the elections in South Africa came off technically and organisationally. But what does one make of their import in terms of voting patterns and support bases? Did these support the contention so familiar in analyses of South Africa that South Africa is a racially polarised society where race identity overrides all other interests? We have already pointed out that few observers question the label of South Africa as a "deeply divided" society.

What better confirmation of this assumption could have emerged than the empirical fact that less than 3 per cent of whites voted for the ANC and less than 5 per cent of Africans voted for a tradi-tionally white party such as the NP in the first nonracial election. Prudent analysts such as David Welsh, Bill Johnson and Lawrence Schlemmer agree that the 1994 election amounted to a "racial census" in which racial demography largely determined the out-come. Hermann Giliomee draws the logical conclusion that in such frozen voting permanent racial majorities and permanent minor-ities prevent the rotation of government. Its performance hardly matters if race predetermines election outcomes.

From this perspective, the fact that the "white" National Party, in absolute numbers received slightly more votes (51 per cent) from non-whites than whites (49 per cent) is dismissed, because colour-eds and Indians who voted with two-third majorities for "white" parties are said to feel equally racially distant from Africans. In the absence of overlapping common bonds, particularly minimal social integration and intermarriage between Africans and the other 25 per cent of ethnic minorities, South Africa would indeed seem to be a deeply divided society in the classical sense first described by Furnivall.

Against this emphasis on a racial competition stands the opposite interpretation of some observers, such as Rupert Taylor: "Generally, the election was not contested on a group basis and voting did not follow neat racial or 'ethnic' lines."[4] This assessment is certainly correct in as far as the coloured and Indian vote is concerned. The fact that no coloured or Indian party contested the election testifies to the hegemony of political nonracialism, although coloureds and Indians are certainly highly group-conscious. However, in both the African and white groups, overwhelming majorities voted for traditional "black" or "white" parties with a black or white president, although the main parties (ANC, NP and Inkatha) had made great efforts to present themselves as nonracial organisations. Surveys indicated a volatile coloured electorate with a large proportion of floating voters. One-third of coloured voters classified themselves as undecided just before the election. The trend was even more visible among Indians. Tom Lodge suggests "that more than half the Indian electorate were swing voters".[5]

The dependence of the major parties on at least 15 per cent of their vote from other than their traditional constituency (in the case of the NP more than 50 per cent of its vote) militates against racial mobilisation. Overlapping racial party support stimulates moderation. It is mostly through votes from ethnic outsiders that a party can expect to grow. Of course, a party can also lose support among its ethnic community if it is perceived as too accommodating towards others. On the whole, however, Liphart is correct when he states: "Leaders of organisations with heterogeneous membership will be subject to the political cross-pressures of this situation and will also tend to assume moderate, middle of the road positions."[6] Such was the fortunate constellation at the first democratic election that prevented parties "articulating the communal cleavage", although in the case of the ANC and IFP the dependence on cross-racial support was small. Barry views the temptation to reinforce cleavages as the main danger of consociationalism. But as long as party leaders see the need to appeal to cross-cutting support, exclusivist mobilisations are by necessity undermined and diluted. However, once such a system has shifted from inclusivism to frozen exclusivist perceptions of who constitutes the eligible insiders, it appears indeed impossible to reverse, "because of the primitive psychological strength of communal identification".

A more nuanced perspective on voting behaviour that focuses on interests rather than identity alone can shed a different light on the conventional interpretation. To be sure, class interests and identity concerns cannot be separated easily. People interpret their worlds and perceive their interests subconsciously on the basis of their distinct group histories, particularly after legally enforced separation. Nonetheless, it is illuminating to pursue the relationship between interests and racial identity in more detail because of its obvious implication for South African democracy, the nature of the proclaimed nonracialism and the character of the ANC.

It is obvious that legal racial discrimination created interests that happened to coincide with race. In the same way, racial privilege determined interests on the part of a racial minority and racially defined middle-groups. To conclude from this constellation that it is racial identity that shapes voting behaviour clearly means overlooking the interests that lie behind skin colour. It is those interests in equal treatment and the fear of losing racial privilege that can be held at least as significant in influencing voting behaviour as the racial mask in which those interests express themselves.

In addition, the racial compartmentalisation produced subcultures of information and perceptions of politics that reinforce seemingly neat correlations between voting and race. Yet it is hardly the desire to protect or advance a racial status that motivates a specific voting behaviour, but the space people occupy and the information, contacts and world-views they hold that result from racial ghettoisation.

Undoubtedly, racial identity and material interests in such an interwoven context appear as a package. The voters themselves may not be aware why precisely they voted for a party – a decision that always bundles many motives with complex origin. Yet if race or ethnicity were the primary motive for voting, people would most likely be conscious of belonging to and cherishing such group membership. Awareness of ethno-racial priorities can be tested empirically. Therefore an open ended question as to why people feel close to a political party does elucidate the reasons for party identification. Such a question was asked in an IDASA-sponsored post-election representative survey. Its author concludes: "The principal and perhaps surprising finding here among the entire sample is that the vast majority of South African voters do not recognise race or ethnicity as a primary reason for their party support."[7] Only 12 per cent mentioned race or ethnicity. Virtually no difference between black and white voters showed. Other reasons such as ideology, policy, performance, competence, trust and reliability outweighed race. With the exception of the Zulu-based IFP and the Afrikaner nationalist Freedom Front, most voters view the main parties as inclusive in the sense that they represent citizens from more than one ethnic or racial group. Only 12 per cent of the sample perceive the ANC to be a black party and only 1,5 per cent as a "Xhosa" party. Although the ANC receives most of its votes from blacks, it cannot be argued that the ANC represents a black party in the sense that voters consciously flock to the ANC because they prefer a black party. Had this been the case, ANC supporters would hardly have elevated Joe Slovo to the second most popular politician after Mandela during the 1994 election campaign. Racially motivated African voters would not tolerate a party in whose leadership Indians are overrepresented and some whites also occupy high profile positions. While there exists an Africanist sentiment in the ANC that is occasionally stirred by ambitious politicians, it does not nearly amount to the current of dissatisfaction that led to the PAC splitting from the ANC in 1958. Had there been widespread rejection of the ANC's proudly proclaimed non-racialism during the first democratic election in 1994, the Africanist PAC surely would have benefited. To the surprise of most observers, the anti-white uncompromising image of the PAC attracted only 1,4 per cent of the popular vote. For all these reasons, ethnic voting played a less prominent role than is commonly assumed, yet frozen ethnic voting is identified as the major stumbling block to a liberal democracy by the analysts of deeply divided societies.[8]

Lawrence Schlemmer interpreted survey findings about voters' priority of concerns that "charisma, fear and communal interests superseded otherwise important, more specific, material concerns in the election".[9] However, the identification with an idolised leader could also occur because voters expect the strong figurehead and celebrated party to deliver material goods. While it is impossible to separate such motivations accurately, there is no doubt that the symbolic rewards of having achieved liberation overshadowed any other concerns in this first democratic election, as Schlemmer rightly points out. The assumed lack of fluidity of voters' loyalties has to be reassessed if Mattes, Gaus and Kotze's empirical findings "reveal a surprising lack of an explicit, conscious connection of race or ethnicity to partisanship".[10]

This does not deny that voters everywhere prefer to be represented by people like themselves. An ANC without an African president would hardly have been conceivable, particularly since Africans were denied political representation for so long. The pride in a president of "our people" and the automatic trust that such ethno-cultural affinity engenders, however, does not prove racial exclusiveness. It means that a potential supporter from another ethno-cultural group has to overcome an initial scepticism of unfamiliarity among the African majority. Once those credentials have been established, equal membership is extended to ethno-racial "outsiders". They can feel at home in a party whose numerical majority and leadership differs in cultural background by the sheer demographics of the population. Non-Africans have joined for ideological reasons and are welcomed for that commitment by like-minded fellow travellers for whom skin colour is overshadowed by policy support. This openness towards every citizen, regardless of ethno-cultural background, remains the true test of nonracialism.

The fact that few whites at present vote for the ANC and few Africans vote for the National Party not only reflects the historical legacy of segregation and liberation, but above all the different interests that the ANC and NP represent. The social-democratic ANC clearly advocates the priorities of the impoverished majority. It does so more convincingly than the policies of the National Party or DP, which increasingly represent a multiracial middle class reluctant to pay for the advancement of the have-nots. Such conflicting class interests are the normal core of party politics in every democracy. Nonetheless, they are always overlaid with other preferences. Whether the personality of the party leader appeals, how much a party is seen to embrace special interests (religion, ecology, women's advancement) can all go into the calculation of party support and often subvert an objectively discernible class interest. Indeed, as Max Weber has stressed, people act not only upon their material interests, but their ideal interests as well.

From all empirical evidence, it can be concluded that ethno-racial identity ranks low among the ideal interests of South African voters. Status needs on the basis of race and the psychological security that ethno-racial membership in an imagined community of kin provides have not been mobilised by the leading opinion makers in post-apartheid South Africa. Unlike Yugoslavia, where all politicians played the ethnic card in a deadly game for power, in South Africa an ethnic demographic majority need not rely on ethnic mobilisation. On the other hand, an ethnic minority cannot afford racial exclusiveness either if it wishes to make inroads into the black voting constituency, as the reforming National Party has clearly realised. To be sure, the ANC faces little objective pressure to reach out to non-African voters, given the high level of partisan loyalty that the party under Mandela enjoys among black voters. Seventy-five per cent of black voters identified with the ANC in 1997. Since black voters constitute about 69 per cent of the electorate, this accords the ruling party a seemingly unassailable built-in majority. The spectre of long-term one-party predominance cannot therefore be dismissed out of hand.

Chapter Five

Is South Africa a liberal democracy?

In the 1980s one could immediately divide a South African cocktail party into hostile camps with one's definition of democracy. Arguments raged about the merits of "participatory", "people's", "social", "liberal", "one party" and "workers'" democracy. The left developed instant solidarity of purpose in dismissing liberal democracy as a political facade for capitalist exploitation. Yet it is the dominant paradigm of what a democracy should be today. As Pzreworski puts it, the preconditions, context and universal applicability of a liberal democracy have become the major export commodities of North American academia.[1] In fact, democratisation and the expansion of a competitive market economy are the two most dominant international trends in the last decade of this millennium, i.e. liberal democracy and capitalism.

R.A. Dahl,[2] arguably the doyen of American political scientists and perhaps the most authoritative scholar on the virtues of liberal democracy, draws a distinction between "assembly democracy" and "representative democracy". The former originated in the Greek city states in 500 BC, but its manifestations can be found today as well. This is direct or instantaneous democracy where mandate, execution and accountability can be easily organised by assembling the community of citizens at a particular venue. The spirit of assembly democracy is captured by phrases like "the will of the people", "the majority", although the majority of the population, women and slaves, were excluded from the definition of citizens in ancient Greece. As Dahl points out, the conditions for "assembly democracy" are impossible to realise in large, complex industrial societies and attempts to persist can lead to serious distortions and even pervert the intentions of assembly democracy. This is the danger of populism, referenda politics or shop-floor democracy where continued popular involvement is difficult to sustain and can lead to elite manipulation and abuse. Parliamentarians as the elected representatives of the people are supposed to constitute a rational screen for the potential irrationality of agitated masses.

Representative democracy evolved with the development of complex, urbanised, industrial societies and consists of elected representatives who are given an extended mandate to pursue the interests of their supporters in structures and organisations remote from the immediate environment of those who elected them. Out of this process evolved the distinctive characteristics of liberal democracy, or polyarchy as Dahl calls it. The advantages of representative democracy lie in its extended mandate which provides greater continuity in pursuing policy objectives. Among the disadvantages must be counted the fact that it is more impersonal and distant from the nature of decision making, which often alienates parliamentarians from the general constituents who can only vote once every few years. Regular and more spontaneous accountability is thwarted unless there exist recall procedures or report-back duties. Various techniques and procedures are constantly explored to introduce elements of assembly democracy into representative democracy to increase a sense of popular participation and involvement.

Schmitter reduces the key principles of liberal democracy to two: *contingent consent* and *bounded uncertainty*.[3] Contingent consent is the principle that the party that wins a decisive election for government will not abuse its victory to deny those who lost the opportunity of winning next time. This is contingent on the willingness of the parties who lose to accept the right of the party that wins to take binding decisions over them until next time. Essentially, this principle has to do with the role of opposition in a democracy. Bounded uncertainty is the principle that certain critical issues or rights are removed from the arena of political contestation and protected from the capricious will of politicians. The uncertainty of democratic politics is thus bounded to the extent that fundamental rights are protected by a Bill of Rights and the Constitution. Bounded uncertainty is essentially the principle that vetoes unrestrained majoritarianism and protects the rights of individuals and minorities. Thus the dictum that a liberal democracy is measured not by how it treats majorities but by the fate of its minorities.

Together with these principles flow the conventional procedures of a liberal democracy, e.g. all adults are entitled to vote and can stand for election, provided they are sane and without a criminal record; the secrecy of the ballot is ensured; there is freedom of access to information; all constitutional parties can register and raise funds under the concept of freedom of association. These principles and procedures constitute the formal characteristics of a liberal democracy.

Well, is South Africa a liberal democracy? Formally and constitutionally the answer must be in the affirmative. Most of the classical elements of a liberal democratic polity can be found in both the interim and final constitution. There are ongoing debates about some of the features of the constitution, e.g. the independence of key institutions and positions such as the Public Services Commission, the Electoral Commission, the Public Protector and Auditor General. The general trend is more to observe and interpret the spirit of liberal democratic principles than to subvert it.

However, it is one thing to concede that formally and constitutionally South Africa resembles a liberal democracy. It is quite another thing to state that a liberal democratic constitution can be sustained or be accepted and practised by the South African electorate. Is there an appropriate democratic culture or can it be nurtured? Are the centrifugal tendencies characteristic of deeply divided societies not too strong in South Africa to tolerate the constraints of a liberal democratic constitution? What about the political intensities of permanently excluded minorities? It is one thing to state that a liberal democracy must enable opposition to come to power. But what if opposition is too fractured or small to challenge a more or less permanently entrenched dominant majority? Thus, South Africa may formally and constitutionally prescribe a liberal democracy, but has it got the capacity to become one substantially and practically? Some critical issues have to be considered in coming to grips with this question.

As was pointed out earlier, the leadership of the ANC, and the NP for that matter, would be the first to concede that they were not liberal democrats by historical record and inclination. Jannie Gagiano and Pierre du Toit[4] argue that the bulk of ANC support still confuses "liberation democracy" with "liberal democracy"; that it has still not abandoned the idea that the state is a site to be captured permanently by the dominant party and then used as the key instrument to "liberate" the economy "for the people". There is said to be a fundamental hostility towards the separation of powers demanded by a liberal democratic state, particularly among some trade union and SACP ideologues in the ANC alliance. However, it is difficult to sustain this argument in the light of the manner and content with which the ANC leadership has negotiated the Constitution and has conducted itself since its adoption. The separation of powers has been constitutionally entrenched and the Constitutional Court has already exercised its sovereignty against Parliament and the President on several occasions. The court has even rejected crucial sections of the draft constitution and referred them back to the Constituent Assembly to be rewritten. Combined with intense international scrutiny of the emerging government's commitment to "democracy", the tendency on both the ANC and NP leadership side has been to outbid each other in their observance of liberal democratic principles and procedure. It is difficult to think of contemporary examples of democratisation in Central and Eastern Europe, Latin America and Southeast Asia, where in terms of process and product of democratisation the trappings and rhetoric of liberal democracy have been more prevalent than in South Africa.

However, the dynamics of transformation may prove a far more serious threat to consolidating a liberal democracy in South Africa than the intent of those who negotiated it and now have to practise it. By consolidation is meant the extent to which people and interest groups increasingly accept law, regulation, statutes and ordinances as the preferred way to settle their disputes and pursue their objectives. This rather abstract definition covers a wide range of actualities, e.g. accountable budgetary procedures, due process of law, paying taxes, rates and speeding fines, *audi alteram partem* – respect for the other party – in short, establishing a democratic culture. Adam Pzreworski makes the telling point that when a regime moves from repression to democracy it becomes weaker. In other words, the institutions that supported a repressive regime – courts, prisons, police, defence, practically the whole civil service and different tiers of government – themselves have to go through a process of transformation before they can adequately sustain a new democratic regime, if they ever can. This fact alone fundamentally affects the capacity of the new regime to deliver the normal services associated with a modern industrial state. Symptoms of this are

escalating crime and slow and erratic implementation of new policies in housing, education and electricity supply. We will consider
some of the problems of delivery later on. Suffice to say that the
transition from repression to democracy makes the art of government infinitely more complex and is sufficient to undermine the
intentions of even the most committed liberal democrats.

But what about the probability of vibrant opposition politics developing in the South African constitutional context? Analysts of the
South African transition have expressed grave concern about the
space and clout of opposition in the negotiated arrangement of a
Government of National Unity (GNU). The power-sharing arrangement negotiated between the reformers of an outgoing authoritarian government and the moderates of the ascending populist forces
is suspected of circumventing strong democratic opposition by its
very compromise. Cosy deals at whose expense? Political scientists
identify different ways in which democracies can emerge. In the
American tradition, analysts compare negotiated transitions with
imposed democracies or whether the initiative comes from those in
power or from opposition groups. Some analysts conclude that negotiated transitions tend to undermine the development of institutionalised opposition required by a liberal democracy. Thus an elite
cartel such as a GNU would undermine the role of institutionalised
opposition.

This conclusion would be premature in the South African case for
a number of reasons. First, the power-sharing arrangement which
ended with the 1996 exit of the NP after two years was clearly
confined to five years with all expecting a "normal democracy"
thereafter. A "normal democracy" would be majority rule without
minority participation in government. Second, the transitional
compromise was not a "constitutionally enforced" grand coalition.
Minority parties were merely constitutionally *entitled* to representation in the executive but free to withdraw from government responsibility if they viewed their interests better guaranteed as a
legal opposition. This was precisely the argument used by De Klerk
when he withdrew from the GNU in 1996.

Thirdly, there is evidence that the power-sharing arrangement
did not constitute a pact of ideological allies but one of competitive
foes. In this pragmatic government of political enemies, rather than
political partners, opposition forces can be more effective inside

than outside the executive. They command easier access to information. If the opposition is formally part of the executive, it can expose the shortcomings of its rival more easily than if it has to rely on question periods in Parliament or leaks from sympathetic civil servants. The so-called shared cabinet responsibility exists in name only. Cabinet ministers from different parties blame each other. Government secrecy is a futile demand under circumstances where embarrassing details are leaked. Well before De Klerk left the GNU, the parties in it caucused separately before Cabinet meetings.

Another source of indirect opposition to the majoritarian designs of the dominant party in government can be found in the form of a watchful and wary Afrikaner-dominated civil service. Critics of the interim constitution overlook the fact that the ANC had little choice but to enter into a temporary pact. Inasmuch as the NP could no longer guarantee stability without legitimacy, the ANC too could not have ruled alone, given its own shortage of skilled administrators and its reliance on the legally entrenched NP-oriented civil service. Short of civil war, it is one thing to acquire the legal power of hiring and firing director generals and colonels and quite a different task to exercise such a legal right in light of absent alternatives and the inability to enforce them. Pensioning off ideologically hostile personnel could be feasible only in the case of a few top diplomats or generals. General bureaucratic cleansing would have been too costly in economic terms, legally difficult in the light of required rights of tenure, and politically disastrous for stability. Apart from incorrigible racist insubordination, a "clean slate" policy could not have been pursued throughout the administrative hierarchy. Given the nature of the negotiated constitution as well as the practicalities of governing the negotiated transition, it was extremely difficult for an ANC government to impose its unrestrained will on the South African situation, however offensive that may be to purist liberal democrats. To wail about an absent opposition in the Government of National Unity constitutes an academic infatuation with abstract democratic model-building but is unreflective of South African realities.

It is true, however, that the formal constraints of a liberal democratic constitution do not make practising democrats of those who operate under it. Far more worrisome than weak *inter*-party competition remain the autocratic *intra*-party trends. Mention of this in

NP ranks has already been made. The transitional constitution granted far too much power to the party leadership by forcing members of parliament to resign should they no longer wish to adhere to the official party line or were expelled as in the case of Bantu Holomisa. As Andre du Toit first pointed out, the restrictive Article 43(b) stifles intra-party dissent and enforces group conformity. Individual conscience and independent judgement of MPs are undermined if members lose their parliamentary privileges should they cross the floor. The prohibition of floor crossing, retained in the final constitution after much controversy, benefits the smaller parties whose members are more likely to be enticed by the patronage of their bigger rivals.

An additional factor strengthening intra-party conformity is the list system in proportional representation which grants the party hierarchy or bosses rather than the local constituency the final power to decide the fate of candidates by their ranking on the party list. Although the ANC determined its list according to an admirably democratic nomination process by its branches, the final list and ranking was decided by the national headquarters. Its difficult task to ensure a balanced representation of regions, women, races, allied groups and other lobbies ought to be acknowledged. With direct constituency selection of party candidates, the ANC slate would most likely be dominated by the majority ethnic group without the leadership being able to engineer a broad-based multiracial list on which minority candidates were in fact over-represented. However, it would have been more democratic had the final list for the first democratic election been referred back to the branches and members for ratification.

At the time of writing the final Electoral Act has not been ratified. One does not know what kind of electoral system is to be institutionalised. Certainly at national and provincial level it does not seem as if there will be any serious provision for constituency representation. At local level a combination of proportional representation and ward representation is contemplated. Perhaps at this level there may be some experimentation with transferable vote systems which could make opposition politics much easier. This is to be doubted. As Donald Horowitz[5] persuasively argues, it is simple electoral mechanics at the outset which can have far-reaching consequences for democratic electoral politics in the long run.

All the major parties contesting the first elections were in a sense historical parties shaped by the nature of the political conflict in the past. It was striking that when they talked about the future there was very little to differentiate among them. Their actual mobilisation took place by demonising their opponents about their past record. As the emerging democratic constitution matures and new fault lines begin to emerge within established parties, the real test for electoral democratic politics will begin to surface, particularly in the case of the ANC which is a political house of many mansions. It could be argued that as long as the ANC is secure in its electoral dominance it can afford to be tolerant of such opposition as exists and to defer to the constraints of a liberal democratic constitution. However, the real test will come when the alliance breaks up and new political alignments begin to emerge. What will they be and will they be liberal democratic in intent and practice? It is unlikely that answers to these questions will be found before the second national elections in 1999. The electoral system in place by then and the manner in which the new Independent Electoral Commission manages both the electoral system and the elections could have an important impact on democratic practice.

It is premature to argue, as R.W. Johnson[6] does, that "the new rulers have little regard for liberal constitutionalism. The government legislates with almost no regard at all for what the constitution says." This indictment cannot be justified in so stark a formulation. In the few instances where government actions were rescinded as unconstitutional, they resulted more from autocratic bungling by overlooking the letter rather than intentionally violating the spirit of the constitution. That the government aimed at centralising as much power as it could get away with during the final constitutional negotiations may appear offensive to federalists, short-sighted for reconciliation with Inkatha and imprudent for political stability as a whole, but shows in itself no disregard for liberal constitutionalism. Not all liberal democracies are genuine federal states. John Kane-Berman[7] who is usually not shy to castigate the smallest indicator of illiberality, concludes: "Not only does the constitution lay the foundations of a liberal democratic state, but the country also at present enjoys a free and critical press, robust institutions of civil society, and a strong private sector."

Compared with the totalitarian systems of Eastern Europe, the existence of a limited racially entrenched white democracy paradoxically facilitated the transition into a genuine democracy. Democratic institutions did not have to be established from scratch, but merely extended to the entire population. Unlike the total absence of a civil society in the former Soviet Union, the culture of criticism and public dissent was never totally silenced in the apartheid state. It was not a totalitarian system that managed to impose its ideology on the entire society despite censorship laws and media manipulation.

The apartheid state constituted an authoritarian system that was nevertheless accountable to its racial constituency upon which the ruling party depended for periodic re-election in competition with more liberal groupings with different strategies for white minority survival. In this respect, the enfranchisement of the entire population could fall back on a democratic tradition that was absent in Eastern Europe. This was particularly evident in the technical organisation of elections when, specifically in the local ones, returning officers and other election officials who for years had administered racially exclusive elections simply extended the same procedures, rules and regulations on a nonracial basis. It was quite extraordinary to see white Afrikaner town clerks in hundreds of small towns and villages meticulously administering election regulations to ensure an acceptable outcome.

On the other hand, the "Herrenvolk" mentality (Pierre van den Berghe[8]) certainly hindered democratic transition. Compared with communist states, Bantu education deliberately fostered political illiteracy. It aimed at depoliticising those whose rights of citizenship were denied. Liberal democrats in whatever party are still challenged with the huge task of the political education of the formerly disenfranchised. A culture of tolerance for competing parties has not really been established in the townships. Even among some ANC leaders the concept of "a loyal opposition" is viewed suspiciously. A constitutional Bill of Rights remains confined to expensive lawyers' discourses if it is not backed by the sentiment and political practice of the people.

Liberal analysts have described South Africa as a "one party dominant state". They deplore the lack of a strong opposition that would have a realistic chance of replacing the government in power. This is considered a precondition of a liberal democracy by most democratic theorists. Indeed, the absence of a strong opposition can make a ruling party complacent and arrogant. Without effective scrutiny, corruption spreads. However, the much greater problem in South Africa at present is not democratic one-party rule, but post-apartheid restructuring. A strong broadly based government may be able to tackle this task more effectively than an executive which has to worry about being re-elected. However, even a one-party dominant state is not necessarily a stable and cohesive one.

We have already mentioned that the transition from repression to democracy can weaken, not strengthen, the state initially. A few random indications of social and institutional disintegration can illustrate the worse alternative of a collapsing state. The ANC government with its 63 per cent mandate is unable to persuade large parts of its township constituency to pay rent or service fees. Attempts to tackle an escalating crime rate are fraught with obstacles of which widespread corruption in parts of the criminal justice system is perhaps the most important.

In 1997, the safety and security minister revealed that almost 20 000 convicted criminals had been granted licenses to own firearms. Close to 200 000 firearms were lost or stolen in South Africa over three years. About 100 prisoners are allowed to escape each month, mainly due to corrupt officials. An underpaid, demotivated and inefficient police force works within a criminal justice system that can hardly cope with an apartheid legacy of brutalised criminals. Interpersonal violence affects helpless children and women in particular. Sexual violence against women has reached unprecedented heights, although only a small proportion is reported. Abuse of black females under eighteen is said to number close to half of the township population. A member of the gender forum at Wits University reports:

Last year I ran workshops in the townships on rape and sexual harassment, under the auspices of People Opposed to Women Abuse (POWA). These workshops were aimed at matric and pre-matric students, both female and male. What came out of these workshops indicated that women were seen by a significant proportion of young males as simply receptacles or vehicles for the gratification of sexual need. It was seen as sport to select a girl who was deemed hot, or attractive sexually, get a few friends together, abduct her and in many cases gang-rape her. The idea that a woman was an equal and was as worthy of respect and consideration as a man was openly scorned and derided in these workshops by some of the participants. (G. Bailey, Letters to the editor, *The Sunday Independent*, November 10, 1996.)

Rising incidents of rape are certainly not confined to townships, but a culture of women abuse is less ostracised in townships than in other communities. The number of reported rapes countrywide increased from 20 321 in 1990 to 35 888 in 1995, precisely during the period of political liberalisation. It should not be forgotten that most of the victims are black women and children raped by black juveniles, while interracial rape is still a rare event. In a survey, Soweto residents rank murder (81 per cent) as the most serious problem, closely followed by the rape of children and women, teenage pregnancy, car hijackings and vehicle theft with 80 per cent and 77 per cent respectively (*Business Day*, 30 May 1996).

The government barely manages to collect taxes. The head of a tax commission describes the country's collection system as "basically voluntary". Should the 12 per cent of whites who pay most of the taxes withhold their dues in protest, it is not clear how the government could enforce the law when it has capitulated to the habits of boycott by the majority. The South African justice system is in severe disarray. An understaffed and underpaid police service and an overloaded and overworked judiciary led to a decline in prosecution and conviction levels. Of more than two million crimes reported to police in 1993, only 22 per cent resulted in prosecutions and only 17 per cent in convictions. Prisons are notoriously overcrowded, although only 16 per cent of offenders were sent to prison without the option of a fine.

To all intents and purposes, customs control at South African harbours and airports has broken down. Huge quantities of drugs and weapons enter South Africa freely, while overworked and frequently corrupt officials release containers of cheap textiles to the anguish of a protected local industry. In the NP-dominated Western Cape, massive fraud in the administration of pension and welfare payments amounted to "tens, maybe hundreds of millions of Rand", according to Pieter le Roux's forensic task group investigation. Convicted fraudsters had been promoted to positions of financial responsibility and a dozen clerks collected payments for dead people by reusing their pension numbers. In short, South Africa remains far more threatened by administrative anarchy at present than by a too powerful, conspiratorial, anti-democratic state executive.

Furthermore, while electoral rotation may be a useful spur to party responsiveness in mature Western democracies, the danger of being unseated may tempt a ruling party to engage in racist populist mobilisation or to consider suspending democratic practice. It is a moot point how much vigorous demagogic inter-party competition a fragile emerging and unconsolidated democracy can bear. Knowledgeable analysts predict that in quite a few East European and former Soviet Union Republics, nationalist dictatorships may replace democratic politics.

In South Africa, voting determined by demography may be a blessing in disguise as long as it allows the strongest ethno-racial group to extol nonracial tolerance, which it can afford to do without undermining its own power base. The smaller parties and ethnic minorities also benefit from this structural generosity compared with a situation of ethno-racial mobilisation that is likely to victimise minorities. Thus, possible government rotation may indeed constitute a precondition for democracy in more culturally homogenous states, but could easily develop into fragmenting racialisation in divided societies. The principle of "contingent consent" if pursued indiscriminately could very well pose a threat to the practice of "bounded uncertainty". By saying this, we are certainly not advocating the virtue of frozen eternal majorities that can indeed relegate ethnic minorities to permanent losers, as the one-third Catholics in Northern Ireland can testify. In the long term, given the pressures of emerging faultlines and realignment, this may be highly unlikely in South Africa. However, in the short term, the unintended benefits of a much exaggerated "democratic despotism" may indeed outweigh its oppressive potential in specific circumstances.

We return to the question: Is South Africa a liberal democracy? From the preceding analysis, it is clear that judgement has to be reserved. But it has to be reserved not because of the undemocratic intentions of the new government, or the leadership of the ANC, as some analysts would have it. If anything, the bulk of the ANC leadership and representatives in Parliament have become more liberal democratic, although in some cases very reluctantly, than those who remained unrepentant democratic centralists. Many "assembly democrats" by inclination have become more and more embroiled in the constraints and imperatives of "representative" democracy. What we have tried to show is that even if the new government consisted of dedicated, convinced and highly competent liberal democrats, they would have been confronted with formidable problems in making South Africa a functioning liberal democracy in the space of a few years. We will investigate some more of these problems later on. But one thing should by now be clear: moving from repression to democracy is not just a gear shift from a farm road to a four-lane highway.

Chapter Six

Can a South African nation be built?

"Nation-states are dinosaurs waiting to die" (Kerniche Ohmae[1], successful international business strategist). He argues that not only are they enormously unproductive consumers of capital, and highly inefficient in promoting development, but they are bound to become increasingly irrelevant because of the greater flexibility and transferability of capital, information, technology and consequently consumer preference. Eventually the sovereignty and credibility of governments will be fatally undermined as agents of delivery of needs and thus no longer deserving of loyalty and support.

Adebayo Adedeji[2], former under-secretary general of the United Nations and executive secretary of the Economic Commission for Africa, bemoans the fact that "Among the most unenviable of Africa's colonial legacies is the plethora of minuscule states and borders drawn up in the capitals of Europe. Imperial convenience, not socio-economic reality or political viability, impelled their creation by the colonial masters of a century ago."

Thus one of the writers predicts the demise of nation-states under the impact of modernisation and globalisation, the other the difficulty of making a nation-state viable in Africa because of the politics and economics of underdevelopment.

From a third perspective, Uri Ra-anan[3] declares: "It has been one of the fallacies of contemporary political thought, particularly in the West, as to assume that the international arena of the 20th Century is occupied largely, if not almost exclusively, by nation-states or nation-states to be." He argues that because of the emergence of the nation-state as a fairly recent phenomenon, it has over the last fifty years become increasingly fashionable to "clean up" the ethnic map. This has included genocidal measures: against Jews and Gypsies under Hitler; Crimean Tartars, Volga Germans and Chechen-

Ingus under Stalin; Ibos in Nigeria; southern Blacks in the Sudan; both Tutsi and Hutu in Rwanda and Burundi; Armenians in Anatolia; overseas Chinese in certain parts of Southeast Asia; and Kurds in Iraq. Peoples have been expelled: Asians from Uganda and Germans from most of East Central Europe. Populations have been exchanged through agreement, by semi-voluntary moves, as a result of fear, or in the wake of unilateral measures: Hellenes from Turkey and Turks from Greece; Macedonian Bulgars from Greece and Hellenes from Bulgaria; Turks from Bulgaria and Bulgars from European Turkey – all in the 1920s; most Hindus and Sikhs from Pakistan and many Muslims from India; practically all Jews from Arab countries and about three quarters of the Arabs from the area that became Israel in 1948-9; and some of the few Ukrainians and Belorussians still remaining in truncated post-World War I Poland and many ethnic Poles from former Polish territories annexed to the USSR.

No doubt there are many other examples that will bear testimony to the difficulties of forging a viable nation-state from multicultural/ethnic/racial societies. However, it is necessary to remind ourselves that to pose the question: can a nation be built in South Africa? is to give a somewhat different emphasis to the question we posed and tried to answer in the previous chapter: is South Africa a liberal democracy? The whole concept of a liberal democracy is premised on the existence of a nation-state with a definable geography and clearly determined rights of citizenship. In a sense, both nation-building and developing a liberal democracy have to a large extent to grapple with a common set of problems; it is the selective emphasis that is different. With a liberal democratic emphasis the focus is on constitutions, parties, elections, consolidation and the rights of minorities and citizenship. With "nation-building", the focus is on values, culture, symbolic commitments and transcending loyalty derived from common citizenship. A renowned and respected authority on deeply divided societies, Theo Hanf,[4] concludes that one can usefully distinguish between three general ideologies in deeply divided societies: (1) intolerant and exclusive (exclusive ethnic nationalism); (2) intolerant and inclusive (we must all be the same and cannot be different; Jacobinism); and (3) tolerantly inclusive (multicultural/syncretistic/patriotic nationalism). If a deeply divided society can overcome its own centrifugal tendencies and make syncretistic nationalism the dominant ideology, it stands a chance of becoming successful in nation-building – but then it is a transcending loyalty based on the acceptance of pluralism and diversity, not its denial. In the latter case, if an intolerant ideology of either the exclusive or inclusive variety becomes dominant, then nation-building is simply another name for repressive domination.

Given the reservations expressed about the very idea of a nation-state, it should be obvious that "building a nation" is not simply a matter of using extravagant and conciliatory rhetoric such as the term "rainbow nation", or waiting for the glow of national solidarity that flows from sporting achievements to percolate through to the masses, nor to depend on the clerical injunctions for "healing" and "forgiveness" that accompany sessions of the Truth and Reconciliation Commission. Divorce courts provide ample evidence that truth does not always lead to reconciliation and that it is sometimes impossible for third parties to bring about "healing" between victim and perpetrator. One does not need to look far for such evidence in deeply divided societies either. So what, if at all, makes South Africa special? Why should it succeed in building a nation against all the odds that other societies with similar problems battle to overcome? What does one make of the following in the context of nation-building and cultural identity?

- Right-wing Afrikaners, having lost the battle for a Volkstaat of their own, resorted to negotiating cultural enclaves for "ethnic Afrikaners" as Viljoen, their leader, refers to them. Some of them are seriously beginning to consider withdrawing from society in general and joining Carel Boshoff and Hendrik Verwoerd, son-in-law and son of H.F. Verwoerd, in Orania, a small tract of land in the North West Cape.
- The protection and strengthening of the Afrikaans language by the creation of a nonracial inclusive Afrikaans Council of Delegates, largely in response to the threat perceived to Afrikaans in education, the civil service and business.
- The belated and futile attempt of De Klerk and his party to protect Afrikaans as a medium of primary education in the South African Schools Bill. Prior to the debate De Klerk acknowledged that they had been outmanoeuvred in protecting the cultural interests of the Afrikaner.

- A strong surge of "coloured" ethnicity in the Western Cape. This can be found in the formation of "Coloured Resistance Group" and blatant anti-black bias in Western Cape electoral politics.
- The Griquas, a small indigenous ethnic grouping, refusing to complete census forms because they were not referred to as such and suing the British government for R4 billion for "taking away their land and mineral rights" during colonial occupation.
- The constitutional acknowledgement of traditionalism through a House of Traditional Leaders as well as giving recognition to traditional leaders at local government level. This, however, was rejected as inadequate by CONTRALESA (Council of Traditional Leaders of South Africa) under the chairmanship of Holomisa from the Transkei, as well as Chief Buthelezi who pulled Inkatha out of constitutional negotiations because insufficient recognition was given to traditional leadership and Zulu culture.
- Jacob Zuma, national chairman of the ANC and leader in KwaZulu-Natal, donning traditional leopard skin regalia at Shaka Day celebrations to show solidarity with Zulu culture.
- Black students and black intellectuals determinedly pushing for transformation and Africanisation of all tertiary institutions, by which they mean that they should reflect an "African essence" and the "demographic reality of South Africa"; replacing white academic administrators with black ones, regardless of the political record of individuals.
- The formation of a society of black business executives, the Africanbond, to promote black advancement in the corporate economy.
- In January 1997, a new blacks-only journalists' body, the "Forum of Black Journalists", was formed. The black body stated that it would "serve as a platform upon which black journalists can claim their legitimate space on the stage of idea formation through production, expression and management of information, being active participants rather than mere messengers of news". As Thabo Mbeki and Mandela have emphasised, the urban bias of white editors with a Western mind-set – being like foreign correspondents in their own country – still points to a deep racial gap between different life experiences despite a common immersion in a Westernised consumer culture. Resentment about past racial marginalisation in the newsrooms of even liberal

papers combine with an Africanist vision to assert a new black autonomy from perceived white liberal tutelage and arrogance.

While Mandela has stressed that "the media should not be a lapdog" but a "watchdog to make sure that our famous revolutionaries remain on course", he has also bitterly criticised a number of senior black journalists. Their criticism of some of Mandela's actions has been interpreted by the president as disloyalty by doing the "dirty work" of conservative white media owners. However, by expecting a special obligation from black journalists, Mandela not only racialised press criticism of the government, but impugned the independence of the journalists by implying their willing part in a "secret agenda". An editorial in *The Star* pointed out that the black commentators were part of an honourable "brotherhood of black journalists" who were "neither frightened by apartheid's tyranny nor bought by its gold". By smearing them, it concluded, Mandela "taints both himself and the country". (Cited in *SA Report*, November 22, 1996, 5.)

Are these just "normal" symptoms of dealing with the "legacy of the past", or a vigorous and innocuous manifestation of pluralism in a unifying society; or could this be the beginning of powerful centrifugal tendencies towards ethno-racial competition that could blow nation-building apart under conditions of painful economic reform and constitutional consolidation?

We hold no brief for the primordial theses of ethnicity, i.e. that a person is born with some ethnic essence that is genetically determined. However, the biological base of ethnic awareness is kinship, and powerful primary loyalties and convictions are developed within its structures and rituals. The difference between ethnic awareness in a traditional context and a modern one is the element of individual choice. In other words, the more traditional the customs and practices of an ethnic community, the less choice the individual experiences in matters of childhood, puberty, marriage, status and occupation. However, as Heisler[5] has shown, ethnic awareness does not disappear under conditions of industrialisation and modernity. He refers to the phenomenon of "ethnic nesting" where for specific occasions the individual chooses to behave ethnically, e.g. at Christmas time, or on cultural and religious holidays. This "ethnic nesting", however, has no, or very little, bearing on the individual's life chances in other contexts in modern industrial societies. It is possible, however, that groups of people outside the traditional context, or the nesting phenomenon, can "imagine" themselves into new ethnic communities or revive other traditional markers for expediency.

Many authors, particularly Tom Nairn,[6] have pointed to the Janus face of ethno-racialism. Racial classification and ethnocentric identities function both to exclude as well as to articulate belongingness. Race and ethnicity discourses serve instrumental as well as symbolic ends. Ethnicity expresses identity needs as well as claims to entitlements. Ethnicity can be "the essential building block of all racism", as the British scholar Floya Anthias[7] has argued. Yet exclusion and cultural superiority (ethnocentrism) is not ethnicity's sole ingredient. To consider ethnicity only as a divisive obstacle to state-building remains one-sided. Ethnicity must also be thought of "as a bearer of culture"[8], as the expression of historically evolved specific memories by which the members of a collectivity interpret and give meaning to their worlds. Ake has rightly warned against the trap of only regarding "ethnicity as a problem or a constraint on democracy". He insists that "every aspect of social transformation has to come to terms with ethnicity". Indeed, how can the problems caused by ethnicity for state-building be addressed when its very existence is being denied? The exhortation to "unthink" ethnicity[9] provides an easy escape for the analyst's difficulty in coming to terms with a stubborn reality.

Denouncing ethnic categories as reactionary also ignores the fact that ethnic identity frequently shields the individual from a hostile environment. Ethnicity as a source of self-respect against denigration by the dominant group furnishes the psychological strength to resist and not adopt the victor's definition of reality. The remarkable success of discriminated minorities in insulating themselves from degradations is owed to this cultural narcissism. "If the tenacity with which some Africans cling to certain cultural symbols and a fabricated past seems surprising, one must consider the implications of lacking a sense of self and being lost in a cultural wilderness. More and more people are finding this intolerable and are fighting determinedly not only to assert their cultural identity but also to claim self-determination for it."[10]

Self-conscious ethnic groups in increasingly multicultural states may or may not be a source of conflict. The mere existence of different ethnic groups does not justify the popular conclusion that all plural or poly-ethnic societies are conflict-ridden. Multilingual Switzerland is a haven of prosperous peace. It is useful to distinguish, therefore, between vertical and horizontal pluralisms, or what Horowitz[11] called "ranked and unranked ethnicity". In the latter case ethnic collectivities coexist side by side with equal recognition. This is the goal of multiculturalism in Canada and Australia that aims to abolish an entrenched cultural hierarchy of charter groups by symbolically elevating later immigrant ethnicity to the same level.

In reality, however, vertical pluralism with ethnic subordination is much more likely. The "separate but equal" ideology in plural societies merely obfuscates the inequality in the allocation of resources and life chances in what amounts nonetheless to a ranked ethnic stratification. Unranked ethnicity refers more accurately to multi-nation states where different groups mostly live in their own area with their own complete institutions in what anthropologists have also labelled "structural pluralism". In M.G. Smith's famous phrase, equal versus "differential incorporation" distinguishes between the two situations. With the spread of norms of equality and values of achievement measured by competitive performance, a conflictual relationship between ethnic collectivities can be expected when one group is differentially valued, let alone actually dominated. It is group inequality that engenders ethnically perceived conflict. The German scholar Theo Hanf[12] has emphasised that "social inequality is a powerful revitalizer of communal solidarity".

Group inequality is not confined to material or political injustices. An economic or political determinism often overlooks the far more emotion-laden status inequalities. The work of Liah Greenfield has especially pointed to the notion of *dignity* as the essence of nationalism. "The remarkable quality of national identity which distinguishes it from other identities – and also its essential quality – is that it guarantees status with dignity to every member of whatever is defined as a polity or society."[13] Other analysts have stressed wounded identity or an unbearable sense of shame for the nation's backwardness, or defeat (even in a soccer game), as powerful incentives of nationalist fervour. Indeed, without the humiliating treaty of Versailles, Hitler would not have been able to elicit the feelings of resentment and revenge in so many Germans. Contemporary Arab nationalism and Islamic fundamentalism, too, feed on the imagined humiliation by a cunning West. It is the symbolic claim for status that makes ethno-nationalist conflicts as intractable as they are. Material claims of groups for economic equality can be settled more easily by bargaining. Where conflicting values clamour for equal recognition (for example, on abortion, divorce, sexual orientation or issues of religious doctrine), liberal compromise cannot be expected among true believers. They utter absolute moral claims, in moral language, tied to their identity as principled moral beings.

Nations or ethnic communities are "imagined communities" that adopt their own histories, sense of belonging or purpose. The current popularity of cultural studies at American universities and the preoccupation with slavery and colonial wrongs in Africa and the infatuation with negritude (Senghor, Fanon) and black consciousness (Carmichael, Biko) would be examples of this. The most recent ethnic revival in South Africa is a new imagined community of Afrikaners who wish to mobilise to protect the Afrikaans language and nonracial Afrikaner culture. In short, for us ethnicity, and this includes racial awareness and nationalism, which we define as politicised ethnicity, is a social variable that can vary in its occurrence and intensity over time and has to be understood against changing political, social and economic circumstances. Its social manifestation and reality is a matter of belief and conviction as are the practices and patterns of social behaviour that flow from it.

An important reason for taking ethnicity, ethnocentrism and ethnic mobilisation seriously is that it is extremely difficult to make constitutional provision for them within the structures of a liberal democratic state. Consider simply the case of social welfare, which is premised on a common individual citizenship and the equal provision of services such as pensions. How can ethnic groups define structures within a liberal democratic state in which they can look after "their own"? This becomes acute in times of political mobilisation, e.g. who pays the salaries of chiefs? What, for example, is the relationship between common and customary law and the status of women? How autonomous should church or religious schools be? Should the state subsidise private denominational or ethnic schools?

It is precisely because ethnic communities can prevail on the civil rights of an entrenched constitution that its implementation becomes problematical and can be experienced as a new form of discrimination and oppression.

A persuasive argument could be made that it is because of the centrifugal divisive tendencies of ethnicity and race in the South African context, and the fact that they have so "miraculously" been thwarted in the initial stages of transition, that Mandela in particular has such an obsession with creating a "rainbow" nation and with promoting reconciliation. He has shown extraordinary sensitivity towards "ethnic Afrikaners" like Constand Viljoen, the coloureds of the Western Cape, the Indians of Natal and particularly traditional leaders of all tribal manifestations. So much so that Mandela has been taken to task by members in his own leadership structures who feel he is overdoing it and neglecting his own ANC constituency. Bantu Holomisa, the expelled member of the ANC executive and Parliament, is already stomping on the accusation that the ANC must be careful not to neglect the poor (i.e. black) on the altar of reconciliation and macro-economic reform.

The way in which the "rainbow" nation is being built can, of course, have a determining impact on the disruptive potential of ethnicity and ethnic mobilisation in South Africa. If it is done intolerantly and inclusively in the Jacobean sense outlined earlier, then the very attempt to forge a unified nation could have exactly the opposite effect. There are those who, deeply suspicious of the Jacobin tendencies within the ANC, believe that its professed nonracialism is nothing but an egalitarian veneer to disguise all attempts at undermining cultural and ethnic diversity, i.e. that the ANC is fundamentally anti-pluralist and hegemonic in intent and consequence.

We can postulate two ideal types of possibilities concerning the building of a South African nation given the preceding analyses:

(1) Nation-building, i.e. creating a "rainbow" nation, progressively becomes an ideological facade to impose a form of nonracial (black) domination over all emerging forms of ethnic pluralism. Any attempt by minorities, whether Afrikaner, Hindu, Moslem, Zulu, Xhosa, etc., to protect or promote cultural rights or practices, particularly where they are dependent on the patronage of the state, e.g. education, is opposed or suppressed as threatening "nation-

building" or trying "to preserve racism" or "the legacy of the past". This could create precisely the circumstances which such domination attempts to prevent, i.e. ethnocentrism and ethnic mobilisation which undermines nation-building and reinforces a growing sense of intolerant inclusivism.

(2) On the other hand, creating a South African nation has to do with walking a fine line between politically and constitutionally recognising cultural pluralism and diversity, and developing over-arching symbols of solidarity and commitment transcending particular ethnic loyalties. The "rainbow" nation would epitomise a spirit of tolerant inclusivism in which diversity in unity is recognised. To determine which of these constructs could be most probable for South Africa, one would have to look at trends in the dynamics of transition that bear directly on issues of ethnic identity and their impact on "nation-building".

In the first place, it is necessary to emphasise that "institution-building" rather than "nation-building" should take precedence in a multi-ethnic society. If institutions that can cope with mediating the conflicts and tensions that arise out of cultural pluralism cannot be strengthened, then no amount of symbolic exhortation will overcome them. In the previous chapter we argued that the type of constitution that has emerged from negotiations does not preclude the possibility of a tolerantly inclusive process of nation-building emerging. Cultural, religious and language rights are recognised and protected and there is a recognition of the possible contradictions that may emerge between customary and common law and other tensions between traditionalism and modernity. This possibility has certainly been strengthened by the role of Mandela since his inauguration. Only the most cynical would see his efforts at nation-building and reconciliation as false and manipulative. It is largely through him that old symbols of nationhood such as national anthems and flags have been substituted with new ones in a remarkably smooth and painless process. Very few eloquent prophets of South African doom would seriously have contemplated the situation where a Springbok rugby team, before the commencement of an international game, would clasp their fists to their hearts determinedly trying to sing "Nkosi Sikelele Afrika", whilst the predominantly white crowd waved the new South African flag in delirious support. However, one should not get carried away with such largely symbolic symptoms of nation-building. Constitutional formalities, a charismatic president and new symbols of transcending solidarity are nevertheless positive signs of inclusive tolerance in a culturally diverse society. They are, however, not enough by a long shot.

In the second place, the debate about language is worth following in this context. Language is a powerful symbol of ethnic identity and the manner in which it is dealt with constitutionally and practically can have an important bearing on nation-building. The South African Constitution makes provision for eleven official languages that are "guaranteed equal official status". Not only is this constitutionally exotic, but it is a practical impossibility. Again, one could argue that this provision itself is indicative of a sensitivity concerning the disruptive potential of language conflicts and their impact on nation-building. However, the manner in which this is given effect can stimulate the very conflict it supposedly wishes to avoid. Is it practically possible to give equal status to eleven languages in communication, the civil service, education? If not, what do those language groups who feel aggrieved do? The linguist and educator Neville Alexander argues: "In a truly democratic multi-lingual society, no privileging of any language group vis-à-vis others can be permitted. But what does this mean in the context of the actual inequality of languages? It means that we must be scrupulously honest with the citizens of the country . . . that it will require generations, decades and in some cases perhaps centuries of committed attention to the development of languages of low status in order for actual equality of usage to be realised."[14] One is tempted to add "if ever". Alexander goes on to argue that most black people in South Africa "consider command of the English language to be all that is good and desirable in life". He pleads for a national language plan which will focus on multilingual education at school, accepting the inevitability of English as the current trade (i.e. official) language and observing mother-tongue instruction at least in the pre- and primary phases of education. Obviously, this kind of approach has major financial and personnel repercussions for schools and universities.

But what of a privileged language? Afrikaans that loses "official status" or at least has to share it with ten other languages? What are the political, economic and social consequences of such a loss?

Afrikaner liberal analysts like Hermann Giliomee and Hennie Serfontein are baffled as to why a shrewd lawyer and politician such as De Klerk did not even secure a clear cultural pact on Afrikaans language education. Serfontein wonders "how De Klerk could have allowed himself to be outmanoeuvred by the ANC at the conference table in one of the most sensitive issues in Afrikaner politics"[15] by not ensuring legal protection for Afrikaans schools. Privatising ethnicity, as frequently recommended, remains an unsatisfactory solution because it amounts to double taxation of parents who wish to send their children to denominational schools or want exclusive mother-tongue instruction.

Hermann Giliomee[16] has pointed to the need to supplement the political pact with a cultural peace accord which would entrench state-subsidised own-language educational instruction, provided that no racial exclusion were involved. All qualified students who desire Afrikaans-medium instruction ought to be admitted, but the linguistic and cultural heritage of an education institution should be maintained.

Yet can Afrikaans language and institutional culture be so easily divorced from its association with privilege and past exclusion without generating resentment? Can Potchefstroom simply be laundered neutral by nonracial admission without seriously reflecting on how the cultural strangers feel in the house of their former colonisers? Above all, can heritage maintenance be reconciled with the ANC's view of nation-building, which Giliomee doubts? Similar calls for the retention of the original "Indianness" of the University of Durban-Westville by some sectors of the Indian population, and of the "coloured" character of the University of the Western Cape, express a resistance to the admission of "outsiders", namely black students.

Can this simply be dismissed as a reluctance to share havens of privilege with "others" in which were once apartheid-imposed institutions? It would be too simple an answer. There is a growing sense of cultural insecurity, expressed particularly at tertiary institutions. R.W. Johnson[17] talks about an "ominous pressure on universities to help mould a single common South Africanism". This has to be understood against a growing sense of entitlement and demand for affirmative action by black students and intellectuals. Mamphela Ramphele has deplored "the anti-expertise rhetoric, which has crept into the debate about transformation" and warned that "those who use the legacy of inequity to delegitimise expertise do so at our peril" (*Sunday Independent*, March 9, 1997). The demand that universities in South Africa should be "transformed" to reflect an "African essence" and "the demographic reality of South Africa", is responded to not only as a demand for lowering of standards, and an attack on universities as institutions for advanced learning and protectors of standards of excellence and research, but also as an attack on the "traditional cultural character" of the universities. Precisely because tertiary institutions are a scarce resource and a channel to career opportunities and economic mobility, they have become a hotly contested terrain. If the new imagined communities that emerge at universities in South Africa generate a spirit of anti-intellectual intolerance, they certainly have the capacity to undermine inclusively tolerant nation-building.

However, the actual behaviour of many Afrikaans schools clearly demonstrates the fallacy of the primordialist assumption. Faced with a declining student body and the loss of teaching positions if confined to exclusive Afrikaans-medium instruction, many Afrikaans schools long ago and of their own volition opted for parallel Afrikaans and English instruction in order to attract students from other language groups. Job security and government subsidies clearly weighed more heavily than cultivating an exclusive Afrikaner identity. Most Afrikaans schools and Afrikaans universities integrated a diversified student body smoothly. This changed sociocultural reality pre-empted the initial Afrikaner nationalist strategy to preserve exclusive Afrikaans instruction through language admission tests and religious affiliation.

Giliomee[18] believes that "Afrikaans is ultimately an obstacle to the ANC version of nation-building" (i.e. Jacobean), because the ANC wants to elevate English to the national medium of communication. However, English is not only already the national language, but it also has no rival in uniting the many linguistic groups in a lingua franca. This role of a common language cannot be fulfilled by Afrikaans, Zulu or Xhosa because only a minority of South Africa's population can understand these indigenous languages, i.e. languages spoken only in South Africa.

The designation of an official language in a multilingual state does not solely depend on the number of people speaking the language in childhood. Indeed, fewer South Africans know English as their mother tongue than Afrikaans, Zulu, or Xhosa. However, at least the formally educated in all population groups have English as a second or third language. This is not the case with Afrikaans which, at most, is understood by a quarter of the population, with about 15 per cent having Afrikaans as a childhood language. Therefore, only English and no other group language can fulfil the role of a national medium of communication. The South African situation is similar to India, where regional languages thrive. It would be divisive and impractical to elevate them to national status. Such considerations have not even stressed the advantages of being fluent in a world language. Since language policy goes beyond issues of communication to questions of collective identity, value judgements about the worth of a language are notoriously controversial and should be confined to practical considerations of how best to facilitate optimal communication in a given socio-historical context.

It could be argued that a country is better served with several official languages and does not need a common language to form a mythical nation. Canada and Belgium represent cases of official bilingualism. They have to bear considerable extra costs, as well as having to cope with the divisive potential of linguistic markers for a separate group identity. The more harmonious multilingual Switzerlands of this world are few, while the Sri Lankan cases of exclusion from scarce civil service positions, and other forms of discrimination on the basis of home language and ethnic origin, trigger current regional strife in many parts of the world. The affluent Canadian state is likely to fall apart because it adopted official bilingualism while separatist Quebec nationalists, very much like Afrikaners, considered this policy to undermine a threatened linguistic minority.

The recognition of eleven official languages and a spreading multilingualism indicates an official awareness that the new South Africa has to be multicultural. A few Jacobins in its ranks notwithstanding, the ANC not only tolerates, but practises cultural diversity. Given the composition of its support it has not much choice, and even if it wished to impose a state-dictated cultural uniformity on the population it could not succeed. However, one cannot underestimate the tension that is generated by giving long-suppressed indigenous languages and African symbolism more public prominence and the experienced loss of privilege of Afrikaans and European values. This was to be expected. But rectifying cultural colonialism does not inevitably translate into cultural totalitarianism. It is possible that indigenous heritage supplements and moulds Western tradition into a new South African culture. Even though multiculturalism has been dismissed as a euphemistic term for old style apartheid's separate development, its dynamic nature is often overlooked. This entails the renegotiation of the core culture, thereby providing "space" in the public domain for previously excluded cultures once located on the periphery.

Liberal analysts deplore the ANC emphasis on national identity as a thinly disguised attempt to subordinate ethnic and regional identities. Indeed, the authoritarian history of multi-ethnic African states should serve as a warning against the temptation of ruling elites at the centre imposing their parochial vision of the nation on reluctant subsegments. Pierre van der Berghe's[19] warning that nation-building usually amounts to nation-destroying may sound extreme, but signals a real danger of ethnocide. The issue of language policy and language as a marker of ethnic identification in the context of nation-building in South Africa is, as we see it, in the crucible – it is loaded with the potential for either disruption or unification. On balance, given the initial approaches to it, the GNU government appears to be sensitive to its disruptive potential and is more accommodating than adversarial. Thabo Mbeki has explicitly rejected "linguistic imperialism". Nevertheless, some prominent Afrikaans newspapers (*Die Burger* and *Rapport*) together with influential Afrikaner cultural leaders tend to interpret the loss of Afrikaans of its bilingual official language status, together with the new government's attempt to promote the other indigenous languages, as a deliberate policy to suppress and undermine Afrikaans as a language. If this view becomes conventional wisdom for the majority of Afrikaans-speaking South Africans, it could pose a considerable obstacle to nation-building.

In the third place, apart from the language issue, what role does education play in nation-building? The pessimistic analysts of South Africa rely strongly on the proposition that higher education increases ethnocentrism. Educated elites, not ignorant masses, are said to mobilise group sentiment for selfish purposes. In the words of Donald Horowitz:[20] "Since the mute equation of educated elites with accommodative attitudes is unsupported, there is no reason to think automatically that elites will use their leadership position to reduce rather than pursue conflict." Certainly elites will not opt for reconciliation automatically. South Africa is also cursed with its share of ethnic and ideological entrepreneurs. Expediency in the competition for power often tempts political leaders to mobilise for nationalist confrontation, as the former Yugoslavia has clearly shown. However, political elites also frequently choose accommodation. If the South African "miracle" has proven anything, it is the influence of accommodating leadership. Confronted with the option of civil war, all sides in South Africa pulled back from the brink. The leadership of all major parties exhorted their followers that co-operation instead of confrontation would benefit each party in its own way.

A more far-sighted leadership embraced policies of reconciliation mainly because they could anticipate the costly alternative. However, the sociologically more relevant question is how enlightened leaders manage to sell a rational policy to a seemingly irrational electorate. The assumption of an intolerant constituency, manipulated at will by shrewd elites, must be as much questioned as the assumed belligerence of leaders. Conversely, as Theo Hanf[21] cautions wisely, the alleged relationship "begs the question of how hostile and intolerant masses are going to produce such tolerant and open-minded leaders".

We do not wish to be misunderstood. Certainly South Africa has most of the objective conditions that would support ethnic entrepreneurs to engage in hostile ethno-racial outbidding. This is the kind of conventional wisdom that has informed analyses of South Africa for decades. And there certainly has been, and most likely still is, a fair distribution of such leaders, both educated and uneducated, in the different communities. However, when it really mattered as far as negotiating transition was concerned, the accommodationists rather than the confrontationists came to bargain. Why?

The answer to the puzzle in South Africa may lie not only in its economic interdependence but also in a relatively politically educated populace that flows from it. Although a third of the black voters are still functionally illiterate, apartheid has politicised even

those who cannot read and write. Together with this political education in daily life experience went an understanding of race relations,
particularly the artificiality of state-imposed racial distinctions.
Virtually all South African surveys during the past three decades
show the overwhelming majority of blacks favouring a government
which blacks and whites share. Legal equality, rather than reverse
domination, is desired by black voters the more they escape
traditional life through urbanisation, proletarianisation and better
education.

Horowitz[22] may have a point when he states that "ethnocentrism
increases with education", but this cannot be an unqualified gen-
eralisation. The obverse is also demonstrably true. In support,
Horowitz cites black attitude surveys that "a higher education
qualification was significantly associated with a negative attitude
toward Afrikaans-speaking whites". However, one should not con-
fuse ethnocentrism with heightened political consciousness and
militancy. When black students are found to be more nationalistic
during the apartheid era, this could also prove a higher level of
political awareness rather than ethnocentrism. These two states of
mind are not necessarily synonymous. Even the Black Consciousness Movement and its chief ideologue, Steve Biko, never argued
for an exclusive black republic or a glorified Africanness over
inferior European values. Black Consciousness aimed at psychological liberation from mental colonisation with the goal of equal co-
existence. Likewise, the supposedly racist PAC insists that it invented nonracialism long before the ANC, whom the PAC accuses
of still recognising racial subsections of Indian Congresses.

In short, if ethnocentrism means glorifying one's "in" group as
morally superior over culturally inferior "out" groups, South African blacks demonstrate a remarkable lack of this attitude. In the
population generally, open-mindedness correlates with higher education. Ethno-nationalism is highest amongst the least educated, as
voting behaviour clearly demonstrates. IFP ethno-nationalists come
mainly from rural areas and illiterate Zulu migrant workers. White
right-wing parties are over-represented among farmers and blue
collar workers. The Indian and coloured working class in Durban
and Cape Town voted overwhelmingly for the National Party, while
the ANC found most of its adherents among the professionals of
these middle groups.

This correlation between dogmatism and class and educational status is also found in other divided societies. In Israel, Likud and other right-wing parties find most of their support among the Sephardic section that is generally less educated and poorer than the descendants of European Jews. In Belfast, the reservoir of committed Ulster loyalists is deepest amongst the Protestant working class, that (unlike South Africa) proved strong enough to prevent a controversial leadership accommodation. In short, ethnocentrism decreases with higher education, professional occupations and alternative life chances from which a range of situational identities are derived. Those who are denied these opportunities of alternative identities have the greatest need to embrace ethnocentric self-definitions.

To sum up, it is unlikely that a pervasive threat to nation-building will be generated from an educational system that inculcates universalist values as is the case in South Africa. This does not mean that there will not be those who will mobilise on the basis of race and ethnicity and who have benefited from education, precisely because their actual experience is a contradiction of these values. This may very well be at the core of such mobilisation at tertiary institutions, although it involves a small minority of students and staff.

In the fourth instance, one must consider the role of religion in the context of nation-building.

Czeslaw Milosz[23] and other East European witnesses have pointed to the close ties of nationalism with religion, regardless of creed. "The Serbs' Eastern Orthodox church openly or implicitly blesses the horrors of ethnic cleansing. In Poland, the nationalists invoked Catholicism in support of their doctrine exalting Polishness, and they had the backing of a large part of the church hierarchy." The churches' stance on the relationship between Poles and Jews falsely implied that there could be no Jewish Poles. Indeed, how many Polish Catholics in Krakow could claim indifference towards what the Germans did a few kilometres away in Auschwitz and Birkenau without being in conflict with a staunchly professed faith still remains to be explained. At the same time, many individual Polish Catholics as well as monasteries shielded Jews from the Nazis at great risk to their own lives.

Ironically, religion can both reinforce nationalist aberrations as well as morally sensitise its adherents to their duties toward excluded fellow human beings. Humane charity and immoral callousness co-exist side by side. German Protestantism produced its share of collaborating praise-singers of Nazism as well as its Niemöllers, Bonhoeffers and other luminaries of a "confessing church". South African Calvinism wholeheartedly supported apartheid for a long time and then spearheaded the soul-searching away from racial domination. Likewise, the Israeli rabbinate generally supports a hard line on the treatment of Palestinians in defence of an expansive Zionist state while other rabbis denounce the very existence of Israel as a blasphemy of authentic Jewishness. Many Muslims support the Fatwa of the Ayatollahs against dissidents, while others are deeply embarrassed by the intolerance of holy warriors towards non-believers or emancipated women.

Nationalist ideologies usually mobilise with the semi-religious discourse of sacrifice. Second World War European nationalism portrayed the giving of one's life for one's people as the highest duty. Modern secularised nationalism no longer demands so much sacrifice in return for rewards. For example, Quebec separatists rally under the slogan of being materially better off outside the constraints of the federal state. Conservative Quebec nationalists promise that their flock is being looked after by a threatened welfare state.

Likewise, Afrikaner nationalism always displayed a hypersensitivity to white deaths, similar to Israeli concerns for its Jewish soldiers, as Annette Seegers has pointed out. Martyrdom is glorified among Israel's Islamic fundamentalist opponents but not among the defenders of Zionism or apartheid. Their concern with security and power rather than identity requires a rational calculation of human resources. Compared with the Palestinian suicide bombers in Israel, even the violent part of the South African struggle for liberation remained a rational affair. Nobody ever committed suicide in order to strengthen the battle. It never occurred to MK members to wear cyanide capsules around their necks as the fanatical Tamil Tigers have done in order to prevent being tortured for information in case of capture. The many suicides that are alleged to have taken place in South African prisons were mostly the result of regular torture of activists by security officials.

An absence of fundamentalism on both sides has characterised the South African conflict. Absolute religious values were not at stake. This proposition can again best be illustrated in comparison with the Middle East. For a Muslim fundamentalist in Cairo or Damascus, the existence of a Jewish state on Islamic soil constitutes a religious insult. Dismantling racial domination differed from the perceived battle with alien non-believers. Religious intruders who challenge the core of a collective identity with their very presence provoke an uncompromising resistance. Secularised politicians and generals may strive for peaceful co-existence, but even most Arab intellectuals, far from all being fundamentalists, still refuse to recognise the presence of Israel in their midst. Contacts with their Jewish counterparts rarely, if ever, exist. Even left-wing Israeli writers who wish to engage their Arab colleagues in seeking peace are rebuffed. At international conferences, Arab participants frequently leave when an Israeli speaks. Curious Israelis visit Egypt in droves, but Arab academics stay away from the "enemy country", let alone mourn at Jad Vaschem for a common humanity decimated at Auschwitz. Spielberg's film *Schindler's List* is banned in Arab countries, a ban supported by the intelligentsia. Any journalistic regret for the victims of Hamas bombings would border on treason. When Egyptian Nobel prizewinner Nagib Mahfuz courageously supported the peace process, he was the victim of an attempted assassination. Far-sighted writers like Mahfuz or Emil Habib are the exception to the rule in the Arab world, even in those states that have formally signed peace agreements with the "Zionist entity".

In contrast, white and black South African intellectuals and clergy fought alongside each other. At least they engaged each other even during the darkest days of apartheid. The long-standing tradition of apartheid criticism by secularised English-speaking liberals was eventually strengthened by increasing self-doubt at the heart of Afrikaner power. By the late 1980s, virtually the entire white social science and literary intelligentsia had dissociated itself from the P.W. Botha regime. Some had defected to a greater or lesser degree into the nonracial ANC orbit, even though only a few joined the liberation movement openly. Their common ground was a pragmatic rationality that simply lent a pluralistic dimension to the co-existence of different identities. No conception of contested sacred soil or place of worship provides a reason to engage in a holy war. Even the 2 per cent of Muslims in South Africa adhere to the moderate Sunni version of Islam. Although there are sporadic demonstrations against Israel by a Muslim minority in Cape Town, indifference rather than militant hostility towards Israel characterises the South African Muslim majority, which is more agitated about crime and drugs than religion. The dwindling number of less than 80 000 South African Jews support the Zionist cause but differ among themselves about everything else. The overwhelming majority of South Africans, white and black, belong to Christian religions, although increasingly nominally and less actively, despite a rhetorical adherence to religious rituals.

A common religious outlook, or even secularisation, does not necessarily immunise against ethno-nationalist mobilisation. Many a war has been fought among adherents of the same religious doctrine. In South Africa, however, religious believers of all denominations joined in the battle against apartheid and hence neutralised the divisive potential of religious frictions.

Unlike the Middle East or Northern Ireland with its deep-rooted religious perceptions of the enemy, religious morality united rather than divided South Africa's people, despite the existence of believers of many denominations. South African religiosity not only reflects the global variety of faiths, but an astonishingly open display of beliefs that the secularised Western culture has relegated to the private realm, if not hidden altogether. Hard-nosed, profit-conscious business leaders and cabinet ministers are not shy to be known as born-again Christians. Many Afrikaner households, even those of cynical academics, say the ritual grace with all the guests holding hands before dinner. The former Anglican archbishop talks to God directly as if He were a next-door neighbour separated by a back-yard fence. Desmond Tutu is said even to tell jokes to God. Buthelezi, a practising Anglican, even meets for "guidance" with this politicised bishop from the camp of his archenemy. Inkatha complains bitterly about the partisan stance of the churches in condemning political violence and comforting the victims at funerals of its opponents but not its own.

South Africa's Truth and Reconciliation Commission which grants compensation and amnesty upon confessions of past human rights violation is heavily dominated by clergy and reborn lawyers. Not one of the commissioners is a historian, philosopher or social scientist, because the task of healing the nation is automatically handed over to theologians. Confronting the past through public confessions contributes to public moral education. Had the task been left to historians, as Hermann Giliomee advocated, it would have been confined to an elite discourse among academics. That may have achieved greater analytical depth, but hardly the consciousness-raising sensitivity about a common human morality. However, the Truth and Reconciliation Commission would have benefited from more secularisation with less theological focus on prayer, sin, confession and repentance. Holding candles, praying and meditating in Cape Town's St George's Cathedral beside Parliament includes the agnostic President and Communist Party luminaries in church-led, semi-official rituals. The Cape Town church has become a national shrine, although the Anglican component of the religious flock comprises only a minority of 6 per cent. The South African Defence Force employs a total of 139 permanent chaplains, mostly for its Dutch Reformed Church members, and a number of part-time chaplains for the Muslim and Hindu minorities. Before the Defence Command Council meets, a chaplain-general leads them in prayer and scripture reading. Before regimental dinners, grace is said. The army argues that the practice boosts morale and assures soldiers that good and God are on their side. Even MK – under SACP command – had instituted a religious desk, whose members are now part of the chaplains' force.

This denominational pluralism exhibits a remarkable tolerance. Far from possessing an ecumenical spirit, the believers and their representatives nonetheless respect each other's faiths. When the apartheid regime bulldozed whole neighbourhoods into the ground under the ethnic cleansing policy of the Group Areas Act, it exempted the mosques and Hindu temples. They stand as forlorn survivors of religious respect in the devastated landscape of human disrespect. Without a state church, the men of the cloth nonetheless play an important role as protesters, mediators and reformers of public policy. The apartheid regime reeled under the constant attacks of its legitimacy by the South African Council of Churches with its worldwide support network. When the Calvinist synods finally concluded an agonising debate with the condemnation of apartheid as heresy, it robbed its apologists of their biblical justifications. Apartheid as sin and heresy amounted to its last death stab, albeit rather belatedly.

Similar liberation from cherished doctrine applies to the collapse of political ideologies. The end of the Cold War not only freed South African whites from their "total onslaught" hysteria, but also liberated the ANC unwittingly from their burdensome Soviet sponsor. Two unrecognised advantages for the ANC resulted from this break. No longer being allied to a vanished terror system made it easier for Western liberals to support a genuine liberation movement. Even more importantly, an ANC/SACP cut loose from a stifling doctrine of democratic centralism allowed the rulers-in-waiting to search pragmatically for feasible alternatives to a discredited command economy. Several prominent ANC exiles let their membership of the Communist Party lapse quietly. In short, what previously amounted to a reluctantly embraced asset, when no Western powers were ready to back the ANC cause, had turned into a liability that could finally be shed. Most were relieved, even many in the pro-Stalinist SACP. They vowed to replace vanguard authoritarianism with democratic socialism.

In short, with religion being reduced to a ritualised celebration of legitimacy, the steam has gone out of exclusive ethnic mobilisation. The few remaining true believers and dogmatic ideologues are open to counter-messages of unity and individual happiness outside a stifling doctrine advocated by a political ideology or an imposing clergy. Ethno-nationalism is only one among many identities on offer. Whether ethno-nationalism is embraced or rejected for a wider, more inclusive identity (patriotism), depends not only on collective predispositions but on material opportunities as well as status securities offered by the competing definitions of identity. In South Africa, the patriotic project of nation-building still awaits its test beyond its rhetorical proclamation.

Finally, within the context of nation-building, one can consider the role of the economy.

The most formidable objective force against communal strife in South Africa has always been a thorough economic interdependence. Nonetheless, Donald Horowitz,[24] among many other academic analysts, has explicitly doubted the significance of this bond for pragmatic accommodation: "The economic interdependence of South Africans is hardly different from the interdependence that characterised many societies later shattered by ethnic violence, among them Lebanon, Cyprus, Uganda and Sri Lanka."

This is a questionable conclusion to draw. The interdependence of Lebanon, Cyprus, Sri Lanka or Yugoslavia (not to speak of an agrarian society such as Uganda, where the majority is still engaged in subsistence agriculture) differs from the interdependence in South Africa. In Lebanon and the former Yugoslavia, separate communal economies exist side by side. The civil war harmed the overall state economy that relied on the co-operation and exchange of goods and services from the different ethnic regions and enclaves of the state. While disrupting those intercommunal economic ties, the strife did not destroy the communal economies onto which nationalists could fall back upon in their own territory. Hence Croats employed only Croats, Sinhalese only Sinhalese, and Greeks only Greeks in the territorially divided economy of Cyprus. Such exclusive communal economies caused a lower living standard, but they still allowed for the indefinite survival of the ethnic group, albeit with a reduced or negative growth rate, inflated prices, soft currencies and other indicators of long-term economic retardation.

In South Africa, on the other hand, there is no black or white economy. The number of blacks employed by black business remains negligible and there is hardly any white-owned business that does not rely heavily on black labour for its very existence and profits. This mutual dependency has always limited the potential ruthlessness of racial exploitation and dampened the militancy of the subordinates. When you go hungry the next week or you lose your only shelter in a hostile environment, you think twice about striking. Contrary to the Leninist immiseration theory – that radical actions increase with misery – impoverishment induces reluctant compliance. People struggling to survive the next day do not have the physical energy to think about alternative strategies. Political consciousness of the correct kind remains the luxury of a privileged and unionised labour aristocracy. This is confirmed by South Africa's history of labour conflicts. The longest and most bitter strikes in South Africa's labour history occurred among the best paid and most secure segments: the auto industry in Port Elizabeth and municipal employees in various towns. Conversely, corporate management had to take account of the grievances of its workforce well beyond the factory gates. As long as insecure transport, crime, unsafe housing, racial animosities and general political discontent affected productivity and identification with the occupation, no sophisticated employer could ignore such factors for competitive advantage.

It was these mutual interests and constraints on pursuing confrontation that forged bonds of dependency and mutual recognition. The current social-democratic compromise in place of class or racial warfare owes its foundation less to the moral conviction or political will of the antagonists than to this structural interdependence. Notwithstanding the goodwill of the negotiating elites, the objective situation of their constituencies allowed them limited choice in pursuing ethnic mobilisation for civil war. Even committed right-wing ideologues in rural town councils and school boards were quickly brought to heel when consumer boycotts by neighbouring black townships threatened their livelihood. With neither side being economically viable on its own, the political reconciliation amounts not so much to a "good surprise", let alone a miracle, but to an act of collective rationality.

In the Nazi case, ideological obsessions clearly overrode economic logic. Despite the increased need for labour in the war effort, the Nazis killed rather than exploited their slaves. As Gordon Craig[25] aptly remarked: "The Nazis operated officially designated work camps as if economic considerations were irrelevant, forcing their Jewish inmates to work at unproductive, repetitive and demeaning tasks with inadequate food and rest and under constant torture by brutal guards until they collapsed and died." In contrast, South African racism constantly adjusted its ideological rationalisations to economic necessities. Implemented to provide a cost-effective labour force in the first place – although that was not the only rationale – apartheid ideology was bent and ultimately forfeited because it clashed with economic imperatives.

Some analysts have used the concept of an ideological state. In such an entity, political power is geared towards implementing a grand vision. The de facto administrative structure is subordinated to an overarching ideology or a set of ideas that determines all state actions, regardless of other implications. Cuba, North Korea, Israel, the Vatican and Nazi Germany are examples of ideological states where the ruling elite legitimises itself with the myth of a mission that lies beyond normal pragmatic state interests. In its heyday, apartheid South Africa flirted with the notion of an ideological state but could never implement it fully because of economic counter forces as well as the controversial nature of a racial state within the white minority itself.

Industrial interdependence reduced the conflict over land and other non-negotiable issues that bedevil other communal conflicts. In the Middle East, the economic aspect of the conflict is clearly about land and water. Although space diminished as a security issue with the use of long-range rockets, fertile land is scarce and overcrowded. Redistribution of land is also said to be of crucial concern to South African blacks. The PAC made the return of the conquered land to the colonised indigenous people a central issue of its election platform. Not only the poor showing of the PAC in the 1994 election exposed the issue as a myth, but the number of blacks who eagerly wait to become subsistence farmers is generally overrated. Most rural unemployed would rather move to the city, if work were available, than till the soil. Blacks strive to improve their living conditions: whether by peasant farming or wage labour depends on availability and prospects. However, land hunger per se cannot be considered the burning desire it is made out to be. In all opinion surveys, land hardly figures as a high priority among black expectations. This reflects the basic industrial character of South African society, where farming is associated with rural backwardness and the city is seen as the venue for upward mobility.

Commentators have almost unanimously identified inflated expectations as the inevitable cause of mass disappointment and future instability. However, the concern over frustrated expectations may well stem from a European experience of relative deprivation that does not necessarily apply to Africa. Some observers have argued with good evidence that black South African people actually display low expectations. As Moeletsi Mbeki[26] points out: "They're willing to accept low standards, live off subsistence agriculture, wear the same sets of clothes for weeks on end and walk instead of riding a bicycle or motorbike. I would argue that we should in fact encourage expectations in South Africa." While this description fits the traditional peasants in Zimbabwe or Tanzania more than the urban proletariat in Soweto or Kwa Mashu, few ordinary black South Africans compare themselves with their white counterparts in the sense of measuring their satisfaction by having achieved consumerist affluence. With modest expectations, most hope for gradual improvement in the basic necessities of life rather than instant utopia. This colonised mind-set that compares itself to its own group members cushions the ANC's inability to deliver on vast promises.

Arguably one of the most comprehensive and penetrating historical analyses of race relations and the economy is Charles van Onselen's[27] *The Seed is Mine*. He demonstrates how interwoven and involved the economic interdependence of different communities in South Africa are. While the structure of the economy as such does not seem to provide a fertile ground for ethnic and racial mobilisation, one should not ignore the potential for such mobilisation from those who are marginalised and excluded from its benefits.

We began our response to the question: Can a nation be built in South Africa? by concentrating on the potential for ethnic mobilisation and disruption. However, the exclusive focus on seemingly embattled minorities overlooks a crucial benefit that derives from the widespread identification with ANC national interests for the old establishment in South Africa.

When COSATU shop stewards refuse to separate their class from their national identities, they simultaneously forego class confrontation in favour of compromise in the interest of the national good. For example, a survey by David Ginsburg and Eddie Webster[28] reports that "overwhelmingly, respondents expressed a deep-seated commitment to the nation-building politics of the Tripartite Alliance, in which their interests as workers would either be given only parity with – 62% – or would be subordinated to – 32% – the interests of other classes or the nation as a whole". Without this ANC/SACP induced patriotism, reconciliation would have failed. Adversarialism would have triumphed over the envisaged co-determination and conciliation procedures of the Labour Relations Act. The multi-class ANC alliance with all its emphasis on co-operation and economic concessions would shatter if the disruptive potential of black working class militancy were to be encouraged. Therefore, business interests too welcome the "false consciousness" of nation-building. Compared with true workerism in a state with one of the highest inequality rates in the world, national identifications dilute and contain an unrecognised potential for destabilisation. Anglo American has to thank the Tripartite Alliance for pacifying and disciplining its workers with the symbolic reward of national dignity in the absence of the material goods promised. Allister Sparks rightly castigates the complacency of the old beneficiaries when he writes,[29] "I am left with the overwhelming sense that the majority of whites don't appreciate how damned lucky they are."

On the other hand, Sparks may underestimate the Jacobean temptations among nation-builders and the conformity pressure on power-holders and former dissidents alike. In the midst of the elation, the long-term costs of gaining power are forgotten and euphoria blinds them to the dangers of their newly acquired status. Sitting in the chairs of office means losing the critical perspective of the outlaw. Vaclav Havel wittily expressed this predicament shortly after being sworn in as president of Czechoslovakia. He jokingly asked to be jailed again for a day or two each week. Yet as the saying goes, "You stand where you sit". If the new political bourgeoisie let their past as dissidents continue to influence their future public lives, it would amount to a welcome departure from contrary historical experience elsewhere. However, the pressure of office to conform, the drowning routine of tending to immediate problems, together with the need to fend off circling foes is unlikely to allow much space for the vulnerable maverick who thinks against the stream.

The task of retaining and rejuvenating the critical spirit will have to rest with the institutions of civil society. In particular, the alternative media will have to choose between continuing their previous role as cheerleaders of the ANC, or being watchdogs and unrelenting reminders of unfulfilled promises. Some of the liberal English-language mainstream press has been acquired by former ANC office-holders or powerful friends of the ANC such as the tycoon Tony O'Reilly, the colourful chairperson of H.J. Heinz. Other voices have fallen in line out of expediency. The bankrupt South African Broadcasting Corporation is being headed by loyal, card-carrying members of the ruling party. In this constellation, dissidents could easily become as marginalised in the new South Africa as they were under apartheid repression. ANC sympathiser, left-wing legal academic and outspoken media celebrity Dennis Davis[30] has pointed to the homogenising danger of ANC hegemony that has pulled in many elements of civil society in the name of nation-building: "The problem, increasingly, is that if anyone is going to criticise this nation-building process, you are going to be on your own. You are going to be exposed as profoundly treasonous, anti the nation. Any critique is likely to be rubbished as being unpatriotic, and therefore silenced. We have very few elements out there in civil society which are going to resist this project. I think that until such time as we break that concept of narrow nationalism, society is in terrible trouble."

However, the cultural frictions around nation-building in educational institutions and the role of dissidents pale in comparison with the simmering real conflicts of still grossly unequal life chances. A black university vice-chancellor who presses for institutional transformation or Africanisation may upset a corporate culture used to Eurocentric hegemony, but at the same time also distracts from "business as usual". As long as the rainbow nation can be kept delirious with Bafana victories and can wallow in enchanted kinship feelings, even the squatters without electricity and television fall in line. How lucky is an unequal national family with a magnanimous godfather at his helm who announces that "I want to sleep for eternity with a broad smile on my face" knowing that he has united his quarrelling underlings? Whether they are brainwashed in Xhosa, English, Zulu or Afrikaans by an Americanised SABC, whether Stellenbosch remains an exclusively Afrikaans institution or upholds mythical standards in English as well, whether local majorities have the right to insist on cultural security or have to accommodate initial cultural strangers – all these are important issues which excite the participants directly affected. However, in the big picture of political stability and economic growth, the cultural health of communities remains a sideshow. Members of privileged cultural minorities can always opt in or out of their groups according to individual preferences and circumstances. The unemployed in the squatter camps do not face such choices. In order to keep these racially homogenous outsiders in line, the multi-ethnic insiders can ill afford to quarrel among themselves about cultural symbolism. They have to manufacture common national identities.

General theories of nationalism and ethnocentric mobilisation can be enriched and revised by including the lessons from South Africa. An ethnic identity amounts to an awareness of culture in comparison with "others". The apartheid state mobilised culture for divide-and-rule purposes and thereby discredited ethnic identity among the disenfranchised. Elsewhere the political use of a shared historical tradition (ethnicity) correlates with increased economic competition and downward mobility. Political insecurity, status anxieties and doubts about individual identity are translated into a loss of collective worthiness. Nationalism promises to restore dignity and extinguish humiliation, according to specific group histories. Ethnic mobilisers develop myths in constructing scapegoats. The ascendancy to political power by the forces of liberation in the peaceful election in 1994 re-established dignity and identity for the colonised. It diminished the need for ethno-nationalist mobilisation, as apartheid could be blamed for all the misery.

It is generally recognised that ethno-nationalist discourses serve symbolic (psychological) as well as instrumental (economic) ends. Ethno-nationalism expresses claims to entitlement as well as identity needs. Nationalism appeals because it articulates belongingness and bestows meaning, but also because it aims at exclusionary power and monopoly control over scarce resources. The paradox to be explained is why people concerned with their misfortune and economic insecurity embrace nationalism, even if it entails greater sacrifices and material losses. During nationalist wars, whole armies march willingly to their deaths. Bathing in the glory of their collectivity compensates for real losses. Imagined group victories constitute the symbolic gratification that economic reality denies. The more individuals are demeaned, the more they need to borrow strength from victorious group membership, be it through identification with a sports team or by attaching themselves to "superior" religious or political causes. Those caught in the need to join are usually prone to denigrate and demonise non-believers.

In South Africa, a remarkable development in the opposite direction took place. Despite being demeaned by apartheid, blacks generally eschewed nationalism in favour of reconciliation with their oppressors. The oppressors in turn embraced their victims whom they had demonised as terrorists. Given the ideological warfare and the real battles and atrocities that took place in the name of ethno-racialism during four decades of formal apartheid, this pragmatic reconciliation disproves the essentialist and primordialist notions of incompatible ethnic group relations.

At the same time, neither opponent cultivated a culture of revenge. Nor did they merge their ethno-racial identities in an assimilationist fashion. Everyone is aware of his or her "race" after decades of official racial classification. South Africa continues to be a "divided society" in the sense of phenotypical as well as cultural cleavages, reinforced by vast class differences. However, the apartheid emphasis on racial difference made ethno-racial divisions increasingly controversial. The two sides can co-operate not only because they need each other for their mutual wellbeing, but also because they are secure in their self-definition and recognise each other as legitimate citizens with different identities.

This mutual reading of "race" in South Africa differs from the group perceptions in other ethno-racial or communal conflicts. Because the intergroup differences were so entrenched during apartheid, members of each group can transcend their group identity in the post-apartheid era without endangering their self-definitions. Serbs and Croats speak the same language and belong to a Christian tradition with minor ritual differences. Yet Serbs and Croats have become mortal antagonists in their collective attitudes. In South Africa, the very real ethno-racial differences in a so-called divided society have facilitated the emergence of a common state.

At the ideological level, pragmatic co-operation is assisted by mutual group mythologies that avoid inferiorisation. Blacks and whites constructed self-definitions of selected superiority that complement each other without inferiorising the other indiscriminately. The image of whites as technically competent providers of vital goods and services is widely accepted in both camps. The image of moral superiority of blacks as victims of unjust discrimination holds equal currency on both sides. It did not instil in blacks a sense of personal or collective inferiority, since disadvantage could be attributed to "the system". Individual failure – debilitating self-hate and self-racism – thereby was minimised. With whites accepting that amends had to be made for past injustices for which they, and not the blacks, had to be blamed, the ground was laid for the co-operation of equals. Blacks, on the other hand, perceived corrective policy measures not as charity for which they had to be grateful, but as rights long denied.

In these intergroup perceptions of mutual moral recognition, South Africa differs fundamentally from the US and other countries, where a relatively powerless minority remains at the mercy of a dominant majority, with all the psychological consequences that such an unequal relationship implies for members of both groups. South Africa also has little in common with Euro-fascist racism.

Bosnian Serbs and Muslims no longer distinguish between members of the other side, but distrust each other as ethnic group members. Identification of white communists and liberals with the black cause and the need to find black collaborators for the white regime always mitigated against collective stereotyping on both sides. It blurred the boundaries of communalism.

Can a South African nation be built? The potential for ethnic/racial polarisation and mobilisation is ever present. But it has been for as long as South Africa has existed. Ethnic/racial/cultural divisions and differences have been exploited, manipulated and ideologised in the pursuit of power and domination. However, when transition began in earnest in South Africa, these were not the dominant forces that determined the dynamic and pace of change. Another potential is also locked into the body politic of South Africa. We have tried to show how this was possible in constitutional negotiations, language policy, education, religion and the economy. We are not sanguine about transcending loyalties developing in South Africa to help forge a multicultural nation in which unity seeks its strength out of diversity. But we do argue that there is convincing evidence that a South African nation is not only possible but a distinct probability.

Chapter Seven

What about the Zulus?

Very few commentators who have lectured on the South African situation have not at one or other stage been confronted by this question. It is usually posed with an air of sinister profundity as if to suggest that no matter how rational or coherent the analysis, this is one source of lurking irrationality that can undo the best laid plans of mice and men.

We do not look upon "the Zulus" (or Xhosas, Vendas, Sothos, etc.) as homogeneous ethnic groups with unchanging, irreconcilable interests in a multinational society. In fact, to the extent that one can talk about serious inter-ethnic conflict in South Africa it has largely been confined to migrant workers in mining housing concentrations and to some extent in some residential areas in urban environments, usually with single hostel accommodation. Far more serious violence has been of an intra-ethnic nature between Zulus and Zulus or Xhosas and Xhosas in the rural heartlands in the eastern parts of South Africa. The overall nature of the conflict is more a result of modernity versus traditionalism, or traditional versus democratic legitimacy or urban insiders versus rural outsiders. It is in this context that one has to understand also the conflict between the ANC and Inkatha, which, if politically mismanaged, can have very serious destabilising consequences but is certainly not impossible to resolve.

In March 1994, among the high-rise office towers of Johannesburg, a single incident epitomised the unresolved clash of traditionalism and modernity, of countryside and city. It showed insecure resentful migrant workers being taught a lesson by self-confident new political masters, ethnic loyalties being manipulated by self-serving elites, and new urban ethnic legends being constructed for future battles. The ongoing violence between the African National Congress and Inkatha usually occurs out of sight in the Natal countryside with the ANC being portrayed as the main victim. Suddenly the conflict had culminated in an embarrassing reversal of victimhood for the forces of liberation. The new rulers showed everyone that they could behave as ruthlessly towards their opponents as their own oppressor had done for decades. Moreover, the moral high ground that the ANC and Mandela justifiably held in the eyes of the world was momentarily shattered by the incident, better to be forgotten and reinterpreted than thoroughly analysed. The event also revealed why it is impossible to arrive at an agreed-upon truth in an ongoing ideological battle even if dozens of "objective" foreign observers witness the occasion.

On 28 March 1994, a month before the first democratic election in South Africa, about 50 000 Zulu migrant workers converged on central Johannesburg from outlying hostels and squatter camps for an anti-election mass rally in support of the Zulu king. By the end of the day, eight of the Zulu marchers had been killed by ANC guards around the ANC headquarters at Shell House, more were shot randomly by unknown gunmen from surrounding buildings at Library Gardens and scores of injured, both protesters and bystanders, lay in their blood on city streets. Despite hundreds of eyewitnesses, journalists and film crews, statements in Parliament and a 172-page submission by the police to the Goldstone Commission of Inquiry Regarding the Prevention of Public Violence and Intimidation, totally contradictory versions of the events surrounding the Shell House shooting are accepted by the partisans. The Acting Attorney General for the Witwatersrand, Kevin Attwell, says South Africa may never get the answers it awaits, while a researcher for the liberal Institute of Race Relations writes in an institute publication of a "Chappaquiddick-like sore that will fester politically for years to come".[1] Inkatha compares the Shell House shooting to the massacre of fleeing protesters by the apartheid police at Sharpeville 34 years earlier.

The ANC version speaks of disorderly fanatic Zulu marchers bent on attacking the ANC headquarters, defended by guards reluctantly forced to shoot in legitimate self-defence. Indeed Mandela himself in a surprise statement in Parliament several months later revealed that he had given explicit orders to shoot to kill if necessary. Before the event he had telephoned the then State President De Klerk and the Commissioner of Police requesting special security precautions around the ANC headquarters as party leaders were at risk. The police report details the extra forces and soldiers deployed around the city and Inkatha-friendly hostels in response to these well-founded fears. Nobel-prize laureate Nadine Gordimer however states: "No roadblocks were set up around the city; the police outside Shell House that day ran away."[2] Yet film footage shows nervous policemen with guns guarding against snipers kneeling over the bodies of shabbily clad peasants. Gordimer, normally an outspoken champion of poor people's causes, calls these Zulu traditionalists "undisciplined hordes coming to the city with the threat of violence and violence itself". The police, on the other hand, argue "that at no stage were marchers seen attacking Shell House", and that the shooting had, in any case, taken place away from the entrance to that building, when ANC guards opened fire on marchers 50 to 70 metres away "for no reason whatsoever". The police assert that the trigger-happy ANC guards constantly pointed firearms at passing marchers by standing outside and on the balcony of the building and being hostile and unco-operative when asked to withdraw by the police. Another plausible version asserts that right-wing police generals deliberately rerouted the marchers past Shell House in order to provoke inter-black pre-election clashes. This suspicion is backed by the absence of roadblocks around the ANC headquarters. The whole incident was further clouded by Mandela's refusal to let the police enter his head-quarters after the shooting in order to search for weapons, take statements, and arrange for ballistic tests. The investigation was stalled because witnesses felt intimidated and were unco-operative in rendering statements, according to the Attorney General. Another official inquest with public hearings started in 1997.

The events mark an important moment in the history of South Africa's political transition. Competing political forces laid claim to city areas and exclusive sovereignty; the Zulu migrants were mobilis-ed in the name of a threatened ethnicity by expedient leaders who shortly afterwards switched sides: the Zulu king in whose defence against alleged ANC assaults the protesters rallied joined the ANC camp after securing his economic fiefdom. Buthelezi's Inkatha decided to participate in the election at the last minute after the promise of international mediation of outstanding issues. They later worked together in a government of national unity while their followers continued to kill each other. Each Christmas and Easter holiday when the male migrant workers return to their rural homesteads, the killing rate soars as old and new scores are settled among people who all live on the poverty line. Since Zulus fight mainly Zulus, the clashes cannot be labelled tribal or ethnic. As hardly any whites or Indians are ever affected, the conflict is clearly not a racial one either. Nor can it be described as entirely a political competition, in which unscrupulous leaders mobilise ethnic sentiment. Unlike Bosnia, the political elites of South Africa constantly preach peace and sit in the same cabinet. Nonetheless, they deal with each other as semi-sovereign entities akin to nation-states. Since the political heads come from different ethnic groups, their relationship is inevitably perceived as the result of ethnic or tribal animosity.

Inkatha supporters represent the poorer, more rural, more illiterate, older and more traditional section of the eight million Zulu group. Historically, Zulus were conquered last and were therefore considered better organised and more resistant to colonisation. They developed, like the Serbs in their battles with Muslims through the Middle Ages, a "heroic warrior" mythology of bravery and invincibility. Only Zulus cherish the memory of powerful kings. Only Zulus developed a rudimentary state that predates colonialism. This ethnic memory and cultural heritage are bound up with Zulu identity, invoked, manufactured and mobilised by traditional elites who are threatened by democratic modernity. They deeply resent the uprooted, urbanised youth who reject the tribal authorities and embrace the ANC. All Zulus experience a profound value conflict in which the traditionalists are gradually losing out. In the past, they relied heavily on conformity pressure and bureaucratic patronage to keep dissenters in line.

Seeking democratic legitimacy in a multi-party electoral competition would humiliate the pre-modern traditionalists. Theirs is a feudal vision, beyond plebiscite. "I want to state very clearly that I," the King declared in his January 17, 1994 memorandum to De Klerk, "the Royal Household, the Amakhosi and all who are genuine Zulu subjects, cannot accept that any majority in the rest of South Africa has the right to decide on our future." A Zulu king need not contest elections, said Buthelezi. The King merely claims back what has been taken from him: the whole of Natal.

Imagined tradition is invoked whenever democratic legitimacy works against leadership strategies. Scoffing at suggestions by journalists that IFP MPs who walked out of Parliament were "cowards", Buthelezi responded: "Our ancestors would hardly regard participation in debates in the House of Assembly as acts of valour befitting warriors."

The two sides differ on how conflicting visions of the new order should be settled: the ANC considers majority rule as the basic democratic mechanism, while the IFP wants to enshrine crucial features of the state beyond voting. "There are fundamental issues, such as those of federalism and pluralism, which cannot be decided by majority rule, no matter how large is the majority concerned," clarifies Chief Buthelezi in an April 1995 letter to President Mandela. The promised international mediation the ANC's Penual Maduna declares "an undemocratic route," because it would bypass the elected ANC majority in the Constitutional Assembly and "impose the consequences on the nation".[3] In this case, the ANC should never have agreed to international mediation of all "outstanding issues". In principle, both sides are right: majority rule is specifically mentioned as an unalterable, negotiated principle that binds the constitution-makers. However, the IFP's insistence on true federalism is not only politically prudent in a divided society, but constitutionally legitimate in many democracies which contain unalterable principles, such as federalism or divisions of power, that no majority, even a qualified one, can ever overturn without throwing out the constitution itself. In the unresolved debate on the degree of federalism there should be, Inkatha wants an asymmetrical system with different powers than the other provinces. Like Quebec, Inkatha argues that the new constitution should reflect "the unique character of the province", meaning a constitutional monarchy. Inkatha insists on the principle of subsidiarity, i.e. that the centre should not exercise powers that can be administered locally. While this devolution of authority to the lowest level feasible has become respectable in the European debate about overcentralisation and overregulation by bureaucrats of the European community, it is fraught with a different history in South Africa. The divide and rule designs of apartheid have discredited regional rule. Federalism is frequently equated with ethnic "balkanisation", although most new provinces comprise a mixture of ethnic population groups. Despite this territorial federalism, the

ANC insists that the central government overrides provincial powers in the name of ensuring national standards and addressing the backlogs of apartheid through redistributive policies. Given that KwaZulu-Natal comprises 24 per cent of South Africa's population but generates only 16 per cent of GDP, Inkatha's demand for fiscal autonomy backfires. The economic dependency of the province on the rest of the country rules out any possibility of secession with the same living standards.

Nationalism, however, is only partially restrained by adverse economic conditions, as the Quebec separatists demonstrate. It is not only the abuse of ethnicity by apartheid, but the emergent secessionist tendencies incorporated in ethnic claims that traumatises ANC advocates of a central state. Their hostility towards federal designs does not stem solely from the motive to grab all power for themselves at the centre but from the fact that Afrikaner and especially Zulu self-determination could lead to the dismantling of a unitary South African state. Therefore, the ANC would at most concede regionalism, namely the delegation of some power from the centre while denying true federalism, i.e. that the power of the centre derives from the regions. Even territorial federalism, according to Western models, is frequently rejected as neo-apartheid in disguise. On the other hand, Afrikaner Volksfront constitutional spokesperson Fanie Jacobs said that "the Zulus' struggle for self-determination was virtually the same as that of Afrikaners". Volkstaat advocates dream of an independent Boer republic recognising and entering into treaties with a sovereign Zulu monarchy in areas of security and the economy.

In January 1995, Buthelezi defined the relationship with the new "politically estranged" king as a rescue duty for Inkatha. "Our first option is to devise a path which would enable His Majesty to return to his father's people from the spiritual exile to which government's dark forces and those who are working from the demise of our kingdom have relegated him." Buthelezi, part of the "dark" central government himself as Interior Minister, appropriates "the Zulu nation" for Inkatha. He blamed the ANC for encouraging the schism with the King. Not for the first time it was hinted that Inkatha-aligned chiefs might call for the abdication or replacement of the King although the King and Inkatha have subsequently become reconciled. The Amakhosi (chiefs) were concerned that scheduled local elections in their areas would undermine their power. With the ANC being able to organise and canvass in hitherto closed areas of rural Natal, this bridgehead of anti-traditionalists in the heartland of feudal tradition presents a direct threat to the chiefs' hereditary status. Not only could some particularly un-popular chiefs be deposed in election, but the proposed inclusion of chiefs as ex officio members of the local government would mini-mise their basis for patronage and traditional power to allocate land. The conflict presents an almost classical test between the legitimacy and clout of democratically elected authorities and entrenched traditional powers whose popular acceptance has al-ways been assumed but remained untested. Feudal hereditary power as opposed to a democratically legitimated mandate is being contested in Natal.

The ANC faces a similar conflict between democrats and tradi-tional leaders in its domain in the Eastern Cape. It has not resolved the contradiction between declaring chiefs as "part of our heritage" who continue to "enjoy a lot of support", and at the same time support democratically elected structures of governance in the rural areas. Since the ANC national executive overwhelmingly backs the democratic position, the former ANC aligned traditional leaders may well forge an alliance with the Inkatha traditionalists. This emerging coalition of anti-democratic traditionalists transcends ethnicity. As long as rural inhabitants have to rely on autocratic hereditary chiefs for access to strategic resources, backed by offi-cially recognised customary laws of polygamy and women's exclu-sion from power, the conflict will simmer, regardless of ethnicity. Inkatha's threat to exclude 2,5 million people in rural Natal from the opportunity to cast a vote should the chiefs' traditional role be undermined represents an admission of weakness rather than strength. If traditional authority is as widely accepted as its pro-ponents claim, it should not fear submitting its status to democratic approval. On the other hand, Inkatha reverts to democratic legiti-misation when the prospects of winning a popular contest are good or the issue is less important. This is the case with the Inkatha-backed referendum on whether Ulundi or Pietermaritzburg should be the provincial capital. While defending a popular vote on this issue, Inkatha eschews "Western democracy" and hails the "tradi-tional democracy" of chiefly rule as the appropriate mechanism when its own power base is at stake. In similar contradictions of expediency, the organisation used the Zulu monarch for its political goals before the ANC's ascendancy to power, but aims at depoliticising and neutralising the king's role after the royal court backed the ANC for a while.

Ironically, the King's switch resulted from an unintended consequence of Inkatha and De Klerk striving to entrench the Zulu monarchy shortly before the first democratic election. By giving the Zulu king jurisdiction over vast areas of trust land in Northern Natal and a guaranteed higher income, it allowed the present incumbent to free himself from financial dependency on the Inkatha-dominated provincial government. With his own security guard and financial base, Zwelithini, surrounded by hundreds of princely relatives "with their own political agenda, aristocratic intrigues and long-standing personal feuds too complex to be deciphered by commoners", as an Inkatha official explained, could finally distance himself from Buthelezi, the domineering uncle. The King's turn-about in political loyalties has further inflamed conflicts at hostels. For example, the Durban Dalton Men's Hostel recorded 23 deaths at the beginning of 1995 after the KwaZulu-Natal Hostel Residents' Association (Khora) was formed in support of Zwelithini's "neutral" stance. When the IFP responded by launching its own branches in previously violence-free hostels in Umlazi, the heightened politicisation of the cramped living space resulted in new confrontations. The new political identity that previous apolitical migrants had acquired was promptly acted out.

Throughout KwaZulu-Natal, assassinations of political activists on both sides have continued after the election. However, the 50 per cent vote for Inkatha in the province has led paradoxically to an increasing number of its loyalists being targeted. Apart from simple revenge, the stated reasons for these attacks on entire families remain obscure and hidden behind propagandistic rationalisations in a simultaneous media war. For example, the killing of Inkatha chiefs and their relatives was explained by ANC opponents as the work of hard-line Inkatha members who objected to their colleagues' peace overtures, including their advocacy of the return of ANC refugees to the area under their control.

Many English-language South African journalists, as well as most foreign correspondents writing for a liberal opinion abroad, are more favourably inclined toward the ANC's interpretations than "tribal" Inkatha or Africanist visions. In South Africa, liberation politics is largely conducted in English, which paradoxically makes it more accessible to outsiders than to the two-thirds of the locals who have only a Standard 6 education and a minimal understanding of English. Few journalists or liberal academics bother to explore the views of rural people, migrants and squatters who are thought to be ably represented by a popular sophisticated elite.

James Fenton[4] has pointed to the example of French and European support for the efficient Hutu regime before the genocide in Rwanda in 1990. Its dictatorial features notwithstanding, the people's government was encouraged by foreign infatuation. "This proneness to infatuation – with a people, with a regime – is typical of colonialists, missionaries, aid workers and certain kinds of foreign correspondents. It is natural perhaps for anyone living the lonely life of the outpost, but it poses problems when the infatuation for one people is at the expense of another." A similar kind of uncritical adoration by left-liberal observers benefits the Mandela government while the international conservatives extend the same blind loyalty to Chief Buthelezi. Prone to adopt African clients upon whom they can bestow their material or rhetorical largesse, the "objective" outsider turns into a propagandist.

The failure to understand accurately Inkatha-ANC differences adds to the prospects of more violent clashes wherever Zulu nationalists and ANC supporters live together. The main fallacy considers KwaZulu as merely another artificial apartheid creation, an unpopular Bantustan propped up by Third Force elements, a tribal relic, with Buthelezi a surrogate and dependent client. Therefore, it is falsely argued, the centre tightening the screws would easily eliminate "the Zulu problem". The ANC took it upon itself to deal with its aberrant offspring in similar ways as it had used to defeat the corrupt and unpopular Bophuthatswana and Ciskei regimes through easily instigated uprisings. Cyril Ramaphosa, contrary to his reconciling pragmatism in negotiations with the National Party, compared Inkatha to "howling dogs" which will eventually fall silent or will have to be forcibly silenced when the democratic caravan inevitably moves on.

Even conservative international opinion that once hailed Buthelezi as the nonviolent, capitalist hope, turned against "the spoiler" who refuses to come on board. The liberal South African press perceived Buthelezi's rule as based mainly on force and patronage. Ken Owen[5] urged De Klerk to cut off all state support immediately: money, personnel, facilities and access to credit. "Only when Chief Buthelezi's reign of terror in Ulundi is brought to an end will we know how many Zulu people support him. Only when his administration is allowed to collapse will the Zulu people be able to join the rest of South Africa in the march to freedom." The war talk and sense of invasion was further accelerated by former ANC youth chief Peter Mokaba saying that "the ANC will march into the KwaZulu capital Ulundi to show that it is not afraid of IFP leader Mr Buthelezi" (*Weekend Argus*, 7 April 1994). Mokaba said that his organisation was becoming tired of demands made by Inkatha. Former Transkei leader Bantu Holomisa offered his forces to subdue Zulu feudalists. SACP candidate and TEC co chairman Pravin Gordhan called for the state of emergency to be intensified and the Zulu government to be axed. "It is time that political and economic clout was brought to bear" on KwaZulu. Buthelezi should be stripped of his position as provincial police minister, the ANC argued before the 1994 election.

It is no wonder that the targets of the threats found their tribal paranoia of Zulus being dominated by Xhosas confirmed by the ill-considered verbal warfare. Indeed the sticks, axes and shields that the illiterate Zulu migrants wield during the hyped-up marches constitute less of a dangerous weapon than the incitement to violent escalation in the name of preventing violence. Above all, tanks and artillery columns rolling into the Natal hinterland would be unable to stop the infighting among a deeply divided population. It is not a question of subduing a mutiny or defending an area against a foreign invader, but pacifying a fragmented people. The sight of martial weaponry achieves the opposite. Indeed the mutual killings increased after the state of emergency allowed Inkatha, in the words of Central Committee member B.S. Ngubane, to portray itself as victim of "part of a well-planned strategy aimed at destroying any political opposition prior to the elections" (*Business Day*, 8 April 1994). Zulu traditionalists lament being "raped" with the National Party as an accomplice in the crime by "holding the woman down". At the level of popular indoctrination, nationalist wars were always fought in the name of defending the virginity and honour of women at home against alien intruders. By using emotive sexual allegories for ethnic mobilisation, Zulu traditionalists proved themselves worthy emulators of their colonial masters.

A strong siege mentality had developed in Ulundi. Many Inkatha activists came to regret that KwaZulu had not opted for independence, so that it would have a Transkei-like army to resist what they considered to be an invasion and second conquest. Inkatha would not have to pay the price for having acted in a politically correct manner in the past by defying Pretoria's apartheid scheme of independent homelands. The irony that Transkei military leaders by virtue of their independent Bantustan role could now come out victorious while the KwaZulu homeland as a non-independent part of South Africa was more vulnerable to pressure from the centre was certainly not lost on the traditionalists in Ulundi. It added to the sense of bitterness and betrayal. Simon Barber[6] summarised the prevailing attitude towards Buthelezi on the day of the Shell House shooting: "Nobody even bothers to try to understand Inkatha leader Mangosuthu Buthelezi's position anymore, let alone how he might have come to it. Certainly not now that there are bodies on the street outside Shell House in Johannesburg. Safer to diagnose him as mad, or megalomaniac or both, and watch as his turf is forcibly cleared to make way for free and fair elections. Too bad he got in the way." Indeed, Inkatha's public relations were not helped by the idiosyncrasies of its leader. Diplomats pathologise Buthelezi with a personality problem. However, the medicalisation of an underlying sociopolitical conflict does not solve the issue. Repressive strategies, be they of a military or administrative kind, exacerbate a deep rift that can only be solved politically through mutual concessions in good faith negotiations. Neither side has so far shown the political will to achieve a mutually satisfactory compromise. Hence Inkatha's declining support, ANC triumphalism in the light of a national election victory and NP technocratic designs to save their stakes have combined "to let the Zulu issue play itself out". Few realise that such passive "blame-the-other-side politics" ruins the grand negotiated revolution, even if the weaker Zulu traditionalists are eventually crushed. As long as Inkatha and ANC supporters consider themselves in a virtual state of war, no force can guarantee free and fair elections in the region.

Ironically, inasmuch as the constitutional compromise was negotiated, so were parts of the 1994 election results, particularly in northern Natal. The practice made a mockery of the slogan of voters' education. "Every vote counts": many votes were neither counted nor cast according to prescribed procedures, although this portion of disputed votes constituted a minority and not more than 4,5 per cent of the total votes cast in Natal. Similar widespread irregularities occurred in the Eastern Cape, which gave both the ANC and IFP leadership reasons to avoid a challenge with the likely prospect of renewed violence. However, the failure of both parties and the Independent Electoral Commission to inform the public about their secret deals has undermined the acceptance of election results in certain circles and affected voters' confidence in future elections. R.W. Johnson aptly concludes his comprehensive account of the 1994 election:[7] "In a country where social and political peace depends upon a respect for all substantial minorities, it was literally dangerous to life and limb to so shroud the electoral result in mystery that it was possible for one party to claim that the votes gained by others were so fraudulent that effectively they did not have constituencies that needed to be respected."

Ken Owen has identified "a powerful sense of their own virtue"[8] among the ANC leadership. He speculated that this attitude stems from the exiles being lionised overseas as the refugees from an immoral system now occupying the moral high ground. However, what Owen exaggerates as "profound dislike of dissent" and "hostility to rival power centres, whether province or Press or business itself" shows itself mainly towards Inkatha. Since its split with Inkatha in 1979, the ANC as a whole has basically denied the legitimacy of the rival organisation, minimised and ridiculed its support and aimed at destroying its remnants by all means possible. The notion of Inkatha as an artificial creation of the apartheid state originated in ANC strongholds in Natal. Once state support was withdrawn and the patronage of Inkatha drained, the organisation was supposed to collapse. Later it was believed that if the Zulu king could be enticed to switch sides, the symbolic power of the monarch would achieve the same end. When this did not occur, despite the king's condemnation of his autocratic uncle Buthelezi, the ANC put its hope in buying off the chiefs whose majority constituted the mainstay of Inkatha support in rural Natal. By paying the three hundred chiefs the same high salaries as the members of parliament together with car allowances, secretaries and bodyguards, the ANC government intended to erode the alliance between Inkatha and the Amakhozi. Instead of heeding the lessons from the same failed attempts of blatant bribery of traditional leaders by the apartheid state, the new rulers repeat the discredited politics of co-optation and blackmail. Alexander Johnson[9] has commented: "Though by no means the only factor inhibiting the growth of 'normal' political competition in KwaZulu-Natal, this strategic mind-set is a particularly aggravating one."

The NP and ANC together have facilitated Inkatha's sense of exclusion and rejection. Buthelezi, who always considered himself an equal player to De Klerk and Mandela, was shunned by both. The National Party turned away from a potential alliance with Inkatha when it became clear that it could not deliver the votes. The constitution initially even omitted the name KwaZulu. However, a more fundamental error was committed by the ANC and the NP at the end of 1992. Frustrated by the slow progress of the negotiations after the breakdown of CODESA, both self-appointed "senior partners" decided to engage in bilateral negotiations. While this is understandable and was subsequently practised by other parties, the ANC and the NP also resolved that the outcome of their bilateral talks would in future not be allowed to be undermined by multilateral negotiations. This reduced the Kempton Park negotiations to a rubber-stamp function, to a take-it-or-leave-it role for the smaller parties. Inkatha together with the right wing walked out. They can now claim that they had no part in designing the new order although Buthelezi promised to abide by the new constitution. A process that should have been as inclusive as possible had turned into a fatally exclusive exercise. Had Inkatha been part of the "sufficient consensus" of modern constitution-making, it would not have had to fall back so much on feudal rationalisation for its continued existence.

In this constellation, Zulu nationalists perceive their very survival at stake, apart from being humiliated. "Can you imagine," the then Inkatha-aligned king implored De Klerk, "the hurt that you, as Head of State, have inflicted on us Zulus, Mr President, in allowing us to be humiliated in this way, by people who have never conquered us in any war? People who would never conquer us if we were to engage in any such conflict. Can you imagine?" Nationalism everywhere feeds on wounded identity. Not even being allowed to entertain the option of a Zulu semi-autonomy, which the ANC theoretically has granted its right-wing opponents, and the feeling of being deceived by the abrogated promise of international mediation, the threatened traditionalists turned to active resistance and boycotts of the democratic process. Ethnic mobilisation from above falls on fertile ground as long as nationalist identity remains the only security deprived people can achieve. Ethnicity provides a sanctuary when other identities are denied.

The ANC has treated the IFP more as a security problem than as a political opposition with which the ruling party has to co-exist. Calling the IFP a "bandit organisation" (Steve Tshwete of the ANC) or dismissing Buthelezi as a "mean-spirited, gutter mouthed politician"[10] may escalate the verbal warfare and delegitimise the party in the eyes of its detractors. However, the fact remains that the party received 50 per cent of the 1994 votes in South Africa's most populous province, even if the result continues to be suspect as a negotiated one.[11] Instead of hoping that the IFP would cease to exist "after Buthelezi", the new power-holders would act more wisely if they were to strengthen the moderate elements in the IFP who share much of the ANC's concerns about avoiding the ongoing strife in a province that desperately needs economic growth. With a declining support base due to continued urbanisation, the IFP-oriented chiefs could well be driven into more regressive stances unless the stronger ANC accommodates the feudal remnants in a similar prudent compromise as the dangerous white right wing has been neutralised. Concessions towards an imaginative federalism and sincere efforts to include the boycotting IFP promise to be more effective long-term solutions to the ongoing political violence than deploying more soldiers and policemen.

Some unexpected progress in reconciliation has been achieved in recent times. Inkatha moderated its demands, dropped the call for international mediation and participated constructively in the GNU and parliament. Mandela, on the other hand, repeatedly appointed Buthelezi as acting president during his absence from the country, and some regional ANC leaders under the affable Jacob Zuma have also established good relations with their IFP counterparts. A genuine reconciliation or even a merger of the ANC and the IFP could also be conceivable in future.

Chapter Eight

Corporatism: Business-union-state relations

New constraints on any government's freedom of action at the turn of the millennium are imposed by the incorporation of the South African economy into the global market. Globalisation has not only undermined the power of national governments in Western industrialised economies, but has particularly affected the autonomy of semi-developed states to shape their political economy in a protected domestic market towards a supply-side economy, stimulated by export-driven growth. The need to be internationally competitive and to attract foreign investment forces a fundamental restructuring at home. The scope, pace and context of this shift, particularly the reduction of traditional public activity towards privatised services under profit imperatives, is of course highly contested.

In order to manage such conflicts more rationally, corporatism provides a more effective form of decision making than adversarialism. Corporatism represents the national institutionalisation of global imperatives, articulated by business organisations and state bureaucrats. Regulated bargaining between labour, business and the state replaces adversarial relations. Ideally, the force of argument is substituted for the argument of force. In labour relations, trials of strength through strikes and lock-outs are avoided in favour of mediation and compulsory arbitration. Since corporatism relies on consensus rather than the triumph of the stronger party, it provides, at least theoretically, another veto against unilateral decision making. Politically motivated restructuring by the state is dependent on reciprocal consent by labour and business; industrial action by unions is heavily prescribed and regulated, likewise managerial autonomy is circumscribed by expanded and legislated union rights. All three actors are supposed to engage in trade-offs so that all conflicting interests are accommodated in rational compromises through bargaining.

A vast general literature on corporatism exists, dominated perhaps by three prolific writers: Philippe Schmitter, Gerhard Lehmbruch and more recently Markus Crepaz.[1] To what extent are the lessons and insights from thirty years of postwar corporatist reconstruction in some parts of Europe and Japan relevant for contemporary South Africa? Three issues in the literature stand out that directly relate to the quite different history and unique conditions of South Africa with its current attempts of parallel corporatist decision making: (1) the problem of minority influence in a majoritarian democracy; (2) the question of the effectiveness of corporatism to achieve higher growth rates, lower unemployment and fewer industrial disputes than in countries with laissez-faire pluralism of interest representation; and (3) the relative political power and ideological outlook of state, capital and labour. On all three counts, South Africa represents unique conditions.

(1) The Swedish analyst Leif Lewin[2] has stated: "Corporatism is a method to pacify intense minorities by giving them another opportunity to influence politics when they have no chance in parliament." Where the will of the majority decides and in Stein Rokkan's dictum, "votes are counted, not weighed", democracy is faced with a so-called "intensity problem". Permanently excluded minorities with intense preferences opt out of the system or sabotage it. Corporatism fosters social integration by providing additional channels of influence. Interested organisations are formally given a voice, or even a veto elsewhere, be it in boardrooms through co-determination or through representation in state agencies and committees that formulate policies. In this way, the state harnesses extra-parliamentary expertise, resolves potential conflicts and smoothes the passage of legislation. Kenneth McRae has pointed out that corporatism and consociationalism both rely on a "disposition among elites towards collaborative or co-operative rather than authoritative or majoritarian modes of decision making".[3] Lijphart and Crepaz explored the degree of corporatism and "consensus democracy" for eighteen Western countries empirically.[4] They found that "corporatism can be thought of as a more broadly defined concept of consensus democracy"[5] with some of the smaller European countries (Netherlands, Switzerland, Finland, Denmark) leading the consensual states while the English-speaking

Commonwealth countries and the United States are found among the most majoritarian democracies. Jenny Stewart[6] investigated how corporatist and pluralist polities process information and generate support. From her systems approach, she diagnosed "a greater learning capacity" of corporatist states, demonstrated by the postwar success of Germany and Japan on the basis of "rational" interest mediation.

(2) Most European corporatist states, such as Austria, Norway, Sweden and Germany, constitute highly developed social welfare states. In these states, corporatism is also in decline because postmaterial interests (ecology, feminism, participatory democracy) assert themselves in new political parties and a renewed role of parliament. The escalating costs of maintaining social welfare states have caused a shift towards privatising state services. Welfare corporatism can only survive with relatively high economic growth, political parties and a renewed role of parliament.[7] Ralf Dahrendorf, with Germany in mind, concludes: "The appearance of stability which it (corporatism) provided, soon turned into stagnation. In Europe, at any rate, corporatism did not lead to concerted action but to quarrelsome paralysis."[8] Indeed, corporatism appeals to the materialist logic of growth, as Crepaz has emphasised. It was designed for this purpose and fulfilled its function very successfully during three decades of postwar reconstruction in Europe. It may well have outlived its purpose in those societies.

However, Europe no longer commands the resources to solve its problems with welfare state measures and South Africa was never in a position to do so. Improving the life chances of its poorer half can only come through employment creation, massive efforts towards productivity performance, as well as regulated labour relations, orchestrated by what Schmitter, following what German Chancellor Erhard, called "concertation". While unlimited growth is the evil for environmentalists and post-industrialists in the welfare states of the West, growth as a desired goal unites the antagonists in less industrialised states, such as South Africa. Short of divisive and destabilising redistribution, only with economic growth can the enormous inequalities be diminished. Leaving the material cleavages to laissez-faire pluralism, particularly when they overlap with ethno-racial divisions, provides a sure recipe for destructive class warfare that destroys all prospects for growth. Therefore, a country such as South Africa has no other option but to pursue corporatist social harmony.

(3) In South Africa, the degree of union organisation (30 per cent) straddles the lower end between Sweden (80 per cent) and the US (15 per cent). However, unionised labour is highly politicised, due to its having had to step into the vacuum left by banned anti-apartheid parties. Industrial democracy preceded political enfranchisement. Unlike other corporatist states, such as Germany and Japan, the broad political left is formally represented in the post-apartheid government, albeit with a declining influence. This left-wing representation has facilitated corporatist arrangements in South Africa. Leading SACP members pioneered the new Labour Relations Act which must rank among the most sophisticated balancing acts for conflict resolution in the world. Unlike the union-bashing Thatcherites and the open class warfare in Britain, "promoting working-class interests within the framework of capitalism is an essential ingredient for the success of corporatism because it facilitates trade union involvement in a co-operative manner", as Peter J. Williamson has pointed out in a general synopsis on corporatist theory.[9] To what extent social democratic governments with union ties restrain or encourage labour militancy is debated inconclusively in the literature. In South Africa, a union-friendly ANC has clearly dampened industrial action by its alliance partner who did not wish to jeopardise ANC growth strategies. How long this restraint will last remains to be seen and is examined in more detail later. However, all empirical evidence points to a far lower strike rate in corporatist than in pluralist states.

Consociationalism has as bad a name among radical democrats as corporatism is tainted among the left. Both arrangements for political power sharing and joint economic decision making are considered elitist, secretive, exclusive and undemocratic. Some union activists denounce the institutionalised bargaining between business, labour and the state as co-optation into the rules of capital by depriving the labour movement of its capacity for independent action. Others fear the development of a centralised unaccountable union bureaucracy, alienated from the grassroots.[10]

Business representatives, on the other hand, resent the institutionalised union power, particularly when the unions are part of the ruling party as in South Africa. Rather than being pressured to reach agreement with a class adversary, organised capital prefers to lobby state officials directly. South African capital also favours decentralised bargaining at plant level while corporatism implies national agreements to be implemented regardless of local conditions. Moreover, many small businesses which are not members of large chambers or federations feel left out of corporatist deals as are the unemployed, the rural poor, traditional communities and many weaker and less organised interests. In so far as these outsiders are deliberately excluded from corporatist institutions, the vested interests of the big players are strengthened. Collusion rather than consensual, inclusive interest mediation looms as a danger.

Despite these misgivings, post-apartheid South Africa has begun to adopt corporatism while it has implemented a modified form of consociationalism in the temporary power sharing between political parties in the Government of National Unity. While the parties, labour unions and business organisations as part of the pacting are not explicit ethnic entities, their constituencies are dominated by distinct ethnic groups, which adds a consociational dimension to economic accommodation.[11]

The role of the state bureaucracy is neither confined to being a passive bystander nor a neutral arbitrator when business and labour interests clash. Instead, the government actively participates not only in setting the legislative framework for corporate consociationalism but also in taking sides according to its factional parts. The parties are not allies in an elite cartel united by a common interest, except perhaps ensuring economic growth on which their survival depends. In this respect, the Reconstruction and Development Programme (RDP) serves as their common mantra. All parties can pay lip service to the RDP's noble goals because the all-embracing statement of intent avoids hard choices by not prioritising its many contradictory visions. When the RDP was concretised in the government's neoliberal Growth Employment and Restructuring (GEAR) strategy, the debates about macro-economic policy options become much harsher.

Corporatism diffuses and suspends class warfare. By implying a potential class harmony, it denies the fundamental tenets of socialist conceptualisations. Socialists insist that class antagonisms are irreconcilable. For Marxists, the conflicting interests of antagonistic forces cannot be overcome; they constitute the motor of history. At most, business and labour may set aside their mutually exclusive interests temporarily for limited co-operation on specific issues. However, from a socialist perspective, corporatism or social partnerships do not provide solutions because they ignore the terms of co-operation in a capitalist setting. From this point of view, corporatism amounts to sophisticated union co-optation, because the more powerful business sector can dictate the terms of co-operation to weaker and dependent unions which are sapped of their militancy through false partnership models. This deeply entrenched world-view underlies the opposition and suspicion towards corporatism on the left everywhere. For these left-wing critics, South African unions are hoodwinked. Their foreign advisers wonder aloud why class partnership together with racial reconciliation is so widely embraced. Canadian Leo Panitch writes: "The term corporatism is used more positively on the South African left than anywhere else I have ever known in my many years of studying tripartite structures."[12] Other critics assert: "The rule of capital is being re-imposed on labour in the guise of what is called 'corporatism' and 'the adoption of corporatism' as a strategy by the mainstream of the labour movement is parasitic on the state and ill equips it to confront this new situation."[13] The accusation leaves unanswered why labour allows the rule of capital to be re-imposed on itself at the very moment when COSATU assumes part of state power and consequently would be, for the first time, in a position to resist the logic of capital or replace it with its own strategy. The ultra-left critique seldom mentions the trade-offs that unions yield and gain by participating in tripartite relations. By juxtaposing the crossroads of "tripartite corporatism or democratic socialism"[14] the socialist critics postulate an ideal world, as if South Africa could realise socialism in global isolation at the very time when the South African economy is incorporated into global markets and pressures as never before. Nor should the ideology of social partnership obscure continuing conflicting class interests. Corporatism only promises more rational and less costly forms of interest representation, or in the suggestion of the much maligned World Bank for unions: trading "less industrial unrest for vigorous social action".[15]

While left-wing critics fear the integration of independent unions into state structures and unions subordinated under goals wider than mere class goals, conservatives deplore the undue power of unions in tripartite arrangements. Neo-liberal observers lament "that South African unions will keep exercising influence over government not dissimilar to that of British unions in the pre-Thatcher era".[16] This assessment vastly overrates the clout of union leaders with government. It also underrates the alienation between members and leaders and overlooks the fact that many union leaders are themselves engaged in embourgeoisement. When union leaders become partners in profit-making business enterprises, the nature of old-style class antagonism changes fundamentally.

Social-democratic advocates of tripartism, on the other hand, point to the innovative features of the relationship. Indeed, it differs from the Soviet model where unions acted as a transmission belt for the ruling party. Conversely, it would diminish the strategic wisdom of seasoned COSATU leaders to view them as willing dupes of neo-liberal manipulation. Eddie Webster, a union-friendly supporter of corporatism, on the other hand, underestimates the absorbing power of business and overestimates the union clout when he writes: "Importantly, these tripartite arrangements are not part of neo-liberalism – instead, they are a creative challenge to the global agenda of neo-liberalism."[17]

Corporatism has undoubtedly expanded the space and influence of union activity in South Africa. In the final analysis, however, tripartism remains a sensible compromise which amounts to the important equivalent of the political pact on the labour front. It constitutes neither a victory nor a defeat of either opponent but brings both together in more rational arrangements of conflict resolution. However, there remain other dangers of corporatism for democratisation. Not only are weaker, unorganised groups not represented where important decisions are made, but the bargaining forum itself could undermine Parliament.

The state, labour and business have agreed that all legislation with important social and economic consequences should be discussed in the tripartite body, called the National Economic Development and Labour Council (NEDLAC), prior to being tabled in Parliament. The National Economic, Development and Labour Council Act (No. 35 of 1994, Section 5.10) charges the body to "consider all significant changes to social and economic policy before it is implemented or introduced in Parliament". This is supposed to be done in order to "reach consensus and conclude agreements on matters pertaining to social and economic policy". As Pretorius rightly points out, this wide range of competence of Nedlac does not aim at merely giving policy advice or representing sectional interests to government. "Concluding agreements" to which government has been a party imply "authoritative policy decisions" for which the participants take joint responsibility for implementation.

A framework agreement between business and labour is not meant to be a pact or accord. Instead, the national forum is regarded as a third tier of bargaining – "setting options at national level for improving sectoral and workplace level negotiations".[18] The corporatist model assumes that each constituency in Nedlac supports the broad goals of creating jobs, economic growth, equity and participation by civil society in the political and economic reconstruction process. With this long-term vision, co-operation is envisaged on the basis of shorter term trade-offs.

The four chambers of Nedlac (labour market, trade and industry, public finance and monetary policy and development) have an ambitious programme of preparing legislation. According to the institution's executive director, it covers a "new package of support measure for industry, the budget framework and a revised taxation system, a new Employment Act and urban-rural development".[19]

During its first years the Trade and Industry Chamber mainly discussed industrial restructuring, resulting from supply side measures through which firms are encouraged to invest in products that are internationally competitive. A "Social Plan Act" argues for informed worker participation and legal provisions to negotiate and manage industrial restructuring. A social plan reserve fund, to be established, aims at ameliorating hardships accompanying the process. At the insistence of labour, a social clause was negotiated for inclusion in all bilateral and multilateral trade agreements to which South Africa is a contracting party. A government draft bill on competition is being considered by the Chamber and a National Investment Promotion agency was established. Sectoral issues also occupied the group as did initiatives for productivity workshops. The Public Finance and Monetary Policy Chamber focused on the next budget, the tax system, exchange control and civil pension arrangements. The Development Chamber considered urban and rural development strategies, housing policy, job creation through a National Public Works Programme and a redefinition of the Masakhane campaign. The Labour Market Chamber worked on outstanding details of the Labour Relations Act, demarcation of industrial sectors and statutory councils, the appointment of judges to the Labour Court, codes of picketing and the establishment of the crucial Commission for Conciliation, Mediation and Arbitration (CCMA) under the Act. CCMA will ultimately employ 200 trained mediators and arbitrators who will settle disputes quickly on site rather than making the parties wait for a long time for a costly hearing before the Labour Court.

With these vital and potentially divisive issues settled through "careful consensus-building, agreement-making and joint implementation" (Jayendra Naidoo), the unelected star chamber undermines the elected Parliament. Parliament merely ratifies what has been decided elsewhere. Parliament is increasingly left with the symbolic issues that excite the public while the really important policies have long been settled in private bargaining. The arrangement is justified as avoiding costly conflicts.

Even if Parliament retains the final say over corporatist-initiated legislation, parliamentarians are pressured not to undo a "careful equilibrium". To all intents and purposes Parliament could be reduced to rubber stamping the outcome of acrimonious bargaining elsewhere. Alternatively, it would repeat the process which makes the elected chamber look redundant. Since most parliamentarians do not possess the expertise of corporatist negotiators, they are not only handicapped professionally but are also inclined to go along with predetermined legislation psychologically. Particularly if the respective minister, as the party to the corporatist deal, presents it as "in the national interest", it requires independent and strong parliamentarians of the ruling party to upset the passage of a bill through critical scrutiny. Autonomous parliamentarians who rebel against a pre-set government agenda are unlikely to emerge in substantial numbers, given the severe sanctions and leadership control they face in the new South Africa.

Lately, with government's greater confidence to implement macroeconomic legislation without lengthy consultation, the role of Nedlac is being diminished. At the same time, the resolve of union leaders to battle a more determined government has also waned as increasingly more union activists have joined the civil service or vied for political careers. As a general trend, the independence of civil society institutions is increasingly undermined when its office-bearers depend on government favours for their personal careers or the survival of their organisations. Thus the once fiercely independent South African Civic Organisation (SANCO) rescinded a prohibition that its officials could not hold government appointments because the widespread exodus from the poorly paid civics had endangered its existence. Yet the spreading tentacles of government patronage drawing in its likely critics does not bode well for democracy.

While the concept of negotiated compromises is theoretically embraced by all interest groups, it has not yet been established that the negotiating parties carry their own constituencies both for the process and for implementing controversial decisions. While Business SA, for example, successfully negotiated the innovative 1985 Labour Relations Act (LRA), soon afterwards the revived SA Foundation published its "Growth for All" document. This proposal by big business (the so-called Brenthurst Group) was not negotiated through Nedlac. Yet it proposed to establish a two-tier wage system which directly affects the interests of organised labour and ignores the provisions of the LRA. The strategy adopted by the SA Foundation obviously relies on bringing business pressure directly on government with the hope that the ANC will bring recalcitrant unions into line to go along with the non-negotiated business blueprint. Not only does the strategy of circumventing Nedlac undermine union confidence in business commitment to a negotiated compromise, it also led to a predictable rejection by the state.

Doubts exist on the union side as well about the leadership capacity to induce a suspicious constituency to stick to a compromise. If corporate consociationalism is to work in South Africa, it presupposes strong union leadership that can effectively discipline segments who disagree with controversial agreements. Business attempts to weaken union power therefore run counter to the concept of corporatism. In fact, sophisticated business needs to assist a negotiating union leadership to become an equal partner. Unfortunately, much of the strategic thinking on both sides still rests on steamrolling or manipulating the opponent into agreement. Ironically, at present, willingness to negotiate is based on the self-confidence of power and success in outmanoeuvring the other side rather than a readiness to adhere to genuine compromises.

The brain drain of experienced union officials to government and the private sector has caused a weakening of union clout. At the same time, the presence of less experienced union representatives has led to a marked increase in strike actions since the end of 1995. Grievances, as opposed to wage disputes, now account for the majority of strikes. With company restructuring and technology replacing jobs, retrenchment-related strikes are also likely to increase.

Ironically, the implementation of corporatist deal-making is undermined by the very process by which agreements are being reached. On the union side, corporatism leads to organisational elitism. It requires a centralised professional union bureaucracy. Leadership becomes alienated from the grassroots. The former editor of the SA Labour Bulletin has diagnosed the surge of militancy on the ground as a result of the gap between distant leaders: "The involvement of union and federation leaders in increasingly complex interactions and negotiations in industry forums, Nedlac and other institutions has widened this gap and produced a sense of disempowerment at the base. Grassroot activists are keen to assert their militancy and their demands."[20] In particular, public service unions are increasingly militant towards the state as their employer. When senior state officials are perceived as looking after their own interests first through high salaries compared with underpaid nurses, teachers and police personnel, it is doubtful how effective appeals to the national interest can sustain labour peace.

The danger of too close a government-union association was amply demonstrated by the nurses' strike during October and November of 1995. A closer analysis of this event yields insights into the limits of South African corporatism. Thousands of well-organised health workers drew attention to their poor salaries and dismal working conditions by striking against their own union representatives as well as the state as their employer. While the government insisted that wage talks could only take place with recognised unions in a National Central Bargaining Chamber (CBC), the majority of angry nurses turned away representatives from the National Education, Health and Allied Workers' Union (NEHAWU) and the Hospital Personnel Association of South Africa (HOSPERSA). In the end, the nurses formed their own union, the South African Democratic Nurses Union (SADNA) which refused to seek affiliation with either of the country's two major union federations, COSATU or NACTU.

The undertones of the strike revealed not only a mood of disillusionment with the newly legitimatised state by the most important sector of African professional women, but it also signalled the inability of emerging corporatist arrangements to cope with a situation bordering on anarchy. In the illegal strike that amounted to a breach of contract, both sides issued ultimatums and ignored deadlines. The Director General of Health warned that nurses could face criminal charges if patients died as a result of the strikes. The nurses demanded an apology from Mandela for his similar statement on the strike and suggested that the Minister of Health, Dr Nkosazana Zuma, should have been at Baragwanath instead of "staying in comfortable hotels in Beijing" for the UN Women's Conference. Other spokespersons declared: "We are qualified women, not just menial labour. We know our skills are needed to save lives. We refuse to subsidise the government and their fancy cars. Viva RDP. We want some gravy."[21]

While all the established institutions called for constructive negotiations towards resolving problems, "in the labour ward, women were delivering their own babies, sometimes with the aid of patients who were themselves in labour. Post-operative patients were being given over-the-counter pain killers instead of morphine. While doctors, matrons, workers and paramedics helped patients and strove to restore a semblance of order to the chaos ... the nurses toyi-toyied outside."[22] Doctors' reports spoke of life-support systems in a maternity ward deliberately being turned off and HIV infected material being thrown around.

Potential failures of corporatism are revealed in the nurses' confrontation for three reasons. First, most victims of the strikers' ire were fellow Africans. Little empathy was extended to patients compared with the goals of a special interest group. If nurses, indoctrinated with ideologies of service to the community, can act with such callous blackmail, other unions are even more unlikely to accept compromises when the opponent is perceived as a greedy employer of a different race. Second, there are clear limits to government's appeals to take the national interest or scarce resources into account. ANC loyalty is overshadowed by material needs that take priority, regardless of threats or pleas, even by a widely respected figure like Mandela. Government's moral authority is undermined by the different lifestyle and perceived self-enrichment of its representatives. The extraordinarily wide gap between the remuneration of politicians and the poverty of constituents has triggered expectations that sharing in the spoils of office is the right of all state employees. Third, in the confrontation between civil servants and the state, traditional union officials are simply sidelined. They cannot control a militant constituency because they are perceived as colluding with the government in the tripartite alliance. In the nurses' case, the gender difference between strikers and the predominantly male union leadership has fostered an additional element of alienation.

Similar alienation from established unions was evident in a bitter strike at Anglo American's Rustenburg Platinum Mines, where the National Union of Mineworkers (NUM) has a membership of about 30 per cent. After a change of ownership, workers demanded repayment of their pension money, death benefits, long service and bonus amounts as well as income tax deducted. Since the union refused to negotiate with the employer about the uninformed demands, particularly the repayment of pension money (which had previously been paid to other miners from a dissolved Bantustan pension fund) allegiance shifted to a Workers' Committee of five *madoda* (men). Management, with the intention of restarting production, then bypassed the union and negotiated with the Workers' Committee, thus further enhancing the union's rival's credibility. Shop stewards were threatened by angry workers. In their view: "The NUM's leadership is no longer interested in worker's issues, all they are involved with now is the establishment of an investment company and the buying of shares with our pension fund in the Johannesburg Stock Exchange. We do not want to see NUM's leadership here."[23]

As a general rule, it can be concluded that corporatist pacts and leadership trade-offs are not worth the paper they are written on unless the signatories, particularly on the union side, exercise influence over their constituency beyond being their remote spokespersons. Such influence is jeopardised by the very corporatist deals that put its participants outside the interest perceptions of constituents. With internal democracy further fading, without a clearly perceived mandate and without public transparency and the political education to translate necessary trade-offs into ordinary understandings of benefits and cost for members, the social partnership of corporatism remains a delusion in the minds of its originators. Their increasingly technical and legalistic compromises of complex issues further add to the dichotomy, the goodwill and noble intention of all corporatist parties notwithstanding. Only a Gandhian revolution "to walk the talk" imaginatively and patiently would seem to be able to transform a nominal social democracy into a real one. Its test lies in how many actively identify with corporatist trade-offs rather than ignorantly live with its results.

Corporatist agreements have yet to be tested against the reality of increased class stratification within the black majority. As the ANC shifts towards more conservative policies with its firmer hold over the state, business may tend to seek corporatist agreements more than in the past, but union leaders will find themselves increasingly isolated both from their own disillusioned following and their former government allies. How far government can act as an honest broker between conflicting class interests will decide the fate of South African style corporate consociationalism.

In the one-party dominant system – which exists in many African states, Mexico and Malaysia – elections merely reconfirm the ruling party. State and party become indistinguishable. Even if elections are free and fair, a party that need not doubt its renewal in the office exists only in a "nominal democracy". Yet it can also be argued with equal validity that the repeated reaffirmation of a party in power does not negate democracy, provided the election expresses the true will of the people, provided the majority party does not repress or exclude minorities from legitimate influence and, above all, provided the election is procedurally unflawed and free of corruption. It is an empirical question, yet to be answered, whether these provisions will prevail in a South Africa under ANC hegemony. Above all, several constraints on potential one-party dominance exist in South Africa that are absent in Mexico and Malaysia.

The fact that two important provinces (Western Cape and Kwa-Zulu-Natal) voted for rival parties and the ANC barely managed to rule a third (North-West) mitigates against one-party dominance. Although the ANC may well win Natal in a future free campaign with access to the rural areas of Zululand, there remain entrenched pockets of ANC rejection that cannot be eliminated by fiat of a dominant centre. Unlike ZANU in Zimbabwe that first squashed and subsequently co-opted its opposition in Matabeleland, real power bases of opposition in South Africa prevail in both local and provincial administration as well as in outside government institutions.

Vincent Maphai has rightly pointed out that besides consociationalism, other forms of power sharing are practised in divided societies just as in liberal democracies.[24] Federalism, corporatism and the division of power between executive, Parliament and an independent judiciary can all be considered widely accepted constraints on one-party dominance in South Africa. Consociationalism as explicit power sharing between ethnic groups had been wisely diluted in the transitional period of the interim constitution to power sharing among political parties as implicit representatives of ethnic groups. This resulted, as Maphai points out, "in a weaker and more fluid correspondence between party and ethnicity than consociationalism envisaged". All three non-African minorities, as well as Zulu-speakers, dispersed their vote among several parties and the ANC took great care not to present itself as an ethnic party but as a broad-based inclusive movement.

In its self-definition, the ANC does not wish to deprive minorities of an effective say in government. It only wants to limit the influence of minority parties to "a say proportionate to their electoral strength".[25] The ANC views a minority veto power beyond proportional representation as preventing majority rule. However, inasmuch as power sharing during a transition period was necessary for jointly drafting the rules of the political game, so a disproportionate influence of minorities may be a requirement for future stability. Over-representation of minorities as a device for confidence-building is practised in many democratic constitutions, the most prominent of which is the equal representation of less populous US states in the US senate. The equal vote of all member states in the UN General Assembly, regardless of population size and financial contribution, also affirms the principle of over-representation, balanced by the veto power of each of the five permanent members of the Security Council.

Unlike Mexico, vote-rigging and corruption by an institutionalised revolutionary party would also be exposed and opposed by a strong and watchful civil society in South Africa. While there are attempts to curtail civil society – for example the defeated bill to regulate NGOs and divert their foreign funding to the state – the political culture of the anti-apartheid struggle has greatly strengthened civil society. To be sure, liberal components have much to answer for in their betrayal of principles and acquiescence in the often illiberal behaviour of liberation activists, as Jill Wentzel has demonstrated in her distressing account *The Liberal Slideaway*.[26] Nonetheless, R.W. Johnson's warning about the possibility "that the liberal tradition will be snuffed out altogether under the new nationalist hegemony"[27] overstates the threat. Even if the new rulers were to try more forcefully to stifle dissent as in Zimbabwe, they would not succeed in South Africa because of the objective strength of countervailing forces. Such an optimistic conclusion does not rest on the incorruptible staying power of individuals, of institutions that can be sidelined, silenced or taken in by the new hegemony, as Jill Wentzel has shown. The noble intentions of liberal democrats notwithstanding, their opposition alone cannot block a determined illiberal government. It is the objective economic forces that South African liberalism articulates that constrains any government in Pretoria.

The withdrawal of the NP from the GNU in June 1996 has been widely interpreted as giving the ANC a free hand to pursue its own economic policy without the watchdog function and pressure of an in-built opposition. Overseas investors, in particular, are concerned about a populist-inclined African majority party now going it alone. However, far from strengthening the freedom of the ANC, the NP exit from formal power sharing has weakened the government. Not only has the ANC to bear responsibility for failure of delivery alone, it now has to reinforce the impression that it pursues "responsible" policies. Faced with a generalised distrust by a sceptical global audience, the ANC with exclusive power has to be doubly cautious to stay within approved parameters. While no longer saddled with the burden of a conservative coalition partner, the government has been burdened to appear conservative on its own.

The irony of additional constraints on a freer government does not mean that the self-appointed opposition NP has been strengthened in its turn. Not only had the NP become redundant in the GNU, as

Maphai points out,[28] but the party's internally controversial departure produced new rifts and disillusionment. Cut off from state patronage, it could no longer reward followers. As the party had also lost much of its role as power broker, lobbyist for business and other special interest groups, ANC officials became more directly accessible and responsive to new constituencies. When white-dominated business can negotiate all its essential interests in corporatist institutions or through direct contacts with officials, it marginalises political parties as interlocutors and representatives of established class concerns. This "identity crisis" has not only affected the National Party but the DP as well. The loss of historical roles – to look after a well-defined constituency in the public realm and manage the legitimacy crisis of a racially limited democracy – has forced the two historically white parties to broaden their image to attract non-white voters at the expense of their traditional ideological appeal and symbolic messages. Ironically, the NP has managed this transition far more effectively than the liberal Democratic Party. NP inroads into non-white constituencies, however, undermine its traditional ethnic appeal. For Afrikaner representation of educational and cultural concerns, the moderately right-wing Freedom Front has long established itself as a more authentic force. Even Mandela and ANC officials treat the right wing with greater respect than De Klerk.

Regardless of the dominant party behaviour, any South African government is dependent on many other diverse forces, particularly white-dominated business. It could ignore their interests only at its own peril. Inasmuch as the private sector cherishes sympathetic government policies, so government needs the investment, growth and know-how that only business can deliver. Without this symbiotic relationship both sides would falter. With massive capital flight and white emigration, South Africa could join many other African states that did not enjoy the dubious benefits of settler capitalism in the first place. What brought about the negotiated revolution and democratisation in the first place through a mutually paralysing stalemate also guarantees adherence to new rules in the future. When even Ton Vosloo's Nasionale Pers Group contributes to the NP, DP and ANC simultaneously, the stage is set for normal democratic politics with ever more narrowing ideological alternatives, despite shrill party rhetoric.

At the rhetorical level, the ANC indeed asserts "the need for an intense ideological struggle against neo-liberalism for the definition of the context of the changes taking place in our country".[29] The movement indeed presents itself as "people-driven transformation" or even, dead seriously, "as a party of the poorest of the poor" the more its own embourgeoisement proceeds. Since the poor comprise the majority, the party must project a left vocation if it wishes to occupy the centre of South African politics. The SACP's strategy in this respect is: "Pursuing some imaginary centre as defined by the West European political spectrum will gravely weaken the ANC in all respects, including electorally."[30] In short, the ANC cannot water down its left stance by conservative overtures to white, coloured or Indian middle-class voters if it wants to remain credible with its main constituency.

Those worried about this orientation, however, ought to remember that: (a) the party has taken over the state with the connivance, if not the active support, of the more sophisticated sectors of the global and local neo-liberal establishment; (b) only the ANC can guarantee that "the poorest of the poor", i.e. the majority, feels represented and part of the system; and (c) the ANC leadership in reality increasingly resembles a "capitalist nomenclature", noble sentiments for the poor notwithstanding. A far more effective nonracial domination has replaced an outdated system of racial subordination. The different party elites no longer squabble about ethno-racial identity, but about the most effective methods to control anarchy and potential class warfare of which they all would be victims.

The wailing about ANC majoritarianism assumes ethnic minorities as its main victim. This thinking still relies on racial antagonisms as the overriding cleavage in South Africa. In reality, the ANC's historical role is both to represent and control the poor majority. Political stability and economic relationships are not threatened by whites but by impoverished black masses whose lot is unlikely to improve dramatically. Ethnic minorities do not undermine the state or ANC hegemony, even if they vote in their majority for opposition parties. Dissatisfied blacks, on the other hand, pose a mortal danger not only for the ANC dominance but to minority interests in particular. Therefore, only a credible ANC can manage the challenge – very much like union-friendly social-democratic administrations can handle sensitive wage restraints more efficiently than union-bashing conservatives. As Stanley Uys has aptly commented, "ANC majoritarianism is concerned less with suppressing minority ethnic groups than it is with placating and managing the majority black population . . ."[31] Although foreign investors judge the country by its black-white relations, this does not mean that the ANC is leading an "Induna-state, keeping workers in line on behalf of capital".[32] Nor does the ANC government "merely manage the affairs of the bourgeoisie", as another SACP analyst argued. The state is neither an agent of capital nor labour but attempts to reconcile and arbitrate their conflicting interests according to the shifting pressures of the day.

This unique objective constellation makes South Africa a pragmatically united rather than a deeply divided society. The projection of deep ethno-racial divisions on the basis of racial demographics overrates appearance at the expense of underlying forces. Hence, even knowledgeable observers are constantly surprised when their predictions of doom turn out to be overtaken by reluctant co-operation and pragmatic reconciliation. All they can offer is to abandon explanation and relegate the inexplicable to the unquestioned realm of "a miracle". In short, when South Africans and informed outside analysts talk openly about the collapse of public administration; when the net emigration of skills from the public to the private sector as well as to other countries reaches worrying heights; when a soaring crime rate, unemployment and a declining currency engender collective despair, a broad-based stable one-party-dominant democracy may indeed be preferable to a rotating state administration which would add to the uncertainty and discontinuity. The real test for the future South African democracy is whether it is based on an *inclusive* majoritarianism or on *ethnic* majoritarianism.

Post-apartheid South Africa is officially a multi-ethnic and multi-cultural state. Its negotiated constitutional preamble, underwritten by majority and minority representatives, from communists to Afrikaner nationalists of the Freedom Front, says that the country "belongs to all who live in it, united in our diversity". While this noble idealism awaits its translation into practice, it enshrines the opposite of ethnic chauvinism. The vision of the new constitution is inclusive.

Corporatism in the decisive economic realm guarantees the consensual type of democracy that simple majoritarianism lacks in the political sphere. Moreover, given the volatile and fragile state of South African society and its new political institutions, corporatism constitutes an effective and necessary substitute for interest mediation that would be difficult to achieve with electoral politics alone. David Welsh has rightly questioned whether a polity like South Africa can sustain competitive, confrontational and adversarial politics in which alternating government is "normal".[33] In short, with power sharing abolished in the political realm since the unravelling of the GNU, joint decision making and bargaining elsewhere assumes added significance. Single-party dominance in the foreseeable future is balanced by corporatist veto powers. To what extent ANC hegemony is also rendered irrelevant as long as corporatist consensus politics checks basic legislation remains to be seen.

Chapter Nine

Where is the struggle now?

The tension between wish and reality, between ideology and practice, between policy and implementation has, and always will be, a major source of political discontent and conflict. Those who promise in opposition have to deliver when in power, and invariably promises outstrip performance, leading to disillusionment and frustration, which in turn generates new opposition and revolt. This is not only true in democracies but in dictatorships and authoritarian regimes as well, although the opposition differs in quality and scope. In South Africa, "the system" of apartheid and separate development bred the conditions for "the struggle" against it. The struggle has been waged and won, and those who led it are now in power creating their own regime in terms of which they promise to deliver. It should surprise no one that the noble intentions of the "struggle" will be grounded and moulded by the mundane imperatives and consequences of governance. The toughest political challenge anywhere in the world is to "walk the talk" between being in opposition and being in power. There is no reason why the ANC should enjoy special grace in this regard.

The ANC's intentions were noble; from the clauses in the Freedom Charter to the policy goals of the National Democratic Revolution and the Reconstruction and Development Programme (RDP). Foremost among these were the eradication of poverty and inequality and the creation of a government for "the people" which would epitomise austerity and sacrifice and rid the country of exploitation, greed and corruption. There is no doubt that many were sincere in their commitment to these ideals and displayed enormous courage and sacrifices in pursuing them. From sandal-wearing activists to hardened MK veterans it is not difficult to gather evidence of what the situation was going to be once "we were in power". It is not entirely unreasonable to pose the question: where is the struggle now?

In the course of a few years since 1990, the ANC has changed its economic policy from nationalisation of basic industries to a mixed economy, and finally to privatisation of the public sector. An official 1996 government paper, entitled "Growth Employment and Redistribution" (GEAR), resembles a similar business blueprint, called "Growth for All". GEAR explicitly rejects union strategies, although union representatives form an influential part of the ANC hierarchy. In early 1996, the government abolished the special ministry charged with implementing the much propagated Reconstruction and Development Programme (RDP). To all intents and purposes, the policy that almost replaced the sacred Freedom Charter in its vision of a more equal and progressive order has now been shelved. Even its symbolic radicalism is no longer *en vogue*. A Thatcherite discourse of fiscal discipline and market forces has taken over. Growth through deficit financing and an extension of the public service is considered an anachronistic policy of a previous social welfare era that is declining worldwide. South Africa is unable to defy global trends of growth through international competitiveness and foreign investment requiring assurances of conservative stability. These fundamental shifts are deplored by the left wing as a sellout to the global neo-liberal agenda and praised by economic conservatives as the only sensible policy of a liberation movement in government. Regardless of these value judgements, the switches indicate a refreshing nondogmatism. The ANC appears to adapt to economic imperatives and is capable of drawing pragmatic lessons from predicaments that committed ideologues would have ignored to their own detriment.

As late as 1993, there was a firm belief among "progressives" that neo-liberalism was on the way out, to be replaced by sustainable development policies, enhanced by the involvement of organisations of civil society. Thus one reads in a human rights journal: "Mercifully the era of rampant 'free marketeerism' seems to be drawing to a close and calls for the state's complete withdrawal from the market and from the supply for goods and services is now a refrain sung only by a withering band of ideological zealots."[1] Far from withering, the privatisation chorus has been swelled by many a former socialist.

In reality, the ANC in government had little choice but to pursue conservative courses. From a global socialist perspective, the ANC victory came too late. With the Marxist project discredited world-wide after the collapse of the Soviet Union, South Africa would not have been allowed to stray from the Western agenda. It is doubtful that the ANC would have gained office in the first place without the end of the Cold War. The prospect of a Moscow-friendly government in Pretoria has always been a nightmare to Western conservatives and liberals alike. Much of the Western anti-apartheid support was motivated by this threatening scenario and not by empathy with suffering victims of oppression, as was hypocritically proclaimed. Even liberal democrats would have hesitated to back a movement that espoused real socialism. The ANC has received its decisive Western support since 1980 because the option of co-optation seemed increasingly possible. Ingratiating themselves with the potential new rulers, strengthening their "sensible" forces against radical elements, and engineering a smooth transition from embarrassing racial capitalism to nonracial stability, guided the South African policy of all Western governments, regardless of the party ideology of the administration. Social Democratic Scandinavian governments aided the outlawed ANC directly and openly; the more constrained US, British, German and Canadian administrations channelled their funds to ANC-supporting NGOs. Both constituted relatively risk-free investments; most paid off handsomely. The ANC could hardly ignore such noble embraces beyond also praising its Cuban and Libyan friends, to the annoyance of their American foes. Yet such superficial irritations must not lose sight of the overwhelming victory of Western policy vis-à-vis South Africa. Policy makers in Washington, Bonn and London are genuinely delighted with the South African transition. They are at a loss, when pressed to elaborate, as to what Mandela should have done differently.

Dependent on foreign investment and export-led growth, South Africa is locked ever deeper into the global economic rules and dictates. Compared with the scope that the National Party commanded when it assumed exclusive state power in 1948, the manoeuvrability of the ANC fifty years later is severely limited. Defiance of global expectations that was possible with the relatively isolated semi-colonial outpost in 1948 is now immediately penalised by currency fluctuations, higher interest rates on loans or capital outflow and refusal of investments. Such punishment even derives from minor internal policies that violate expected norms and that could be ignored by nationalist Afrikanerdom. In contrast, the ANC has to prove constantly that it is worthy of outside support and that, in the threatening words of a US banker, "the lights should not be switched off". In this respect, the ultra-left critique of the ANC ignores the severe constraints under which any economic experimentation currently operates.

Despite these obvious limitations for socio-economic domestic policy in an age of globalisation, there is some choice. Business support for the ANC internally was, and still is, intensely contested. To what extent conglomerates should "unbundle" by allowing black interests a real foothold in the existing monopolies, for example, and what conditions should apply for black advancement, remain controversial. Likewise, within the government in which official communists and union socialists occupy formal positions, economic policy is being argued on a daily basis or, more frequently, left undecided because of paralysis. Who wins and who loses during this lack of consensus; how a decision is justified and compromises marketed; or why actors switch sides, provide fascinating insights into the real politics of a new democracy. A historical sketch of the gradual embourgeoisement of a liberation movement and its reluctant incorporation by the old establishment sheds light on the paradoxes of capitalism and socialism; of liberation and corruption; as well as the temptations and constraints of political office.

The South African economic debate in the mainstream media reaches hysterical levels when editorials howl at anyone who even mentions that there may be a need for corrective state intervention in an unfettered market. When an ANC lawyer at a seminar floated the idea of a one-time "capital levy" of one third of the wealth of all individuals to be spent on addressing the inequities of apartheid, the mainstream press unanimously labelled the idea as "loony".[2] Affected persons would either sell their property or emigrate. Despite the glorification of postwar West Germany in the South African press, it forgot that the German economic boom and domestic stability rested to a large extent on a successful *Lastenausgleich*, an equalisation between those who had lost everything and those who had retained their property by sheer luck during the war. Trigger words like "nationalisation" or "redistribution" elicit the most vivid apocalyptic scenarios in otherwise sober publications like the *Financial Mail*:

> . . . there will be a massive loss of jobs, shops will empty of goods, housing will fall into ruin, disease and misery will predominate – and Comrade Nelson, like Comrade Nyerere of Tanzania will say: "Sorry, we made a mistake. We've redistributed all we have." That is when the World Bank will take over.[3]

The mass-circulation *Sunday Times* names the culprits for a potential disaster by reinforcing a widespread anti-intellectualism, particularly against social scientists, who are held responsible for indoctrinating an illiterate ANC:

> For ideas, it (the ANC) is largely dependent on academics and professional political workers whose socialist prejudices about the supposed evils of capitalism have survived the collapse of socialism. Such is the penalty of trying, for two decades, to teach economics in the departments of history or political science of the leading universities; the prejudiced lead the blind.[4]

These early warnings soon gave way to a surprised endorsement and delight with ANC attitudes and economic policies. The business establishment was generally pleased with the ANC stance after a year of operating legally. Typical of an emerging opinion is a 1991 editorial in *The Natal Mercury* that praised Mandela for his speech at the tenth anniversary of SADCC in Windhoek, calling it a "milestone in this journey away from the Marxist principles that have influenced his and the ANC's thinking for the past 30 years".[5] While the ANC as a movement and Mandela as leader in particular had never adopted a Marxist position, South African capital could not have pleaded more eloquently than Mandela that a political settlement would not survive unless the economy was turned around, which could not be achieved without a high level of capital formation. It implied that both foreign and domestic investors needed to be reassured. Almost gleefully, the editorial expressed relief concerning the central anxieties of business. "Not a word about confiscatory redistribution of wealth, a centrally planned economy, or nationalisation, the mere mention of which in early 1990 sent inves-

164

tor confidence and share prices tumbling. Even his ritual plea for sanctions to be maintained sounded hollow and out of place." Conservative business executives warmly embraced a changed ANC and celebrated Mandela especially. It was by no means a one-sided overture.

The moneyed classes on both sides of the racial divide were eager to meet each other. The white chiqueria of Johannesburg and Cape Town would no longer give parties without a few black guests demonstrating the host's nonracial open-mindedness. The proliferate women's and fashion magazines began to signal the new trend. The bedrooms of the nation showed much greater openness to the new nonracial order than the stiff boardrooms, if not in the reality of interracial marriage at least in the fantasies of some influential opinion-makers. For example, *Cosmopolitan*, often mainly concerned with how a professional woman could achieve multiple orgasms, acquired a more political focus and chose three ANC luminaries (Tokyo Sexwale, Thabo Mbeki, Sam Shilowa) as "men who get our vote – for their sex appeal and smart talking"[6]. In the same issue, the wife of one of the three objects of political-sexual endorsement claims the sexual liberation of the Robben Island political prisoners for the glossy magazine: "The way in which women, with their wholesome beauty, were portrayed in COSMO gave it the prisoners' unanimous vote. It created a balance in their otherwise predominantly male environment." The editor, Jane Raphaely, added another mostly empathetic portrait of Winnie Mandela. Long before the new political elite took over after the elections, it was welcomed as "inevitable" by the country's more sophisticated establishment.

Even more surprising was the readiness of a liberation movement to be liberated into the bourgeois lifestyle of its opponents. Many ANC leaders raced to catch up with the finer tastes of the former masters. Cyril Ramaphosa's weakness for fly-fishing and single-malt whiskies became the hallmark of his equality with his bourgeois counterparts. Another trade union leader married in a Rolls Royce. The number of prominent ANC leaders living in upper-class suburbs like Hyde Park, Houghton and Constantia or driving German cars far outnumbers those still in the black townships with rusting "struggle cars" or living in the sprawling shacklands. The definition of equality was borrowed from the whites.

Anything less than a white bourgeois lifestyle would have appeared unequal. Among all the ANC candidates for Parliament almost none came from a squatter camp where a sizeable ANC constituency lives. Daring ties, silk and quasi-military style suits predominate among the male liberators, fancy hats and ostentatious dresses among the newly elevated female elite.

The white establishment was delighted with the tuxedoed, perfumed and bejewelled representatives of the toiling masses; the bewildered liberals and shabbily dressed lefties looked the other way when they could not believe their eyes. "There were many changes, of course, but for me, the one most shocking came in the aftermath of the Great Leap Forward when the ANC's top leaders stepped onto centre stage and turned out to be affable chaps in three piece suits with a taste for precisely the sort of bourgeois revelry I had once found so disgusting among white people."[7] Another former UDF activist and author, Chris van Wyk, wrote: "I have come to realise how different my vision for a new South Africa was to the vision of those I rubbed shoulders with. I want to talk about the BMW's, the cellphones, the celebratory parties thrown with hard-earned workers' money while we watch on TV."[8] A business journal reports gleefully under the title "The Left goes right into business"[9] about the successful careers of former activists attending the funeral of a Robben Islander turned merchant banker: "Once Andrew Mapheto's comrades would have arrived in jeans, T-shirts and Indian print dresses. Now they watched silently behind Ray Bans in dark suits and twinsets. A phalanx of BMWs and Mercedes stood on the cemetery verge." A "nattily-attired" former Vula operative is quoted: "I am a good capitalist precisely because I was such a good communist."

In the same week, the ANC placed public advertisements saluting the SA Communist Party on its 75th anniversary. The ANC expressed confidence that its partner would "continue to be one of the driving forces behind the democratic transformation and that the tripartite alliance will persist unflinchingly in its historic task of bringing peace and prosperity to this land". Whether the prosperity is achieved by the capitalist or the socialist route is studiously avoided. Although the salute to the SACP would suggest the Marxist-Leninist juncture, if labels have any meaning the ANC has clearly moved in the opposite direction of free-market policies. Is the ad therefore lying? No, the calculated ambiguity is needed to keep the alliance together. The more "the left moves right into business", the more the sceptics must be assured that the non-racially excluded will also be looked after by the SACP and COSATU.

Private elite schools long ago opened themselves to a few children of wealthy black parents. More amazing was how black activists got away with having their offspring safely tucked away at Bishops or Rondebosch Boys' High while anarchy reigned in township schools that reeled under the demand "liberation before education". Some were even active in exhorting school boycotts while their own children attended unaffected private schools. Other telling signs of bureaucratic embourgeoisement abound. Salary increases in the former homelands were up to 26-32 per cent in the March to June quarter of 1994, amounting to what an editorial called "end-of-empire looting". Another edition of the same paper a year later editorialised: "The rapidity of the conversion of old guerrillas like Defence Minister Joe Modise and his deputy Ronnie Kasrils, to the benefits of big budget weaponry, must count as a modern miracle."[10]

In 1985, the leader of the South African Mineworkers' Union stated categorically, "The experience of the working class dictates that it is too late to save the free enterprise system in this country."[11] Barely ten years later, Cyril Ramaphosa, once widely hailed as a potential presidential candidate for Mandela's succession, and after a stint as ANC general secretary and chief constitutional negotiator, decided to join as a tycoon the same system that survived his prediction of morbidity stronger than ever and has become a member of the main board of the Anglo American Corporation. The move symbolises the successful embourgeoisement of a liberation movement. Visible multiracial capitalism can be sold more effectively to impoverished masses than the racial monopoly of white ownership. The ANC as the guardian and beneficiary of the system that it once denounced as irreformable represents the real miracle of the transition.

Lawrence Mavundla, the president of the Micro Business Chamber, which includes hawkers, shebeen owners and other informal traders, asserts that black empowerment initiatives were only serving "a small group of about 300 black people". Instead of creating jobs or new wealth, Mavundla insists that the initiatives of selling part of conglomerates to black interests means "taking people who are already rich and making them richer". Indeed, it is difficult to ascertain how the much touted "unbundling" and racial transfer of wealth at subsidised loans benefits the average black worker who, in addition, may face greater obstacles gaining ground against an African management board than against more vulnerable executives of the white establishment. It has yet to be demonstrated that black employers pay better wages, refrain from sacking staff at will or flout health and safety regulations less frequently. When the COSATU unions inveigh against "merely replacing white capitalists with black exploiters" they reflect the fear that little except skin colour will have changed in the new order. Instead of exchanging the racial make-up of management, the unions insist on transforming the shop floor, spending resources on skilling workers instead of luring scarce black executives through disproportionate salaries in ill-conceived affirmative action programmes.

In addition, unions are themselves embroiled in an internal dispute as to whether, how and where to invest substantial financial assets. Union-initiated retirement funds have accumulated R20 billion, and influential union investment companies have been established. A correspondent in the *South African Labour Bulletin*[12] argues that union values are contaminated through the union investment companies, "damaging the strategy that unions should pursue". Institutions which manage the retirement funds have little in common with the trade union perspective or are even at odds with union principles. On the other hand, union officials lack the capacity to manage the funds themselves, or if they do, are sucked into the corporate world in similar fashion as the twenty delegated union candidates for the first democratic election were absorbed into government without tangible benefit for their delegating organisations.

While the more sophisticated conglomerates now clamour to give themselves a black face or facilitate partnerships or sellouts to black groups, the deracialisation of a capitalist order did not occur as smoothly as the logic of colour-blind profit making would suggest.

Not long ago, even the more enlightened South African businessmen backtracked from their first exploratory, half-hearted contact with the ANC leadership in Lusaka in September 1985. They not only faced recrimination from a hostile P.W. Botha government, but from their own peers for fraternising with "terrorists". Anglo American CEO Gavin Relly did not see it as his role to bring the government and the ANC together for negotiations.[13] After the Lusaka visit, the private sector was more interested in putting some visible distance between itself and the apartheid regime as a result of the state's disastrous economic performance and the increased threats of sanctions. The visit amounted to a public relations exercise. However, the widely publicised Lusaka encounter (during which the revolutionaries wore suits and ties and the capitalists casual safari dress) legitimised the ANC in the eyes of Western governments. A few months later, Oliver Tambo held his first official talks in London and Washington, whose conservative administration had publicly shunned contact with alleged communist-led revolutionaries until then. Nonetheless, great ambiguity prevailed about the wisdom of engaging the ANC even among liberal businessmen who should have known better. Sampson reports: "Harry Oppenheimer, still outspoken in retirement, remained twitchy about the meeting, puzzled that the atmosphere was so friendly even though Tambo had conceded nothing, particularly over nationalisation"; and in November he had told the American Chamber of Commerce that businessmen should offer "neither moral support nor material support for the ANC" since they want "an economic system that would destroy everything that we in this room stand for".[14]

A few years later, big business subsidises the ANC election campaign and Mandela consults Oppenheimer about his cabinet appointments. The question to be answered is "who has co-opted whom?" The ANC says it succeeded in bringing business on its side and the capitalists say that they successfully taught the ANC crucial lessons. Who ingratiated themselves with whom? Who reneged on its principles – how and why?

In contrast to conventional wisdom, this analysis argues that the relationship between the new "socialist" power-holders and the old business elite is now far closer and better than the alleged racist alliance between apartheid and South African capitalism ever was. Furthermore, as already pointed out, the alleged leading role of South African business in bringing about the transition must be questioned and qualified. Although South African business is not a monolithic group, the case of its largest conglomerate, Anglo American, and its chief executives, can nonetheless illustrate prudent foresight as well as amazing short-sightedness.

In 1982 Harry Oppenheimer confessed that he could not pick up the phone and contact the then Prime Minister John Vorster but had to use his Afrikaner counterparts to communicate informally with government.[15] It has been reported that P.W. Botha even refused to be in the same room with the man whose companies report sales of billions on six continents and control large parts of the South African economy. Louwrens Pretorius aptly comments: "The exclusionary nature of Afrikaner nationalism did not allow consultation between the government and English-dominated business to be seen."[16] There existed no other capitalist country where the political class and the economic elite initially were so divided ethnically and socially, despite common interests and mutual dependence, than during the first two-thirds of the apartheid era. Afrikaner bureaucrats and English capitalists only began to co-operate more closely once an Afrikaner economic bourgeoisie had emerged and the pressure on the rulers heightened through sanctions and internal resistance in the 1980s.

Ironically, sections of the feared new "socialist" power-holders have now forged much closer links with capital than ever existed before. Thus one can read: "It's also no wonder that Mandela briefs Oppenheimer upon returning from international trips, sought his approval for two Cabinet appointments, and even visited his private cricket ground for lunch on the fourth anniversary of his 1990 release from prison."[17] Oppenheimer personally always sympathised with the small liberal Progressive Federal Party (later reformed with other smaller parties into the Democratic Party). Nevertheless, the sophisticated management of his corporation recognised political realities relatively early. Bobby Godsell, a savvy Anglo director, set up a diverse, wide-ranging research project on the country's future in the mid-1980s. Another board member, Clem Sunter, became the most persuasive South African exponent of possible scenario planning; the Chairman's Fund under the shrewd ultra-conservative Michael O'Dowd directly and indirectly sponsored hundreds of progressive projects, including dozens of receptive left-wing academics. An informal think tank ("Synthesis") of tycoons, politicians, academics and journalists, organised by the late low-key Anglo-Vaal chairman Clive Menell, met regularly every two months during the last two decades. Its Saturday meetings became highly prized invitations for leading members of the Communist Party, Zulu traditionalists and Afrikaner nationalists who chatted amicably in the comfortable surroundings of private homes across the country. This relative open-mindedness and accessibility of South African business under siege facilitated the change by providing a valuable learning experience for both sides. To be sure, the conservative Chamber of Mines together with various South African business associations, let alone the cautious Oppenheimer, are far from "South Africa's secret freedom fighters"[18] as a self-serving mythology now asserts. The close-knit circle of associates together with their coterie of supporters in the media and academia now pride themselves on having "weaned off" the ANC of its past economic fantasies, thwarted experiments, kept out foreign competitors and generally "saved the country" from becoming another Bosnia. Indeed when Buthelezi threatened to resist "to the finish" two weeks before the 1994 elections, he was skilfully brought back into the electoral fold after being shuttled around in an Anglo jet for briefings with Anglo-sponsored intermediaries who had carefully sounded-out compromise solutions in their bags. Other well-known business leaders made substantial campaign contributions to the ANC, some to the ANC, NP and Inkatha simultaneously. When Mandela personally phoned the twenty CEOs of South Africa's largest companies asking each for R1 million as a campaign contribution to the ANC for the first democratic election, nineteen complied.

This expedient co-operation, though not social or ideological affinity, between government and the white-controlled business community is not fully appreciated even by observers who should know better. Thus Allister Sparks calls the relationships "uneasy" and concludes: even though many representatives of this group (white-controlled conglomerates) publicly and privately acknowledge the miracle of their survival and express gratitude to Mandela and praise for his efforts, contacts between the two solitudes are noticeably thin.[19] The informal contacts between the old and the new ruling elite, however, are not so thin that several new ministers, including Mandela, were not embarrassed by the revelations of favours to them by controversial figures who clamour to ingratiate themselves with the new power-holders. When the ANC first has to deny and then has to admit that casino magnate Sol Kerzner made substantial campaign contributions, the question remains: what does Kerzner expect and what may he receive in return?

The clout of the private sector in South Africa combines with the need of government to facilitate a better economic performance in order to meet high expectations. This makes the media comparisons with the decline in the rest of Africa journalistic stereotyping. In black Africa, despotic rulers are tempered by what business delicately calls "the softening effects of corruption". The rulers in South Africa are already locked into both the spoils of success and the penalties of failure. The reality of a constellation with limited options has impressed itself even on most of the ardent ideologues of both the nationalist right and the radical left. Only ultra-conservative commentators still fail to understand why South Africa finds itself with communists in the cabinet, "just as nearly every other country in the world has forsaken it". Geoffrey Wheatcroft, author of *The Randlords*, who posed this puzzle in the *Wall Street Journal* compares Joe Slovo to an abandoned Jesuit. "It is as if an ardent Jesuit missionary about to convert some far-flung country heard that the Pope had declared himself an atheist and closed down the Catholic Church."[20] This analogy treats Slovo as a blind follower of a failed doctrine and does not give him credit for comprehending new realities. Despite the Marxist-Leninist rhetoric and the official SACP goal of socialism in the second stage, there is little likelihood that the slogans turn into practice, as even SACP ideologues realise.

If the self-styled communists are not serious about socialism, why has the discourse not changed? Scepticism towards revolutionary integrity does not imply that the party has become an organisation of expedient opportunists. Committed activists of personal integrity abound. However, they are not free to translate their dreams, because other leaders and the party itself are firmly locked into the logic of government responsibility. Furthermore, the more the SACP itself is entangled in the web of power and technocratic solutions, the more it needs the strident orthodoxy to keep restless masses in line.

From the point of view of sophisticated business, what better government could be in power to deal with militant unions and the impossible tasks of satisfying an impoverished half of the population than a liberation movement under a moderate charismatic leader with universal legitimacy, yet also bound to work within the parameters of the economically feasible? Throughout the Western world, social-democratic administrations have clamped down on disruptive unions, introduced back-to-work legislation, rolled back civil servant salaries, or cut welfare spending more effectively than right-wing parties. The social democrats in power were eager to rectify their tarnished image as reckless spenders without regard to a growing deficit. It was usually a conservative administration that "made deals" in the US, in Canada and Western Europe, irrespective of a swelling load of debt. The ANC too has stressed fiscal discipline more than restructuring, to the great relief of business. Such change, of course, did not happen without some heavy prodding and outright threats.

Many South African liberators have finally learned the one great lesson that Lenin had taught his Western sympathisers, which was not how to overthrow capitalism but how to recognise and utilise the greed that generates it. Many former socialists now take full advantage of the opportunities that ruthless capitalist competition provide. They are ideally placed for legitimate embourgeoisement by being in government with great moral credentials and still paying lip service to the plight of the poor. Their record of fighting a progressive cause hides the temptations of self-enrichment which can be presented as being for the noble cause of rectifying racial injustice.

The impact of economic globalisation and the domestic private sector on the ANC has exposed the ANC to a cruel and core dilemma: how does it manage the inevitable political costs and pain of necessary economic reform? It is this dilemma that severely tests the most noble intentions of the struggle and seduces the will of its most prominent leaders. The ANC by force of circumstances has bought into the prevailing economic ideology the idea that a competitive market economy is the most efficient mechanism to generate wealth in society. It therefore has to introduce the reforms necessary to enhance the performance of the mechanism, e.g. get rid of exchange control, privatise state assets, create a flexible labour market, get rid of or reduce government deficit. Yet the very reforms required to generate the wealth that the government wishes to tax create hardship and inequality which manifests itself in political discontent. The ANC spends a great deal of time trying to placate those who demand economic reform as well as those who have to suffer its consequences. The one thing that cannot be done is to drift on in a state of paralysis.

Even the towering influence of a Mandela personality cult cannot indefinitely obscure a development far more dangerous than leadership inaction.

How long can the socialist legacy of the SACP and COSATU cover up for the increased black class stratification in the new order? Already during the last apartheid decade, the richest 20 per cent of Black households experienced a 40 per cent growth in income, while the purchasing power of the poorest 40 per cent of Black households declined by about 40 per cent. The gap between white and black wealth is still vast, but narrowing. Yet the internal economic discrepancies among blacks are widening. State-aligned unions and business lobbies effectively look after the interests of their constituencies in corporatist horse trading. At the same time, the unorganised unemployed, the marginalised squatters and the forgotten, mostly traditional rural population, grow more impoverished.

The group that benefits most from the post-apartheid order is a fledgling black middle class. It consists of a growing number of independent entrepreneurs, a managerial aristocracy in high demand and a new political bourgeoisie eager to join in the consumerism of their former oppressors. Gandhi associated political liberation with an alternative lifestyle. Most ANC officials measure equality by comparison with the affluence of their predecessors. On top of the vast discrepancies in wealth, a thorough Americanisation has penetrated all segments. American habits and ostentatious consumption have become the desired yardstick by which South African progress is measured. When *Sarafina 2* director Mbongeni Ngema was criticised for purchasing air-conditioned luxury buses with public money, he replied: "Why must we be transported in luxury buses in the United States but come back to our own country to be put in the back of kombis? No way! I am proud of our bus." Ngema insists that he creates Broadway theatre of high standards in a Third World environment. His assertion overlooks the fact that it deprives dozens of community groups of state subsidies with which they could spread the AIDS message more effectively. Even the poverty on the Cape flats is Americanised when the Omar Sharif gambling organisation wants to erect a casino complex with the argument that it would help local communities with "upliftment" programmes, promising to create "trained and hungry entrepreneurs" from disadvantaged communities. Omar Sharif sells his casino plans as a "family entertainment and recreation centre". Encouraging the poor to become addicted to gambling by various international sharks circling an innocent prey seems hardly worrisome to a new regime keen to attract any new source of revenue.

An unashamedly elitist self-confidence pervades the new bourgeoisie that claims to be underpaid, compared with the exile experience. "Am I worth R300 000? No, I should be earning at least a million," says the *Sarafina* director. When the state broadcasting corporation launched its revamped TV schedule in February 1996, it presented a glitzy show of flown-in African-American entertainers, including O.J. Simpson's lawyer, Johnny Cochran. With no mention of world-renowned South African literary or arts talents, the new cosmopolitan image of an alleged Africanised service was confined to recycled black Hollywood entertainers. The emulation of Hollywood lifestyles by a new *Ebony* elite resembles the silly glorification of royal titles, quaint British country culture or English dress codes by the old colonisers. It should be of no concern were it not for the squandering of public money amidst a sea of poverty.

At the beginning of 1996, the ANC caucus decided to halve the compulsory contributions to the party. At the same time the ANC whip complained about the monotonous subsidised food in Parliament. Most impartial observers would agree with Tom Lodge's judgement that "Nelson Mandela's cabinet is excessively well paid for a relatively poor country, as are most senior civil servants, whose numbers were considerably enlarged with the creation of nine regional governments each with dozens of director generals."[21] Although the pay scales were derived from the outside Melamat Commission's comparisons between private and public sector salaries, Lodge is also right "that it is most unlikely there would have been serious discord in the Government of National Unity" had the ANC caucus turned down the recommendation. For many years MPs and their spouses – or their nominated "companions" – have also each been entitled to 54 single airline tickets a year to anywhere in South Africa. Once the 54 flights were used up, MPs could buy tickets at just 20 per cent of normal prices. However the 20 per cent privilege was so widely abused that Speaker Frene Ginwala had to suspend it in February 1997. While several new office holders were embarrassed, few said so publicly. Venal self-justification of the importance of public office, laments about financial sacrifices during the apartheid years and a pseudo-racist "blacks must be as well paid as whites" mentality all combined to spread the impression that the new state should be used rather than serviced.

When the same politicians later began a moral crusade against rent and service boycotts ("Masakhane") they were inevitably ignored. Moral renewal lacked role models at the top. Although most new office holders worked tirelessly for the common good, they were not widely perceived as immune to self-enrichment. Although the amounts are small and corrupt self-enrichment among the new elite is still rare compared with the plundering of the state resources by the previous regime, the writing is on the wall and ever fewer of the former idealists seem to care about their deteriorating image. The old elite, on the other hand, adores its new-found disciples. White businessmen even gloat that the African masses love their rulers to display their superior status. In any case, it is said, a little bit of capitalist temptation oils the state machinery by providing influence that fanatical ideologues would deny.

Lack of Gandhian austerity would not be worth criticising were it not for the superior moral claims of the ANC to represent all the people and particularly the downtrodden. While half of the constituency cannot afford a used bicycle, can their representatives afford to wave at them from German luxury cars? As half of the electorate struggle to buy enough food for the next day, can legislators allocate themselves salaries that are justified with the profit making of the private sector? Should politicians be expected to be more altruistic than business people in working for the public interest?

According to a falsely maligned IDASA survey[22] 56 per cent of South Africa's voters feel that people in government work in their own self-interest rather than the public good; 60 per cent say that parliamentary salaries are too high; and a staggering 84 per cent perceive some level of corruption in government. Half of those consider corruption to be worse than in the old regime. It is explosive when 85 per cent believe that people elected to govern should be "more honest" than ordinary citizens, but a sizeable number (34 per cent) feel that, in reality, elected officials are less honest than the average person.

There can be both legal and illegal corruption. While taking of bribes, stealing or misappropriating public money can be more easily identified and exposed, the legal gravy train is far more difficult to combat and carries far more damaging consequences. The former homelands squandered taxpayers' money on a massive scale. Indiscriminate promotions of civil servants for higher salaries together with a lack of internal control measures plague some provincial administrations long after the homeland civil service has been amalgamated. Unauthorised expenditures, neglect of prescribed tender procedures and other irregularities are generally exposed publicly, but little is done to correct the maladministration. For example, Winnie Mandela's quarter of a million rand unauthorised spending while deputy minister has been publicised by the auditor-general. However, Winnie Mandela was fired from her ministerial position not because of administrative incompetence or fraud but because of disloyalty to the ANC and breach of party discipline. It is rare for an ANC member to be expelled because of corruption or admonished publicly for wasteful incompetence.

While concerned democrats worry unduly about weak opposition institutions, they neglect a much more immediate danger of elite pacting, namely the coinciding interests of common financial rip-offs. The new order is less undermined by timid party competition than it is discredited by the common legitimisation of high salaries and perks for its functionaries. In addition, a new provision for cabinet ministers to hire special advisers from outside the civil service at up to R28 000 monthly salaries opened the door for corruption and nepotism. When the vast majority of the black electorate earns less in a year than its parliamentary representatives make in a month, it would be a miracle if disenchantment with the ANC leadership emerges only in the distant future. At present, the relatively high salaries of politicians, senior civil servants, consultants and members of statutory committees lure talents from less rewarded occupations, particularly university teaching and public medicine. Other appointments are frequently made as a reward for past services or personal relationships with officials.

Conflict of interest guidelines on ethical behaviour in such cases are clearly underdeveloped or remain unenforced. For example, many office-holders, in addition to a main salary, draw regular remuneration from other public accounts for their role as committee members or consultants, without perceiving multiple payments as unethical. While South Africa's parliamentary code of conduct is one of the most comprehensive in the world in terms of detailed disclosure of outside interests and benefits, much of this information is kept confidential. A parliamentary committee on members' interests is unlikely to inspire much public confidence, as it is presumed to be soft on the transgressions of its peers. In any case, its sanctions range only from a reprimand to a fine up to the value of a month's salary or suspension from Parliament for not more than fifteen days. A more forceful punishment for violators by an independent judicial commissioner would have amounted to a more effective deterrent, particularly in the many grey areas of conflict of interests.

South Africa also lacks far more important regulations to disclose donations to political parties. The controversial issue surfaced when Mandela revealed that he had secretly accepted R2 million from casino interests. Even though undue influence peddling was denied, undisclosed donations theoretically allow a party to be bought. Forbidden individual bribery pales in comparison with this purchase of collective influence. Yet ANC MP Carl Niehaus declares: "It has been the long-standing practice of the ANC not to make public its financial records, nor details of funders who have made contributions to the ANC. For as long as it is not legally expected of all political parties to make public their financial records, the ANC has no intention of deviating from this practice."[23] It is disturbing that the ruling party has no intention of pushing for disclosure, although the party is committed to transparency.

Foreign donors must share part of the blame for the corruption of several anti-apartheid activists. Foreign governments, foundations and churches thrust large amounts of money into the hands of prominent leaders without insisting on financial accountability. Demand for proper accounting was almost considered a sign of distrust by donors and harassed activists alike. Since the state viewed the activities of hundreds of NGOs with great suspicion, their trustees at least were supposed to oversee and guide NGO activities but in reality hardly ever met. They functioned as the public alibi for letting executive officers do as they wished. Once the taste for embezzlement was whetted by lax control, the practice continued well into the era of legitimate government. Mandela's own school-feeding scheme in the Eastern Cape foundered when its funds were stolen. The ANC's Women's League is riddled with controversies about unaccounted for funds. Although South African corruption in the public sector hardly compares with the former Soviet Union or other African countries where levels of bribery and embezzlement seriously affect the functioning of the entire civil service, the reported South African cases shock because of the gulf between the moral standing and the practice of the individuals involved. As the *Sunday Times* commented: "In the government the spirit of cynical exploitation by the old guard is giving way to profiteering by the new, many tempted beyond reason by sudden opportunities for enrichment."[24]

The argument that public sector remuneration must match private sector rewards in order to attract scarce skills discounts the assumed idealistic motivation of political activists to serve a worthy cause, even if poorly paid. Comparatively meagre material incentives for politicians are also compensated with high status symbolic rewards. While this equation may be increasingly questionable in purely consumerist Western societies, politics as a vocation after a liberation struggle can rightly be expected to spring from a different well. When officials and cabinet ministers in a struggling economy earn more than their US counterparts yet simultaneously preach belt-tightening, the organisation has sown the seeds for its own fragmentation. In fact, the ANC in power has emulated some of the excesses of its greedy predecessor. National Party politicians endorse the new greed not only because they also benefit, but because it exonerates them. It proves that their previous high perks were small in comparison with what the new rulers allocate themselves.

In August 1996, the cabinet and members of parliament voted themselves and their counterparts in the provincial legislatures another 15 per cent salary increase, together with a 30 per cent increase in car allowances.[25] At the same time, the government was calling on trade unions to exercise wage restraints. The brazen rationalisations of alleged "inflation-related" increases across the political spectrum reflected the character of a political class that genuinely believes its rewards should be in line with private sector remunerations rather than their own constituents. The disillusioned public sector had only received average increases of half the amount during the period. The collective plundering of public money is not considered a moral failure or an affront to the poor.

A respected ANC stalwart, Ray Alexander Simons, notes her diappointment "that not a single MP or senator denounced these increases".[26] Mary Burton, a member of the Truth and Reconciliation Commission, found herself alone in publicly questioning unexpected rises for already highly paid commissioners whose salaries are legally tied to judges' remunerations. While the commissioners exercise quasi-judicial functions, the temporary nature of the exercise together with the collective decision making under conditions of great public scrutiny would seem to lessen the need to base expectations of impartiality on financial independence in similar ways as applied to judges with life-long tenure. As different commissions are differently resourced and salaried, jealous resentment has developed between different state bodies. It is not clear, for example, why Human Rights commissioners should receive far less than the generously paid Youth and TRC commissioners. Worse, bad blood is generated when some commissioners openly criticise the high salaries of their own commission, refuse to accept R200 000 car allowances and donate part of their salaries to charity, while others argue that their public work deserves even higher rewards.[27]

In a similar vein, the chairperson of the Gender Equality Commission, Thenjiwe Mtinso, complained that the commissioners' salaries and its budget of R2 million were lower than those of the Youth Commission or the R6 million of the Human Rights Commission. Another commissioner drew attention to her having to fly economy class while others habitually used business class. The idea that it is an honour to be asked to serve on a state commission and that the status bestowed by this honour should be sufficient reward has never been raised in the South African debate. Even those who are independently wealthy cash their judges' salaries, and almost all claim their generous car allowances although their own cars could drive them safely to their workplace. In this case, reimbursement for actual expenses could be instituted and payment made only to those who depend on it or who had to give up other positions.

The political culture in South Africa devalues any public activity that is not being paid for. Volunteer service is frowned upon. The state is perceived as a source of enrichment rather than an institution to be served by citizens who care and receive their rewards symbolically. At times, the state is held to ransom in order to extract individual benefits which are given freely in other countries. In a famous incident, hundreds of ballot counters in Durban held up the final election results in 1994, demanding more pay. (See Johnson & Schlemmer, 1996, for a vivid description of the incident.[28]) Even the euphoria of the first democratic election could not override individual greed. Mercenary attitudes had already been encouraged by thousands of voter-education campaigners and employees of the Independent Electoral Commission being put on the state payroll with benefits that surprised them.

The origin of a culture of selfish opportunism probably lies with successive governments exploiting the state for special interest groups. When one party succeeds the other in power, claims for entitlements to loot likewise come naturally. If necessary, common looting of the public purse is agreed upon between adversaries. When parliamentarians vote on their own higher remuneration few dissenters emerge.

Looting at the top has not gone unnoticed at the bottom. The perception that political insiders are first of all looking after their own interests has not only encouraged a cynical alienation from politics but it has also festered emulation from below in whatever way those not on the inside can achieve their fair share. A white-collar criminal justified his fraud with the excuse that everyone is enriching himself illegally. A member of a car theft syndicate pointed out that this was the only way he could make a living. The large percentage of police personnel who are corrupt are more likely to be inspired by a climate in which common rules are perceived as applying to one poorly paid section but not to another richly rewarded elite. The extraordinary gap between elite remuneration and bottom income erodes cohesion and solidarity in favour of everyone for himself and herself by all means available.

The internal critics within the ANC receive lame excuses from their benefiting colleagues. The fact that the salaries of parliamentarians are now taxed still makes their net pay higher than those in the apartheid era. Deductions for ANC organisational duties also do not justify the high rewards, because taxpayers should not be obligated to finance party political activities via the salaries of their representatives. The most questionable argument was Mandela's retort that without sufficient legal rewards politicians could be tempted to reward themselves illegally. Indeed, nobody would want to see bureaucrats and politicians rely mainly on graft and corruption during an uncertain reign before they are overthrown by the next corrupt elite, as practised in many developing countries. But there exists a vast difference between compensating public servants adequately but not excessively, and enticing their hands into the public till. Even to assume that corruption could become the rule among ANC cadres in office does not testify to great confidence in the moral integrity of the organisation's members by its beloved president. On the other hand, Mandela may have indeed articulated a wiser and more realistic assessment of human nature than ANC struggle literature portrays. The national auditor-general noted that 92 civil servants in the Eastern Cape capital of Bisho had awarded themselves R3,6 million in "unauthorised salary increases". The maverick Bantu Holomisa, known for his populist forthrightness, has described the nepotism of the disarrayed Eastern Cape administration: "I'm just saying that experienced civil servants are being sidelined and certain 'comrades' are employing their in-laws and relatives who have totally no experience".

The apartheid state practised ethnic nepotism on a massive scale – almost by definition. However, its successor cannot afford to continue that tradition because it claims to represent the poor and powerless. When "the average Parliamentarian earns 30 times more than the average citizen"[29] critique of such discrepancies cannot be dismissed as payment according to international standards. The yardstick must be a South African one, not what similar officials in the US or Germany earn, as ANC spokespersons insist. Nor can the critique of the gravy train be rejected as racism when it originates from white quarters. The assumption of racism automatically silences all white critique of black officials. It is a convenient and cheap weapon to employ, although black office-holders also react against the continued dominance and intellectual hegemony of white liberals in the media or academia. But black shop stewards and civic leaders are equally disillusioned about their own representatives in government or on company boards deserting their constituency. The same criticism by blacks of blacks is considered legitimate while branded as racist when it comes from white citizens. For example, Jacob Zuma, the ANC KwaZulu-Natal chairperson, blamed "professional noisemakers" for the debacle about the AIDS play and the criticism of his ministerial wife. The statement insinuated racism when it wondered "whether this hullabaloo is because both the minister and the artist involved are black and the party is targeting the poorest of the poor who are black". Thereby the enrichment of the few or mismanagement is justified with concern for the poor.

Indeed there is a racist assumption that blacks in charge will fail sooner or later. Operating under this self-fulfilling prophecy opens the record of the new officials for exceptionally suspicious and sometimes unwarranted scrutiny. Yet if the new patriotism proclaimed by Mandela is to succeed, the state has to live up to the highest standards, despite the adversarial undertones. Otherwise perceived legal corruption is used to justify more tax evasion and a general culture of public cynicism. It is in the ANC's own interest to prevent such a development even if it is at the cost of its own loyal and hard-working officials. Alienation from the political process undermines the new democracy. Distrust and resentment of distant leaders triggers strikes of comparatively underpaid civil servants. Cynicism leads to what the Germans call *Politikverdrossenheit*, a general apathy and rejection of the public sphere when the propagated patriotism demands the opposite of increased involvement. A spokesperson for an Alexandra squatter association, Ruben Mathe, articulates the typical disillusionment of the poor with the rich. "I do not vote for anyone any more. In this life you've got to survive. I need a roof over my head, not an ANC membership card." Smiling, he said, "You know who came to canvass in this area before the local elections? The IFP – nobody else. The ANC cannot see our problems through the tinted glass of their Benzes. They just drive past."[30]

SACP and COSATU officials so far have managed to be both part of the ruling privileged elite and to present themselves credibly as the champions of the growing underclass. As long as the tripartite alliance keeps the lid on the disillusioned poor in the name of unity of the progressive forces, the "miracle" continues. The old establishment benefits most from this stability. Judging by their anti-socialist crusades in the boardrooms and business editorials, few of the old elite, however, realise to whom they owe the absence of racial populism and potential class warfare.

In conclusion, the relatively peaceful South African transition was greatly facilitated by the vast resources at the disposal of the state and the private sector-led economy. The "good surprise" would not have been possible without the security of pensions and the incentive of vast retrenchment packages. The literature on transition has underrated the availability of options as a precondition for compromise by hard-liners in power. In many ways, the so-called South African miracle is better dubbed the "purchased revolution". The members of the liberation armies who were not incorporated into the official defence force receive a small pension. Many other potential trouble-makers were bought off by being put on the payroll of the public service or the even more lucrative private sector.

For example, when the budget for the intelligence services was drawn up in 1995, a 20 per cent cut was envisaged. This amounted to a comparatively minor reduction, given the absence of foes. However, the ultimate outcome was "a 66 per cent increase from R427,5 million to R710 million – by far the biggest increase for any government department, and this at a time when health and teaching jobs were cut in the cause of the economy".[31] The increase resulted from the integration of over 900 ANC intelligence agents, the PAC security service and three homeland spy agencies so that in the end the National Intelligence Agency (NIA) has almost three times as many staff as the old security apparatus at the height of Afrikaner paranoia. The NIA is only one of five agencies that comprise South Africa's "intelligence community". Similar creative job creation occurred in the South African Defence Force, although with greater transparency and public accountability. Yet despite the money wasted on superfluous civil servants who now spy on each other, it is difficult to disagree with the Suzman Foundation: "If it was necessary to throw a lot of money at this key political problem of making the lamb lie down with the lion, it was probably worth it."[32] However, only in comparatively wealthy South Africa could reconciliation be purchased. Buying off dissent also corrupts the newly co-opted who know that their occupation and remuneration are not justified by the task at hand. How this consciousness of being pacified translates into job performance remains to be tested.

Even purist Azapo and PAC leaders did not prove immune when tempted with offers. The fact that Cyril Ramaphosa could move from head of a militant mineworkers' union and secretary general of the ruling party to chief executive of a business conglomerate and main board member of the Anglo American Corporation indicates an atmosphere of non-ideological expediency, similar to the many shifts of principled ideologues to pragmatic profit-seekers in Eastern Europe. Unique to South Africa is only the need to justify private enrichment with black empowerment that elevates corporate boardrooms to "new sites of struggles".

It was legal continuity and a private sector economy that allowed key security bureaucrats from the old regimes to abandon control of the state peacefully for a golden handshake. Huge payouts were handed out to police generals who retired for "health reasons" or easily found alternative employment in the private sector. Peaceful change is greatly facilitated by such buy-out options. African military rulers and their underlings elsewhere who depend on the state as the main source of income cling to their power because they face not only loss of office, but economic insecurity, unless they have siphoned off revenue into foreign bank accounts. As Michael Holman has aptly observed: "Unlike South Africa's white minority, which when forced to surrender power, could derive compensation from control of the economy, the Nigerian regime and its supporters have no such safety net."[33]

So, where is the struggle now? It would be facetious and an oversimplification to simply say that "the comrades are in business" (although some are), and the "oppressors have been bought off" (although some have), but it would be equally false not to recognise to what extent "the struggle" has been tempered by governance, some ideals abandoned (for the time being?); sights have been lowered; at the same time tired justifications are being used by the new lot to explain themselves to their supporters and admirers and to denigrate their opponents. New conditions for opposition and revolt are being created and new struggles are being born. The current cohort of leadership will come and go as sure as the sun rises and sets.

And yet, despite all of the preceding, the struggle has not been in vain. Fundamentally new grounds of political contestation have been created. South Africa has rid itself of legalised racism and oppression. Scope has been created for new opportunities for development and growth. The challenge to build a new nation in South Africa is not an offence to the intellect as was the compulsion to live in an apartheid state. Above all, the future is far more open-ended politically than it ever appeared before.

Chapter Ten

Is the future what it used to be?

In this penultimate chapter we can begin by answering this question very briefly. The answer is: no; not for the ANC, the NP or for the international community in general. The profound and largely unanticipated changes of the last decade of this millennium underline once again the open-ended nature of change and the future. This is certainly so for South Africa. Consequently we will not attempt to give even a cautious prediction as to the future of South Africa. At best we can try to identify major and minor trends, relate them to one another, locate key actors and interest groups and give speculative projections about the options available. In this way we hope to provide a framework in which the insights and conclusions of the previous chapter make sense.

We have to begin by underlining the predominance of two global trends which have a powerful impact on South Africa's transition: democratisation and reforms towards a competitive market economy. These are two primary export commodities from the consolidated democracies of the West and have had similar influence on the political transitions and economic reforms of countries in Latin America, Southeast Asia, Central and Eastern Europe as well as Africa. The Bretton Woods institutions such as the IMF and the World Bank, as well as international donor agencies and countries, either explicitly or implicitly use the criteria of a liberal democracy and/or a market economy to judge whether a country is moving in the "right" direction democratically or introducing "proper" economic reforms.

The predominance of the drive towards a competitive market economy underpins the globalisation or internationalisation of economic life. Increasingly, mega-corporations are acting in terms of an economy that does not recognise or respect nation-state frontiers or boundaries. This has serious implications for the domestic political developments of particular countries and no less for South Africa. The ANC in power in South Africa cannot afford to act as if it is isolated from the international economy, not unless it wishes to slide into stagnation and greater economic dependency. As one commentator puts it: "The basic situation facing governments of developing countries is one of very strong pressures to liberalise, both from the international community and from international financial institutions, accompanied by strong domestic resistance to reform because of short run costs."[1] No country that wishes to "successfully" democratise or reform can do so in isolation or in an arbitrary manner. There are simply too many international agencies and powerful countries to see to it that they stay on the "right" track or perish. The Bonn Conference on Economic Co-operation in Europe in April 1990 affirmed that "democratic institutions and economic freedom foster economic and social progress . . . that the performance of market-based economics relies primarily on the freedom of political enterprise" and that "economic freedom for the individual includes the right to freely own, buy, sell and otherwise utilise property".[2] Similarly, the Charter of Paris for a new Europe in November 1990 saw the leaders of the CSC's (Conference on Security and Co-operation in Europe), proclaim the end of the Cold War and affirm the link between politics and economics by stating: "Freedom and political pluralism are necessary elements in our common objective of developing market economies toward sustainable economic growth, prosperity, social justice, expanding employment and efficient use of economic resources."[3] These are powerful sentiments that no doubt helped shape the minds of negotiators in the ANC and NP when they eventually became pragmatic bedfellows. It is well to remember too that this was essentially a marriage of convenience rather than one rushed into with unrestrained passion.

The "victory" of liberal democracy and capitalism is too recent not to remind ourselves that this was essentially an ideological victory about the "best" way to be democratic and bring about economic development. An ideological statement is simply a value judgement parading as a statement of fact. Therefore, when a respected analyst like Peter Berger unequivocally states that "Democracy depends on a market economy",[4] and is joined by Kyong-Won:[5] "It is in the nature of capitalism that it secretly nurtures and eventually unleashes democratic forces", they are quickly challenged by Claude Ake:[6] "In the end, the bourgeoisie succeeded in replacing democracy with liberal democracy, which was not so much a political morality as an economic convenience – the political correlate of the market necessary for optimising its sustainability and efficacy", or Ralph Milliband:[7] "Liberal democracy equals capitalist democracy – a contradiction in terms – it is oligarchic rule tempered by democratic forms, democracy is an intrinsic part of socialism." Somewhere in this debate one can be sure that value judgements will be defended as self-evident statements of fact and therein lies a new and powerful source of political tension, particularly in South Africa.

It seems to be the nature of political ideologies that, at some or other stage, they get increasingly out of touch with prevailing socio-economic and political circumstances and, if they are clung to too dogmatically, generate all kinds of tensions. This undoubtedly was the case with apartheid and separate development as well as democratic centralism and socialism, and may even have facilitated the process by means of which the ANC and NP embraced a common ideology consisting of nation-building, liberal democracy and economic reform. In so doing the ANC brings itself "in tune" with the prevailing international climate and now faces the challenge of making this ideology "work" for the new South Africa.

In a brilliant, short and incisive article, Dahl[8] has pointed out that there is a persistent tension between the central tenet of a liberal democracy and that of a competitive market economy that cannot be resolved without some form of state intervention. This flies in the face of the conventional wisdom of free marketeers. The core tenet of liberal democracy is that of an egalitarian rights culture, whereas the core tenet of a competitive market economy is that of inequality in the capacity to risk, generate wealth and to own the means of production. There are circumstances where "competitive markets may be excessively harmful to the processes and institutions of democratic government". He is backed by Pzreworski[9] who shows why markets do not necessarily produce the most efficient or justifiable outcomes and may result in state intervention. The dilemma is obvious: if competitive markets generate wealth and growth most efficiently, how is the subsequent economic inequality mediated/managed by a political system that promotes equality and egalitarian rights? This is what we referred to as the core dilemma facing the ANC in government: how to manage the inevitable political pain of necessary economic reform.

The central thread in our analyses revolves around this core dilemma. The way in which the ANC manages this is its primary political concern. It informs the manner in which it engages in nation-building, responds to demands for minority group recognition, copes with traditionalism, reacts to internal dissent, etc. We do not deny the relevance or importance of these other dilemmas, but they are for the time being secondary to this central concern. If the ANC fails somehow to manage this core dilemma it risks its own legitimacy and exposes its own inability to deliver on the promises it made. Even if it wished to, the central concern of the ANC in power cannot be to impose some form of ideological hegemony on South Africa, e.g. Jacobin conformity to only one version of nation-building. It has neither the power nor the resources to do so. Its central concern is to develop the capacity to manage the complexity of its own adopted political programme.

Many commentators have stressed the point that there is no necessary relationship between the type of regime and the success of economic reform. It is possible to have democracy without reform, reform without democracy, reform and democracy, no reform and no democracy. As Pzreworski puts it: "We still know too little about markets and democracies and the little we do know, does not support any ideological blueprints."[10] However, what is recognised is that to pursue democracy and reform at the same time in emerging or developing countries generates extraordinary challenges. This is known as the problem of simultaneity. Those who govern South Africa at the moment believe it is possible to pursue four overarching goals successfully and concurrently: to complete the process of democratisation by 1999; to stimulate economic growth through a competitive market; to develop a strong human-rights culture; and to satisfy the socio-economic needs of the citizens.

Throughout our analyses we have shown how the concurrent pursuit of these goals generates paradoxes and unintended consequences: the tension between traditionalism and modernity; the imperatives for growth and industrial democracy; human rights and transforming the criminal justice system; democratic stability and political populism. From one perspective one could argue that contrary to popular perception, the new regime's ambivalence and apparent inaction does not arise from doing nothing, but from trying to do too much. So far there have been very limited attempts at alignment or prioritisation between these goals. These goals need not necessarily be incompatible with each other, but neither is the practical or concrete relationship between them self-evident. Increasingly these will have to be articulated through a series of clearly defined policy trade-offs. Failure to trade off reinforces the perception of inaction and paralysis because of the apparent contradictions generated by the simultaneous pursuit of those goals.

So, if the ANC has to choose between consolidating democracy by slowing down the pace of economic reform or, vice versa, speeding up the pace of economic reform at the cost of slowing down the consolidation of democracy, what is it most likely to do? Our guess is that if the ANC has to choose on which side of the conundrum it has to come down, it would prioritise democracy over economic reform, although it is likely to do everything possible to postpone making this choice. This does not mean it would abandon reform for democracy: it cannot afford to, but certainly it would concern itself more with consolidating the democratic infrastructure that it has created, including its own support base, rather than risk that by embarking on too painful economic reforms. This may "irritate" the local business sector and "alarm" potential investors from abroad, but the simple point is that if the democratic infrastructure such as it is, is destroyed, it is not quite clear what type of regime would take its place, nor is it clear how friendly it would be to business and other disgruntled minorities in the long run. There certainly is no Pinochet (Chile) or Jaruzelski (Poland) waiting in the barracks to impose a military-controlled capitalist or socialist growth path on South Africa, or an ethnic minority with sufficient coercive resources at its disposal to claim South Africa once again as its own.

Historically, in a sense, South Africa is condemned to democratise or face disintegration. In this transition, certainly in the initial phases, the ANC has to play a definitive role. It is vital for successful consolidation. If consolidation is successful the ANC becomes redundant in terms of the political system it has helped to institutionalise. If consolidation is not successful South Africa regresses into all the dilemmas of a deeply divided society we identified in the opening chapters. Therefore, to conclude with a speculative analysis of the state of the ANC facing the dilemmas and challenges we have outlined is entirely appropriate.

Three latent cleavages threaten the unity of the heterogeneous ANC: (1) The contradiction between socialist ideologues in the union movement, and more liberal or social democratic factions in the state bureaucracy, including a fledgling black bourgeoisie. The current conflict centres on the extent and pace of privatisation, the independence of unions in the tripartite alliance, as well as adherence to a global neo-liberal agenda in general.[11] (2) Antagonisms between racial populists or African nationalists on the one hand and more nonracial pragmatists on the other have flared up occasionally. The racial populists whose past figureheads included Winnie Mandela, Bantu Holomisa and Peter Mokaba have been silenced or marginalised for the time being but command considerable potential support. (3) The rift between traditional leaders and democrats does not only divide Inkatha and the ANC but remains highly controversial within the ANC as well. Its constituency comprises both, but its official ideology is shaped far more by an urban elite in the enlightenment tradition of democratic legitimacy. Women's emancipation, for example, clashes directly with traditional notions of patriarchy and polygamy.

All three cleavages are unresolved or unresolvable within current ANC structures. They exist more or less as taboos that are not thoroughly debated but referred to in coded terms. The divisive nature of the controversial issues is evident to all. This analysis sketches only the likely development of the first two tensions in order to arrive at a speculative worst-case and best-case future scenario.

One of the enduring crises that the ANC in government faced during its first year in power was the revolt of its own soldiers. In October 1994, over 7 000 Umkhonto we Sizwe (MK) members absented themselves without leave from their training bases at Wallmannstal over grievances about low salaries, poor food, racism of trainers and administrative delays in their placement. The former guerrillas, above all, expected to be recruited at much higher ranks than a joint commission of officers from the SADF, MK and a British Military Advisory and Training Team (BMATT) were willing to grant. In the perception of the MK members, they had achieved a victory as a result of the April election and expected their year-long sacrifices in exile to be duly rewarded. In contrast, their own commanders, including former guerrilla chief and now defence minister Joe Modise and his deputy Ronnie Kasrils, insisted that they either had to submit to military discipline in the new South Africa National Defence Force (SANDF) or choose another career. The harsh Military Discipline Code (MDC) that previously applied to a conscript army was criticised as inappropriate for a volunteer professional military. MK soldiers challenged the very core of military expertise and discipline on which the leadership of all parties had agreed as the basis for integration of the disparate armies. A view of one disgruntled mutineer, as articulated in the ANC-supporting *New Nation*, typifies the sentiment of the many eager recruits:

Who qualifies? Racist soldiers who had defended the oppression of the majority by the National Party government, who had supported the corrupt homeland governments? They are said to be better trained and hold more senior ranks than our soldiers who fought for freedom. What is better training? Is it the destruction of Angolan villages and infrastructure? Is it the rape of Namibian women in the war zones? Is it the dismemberment of Mozambique's population by land mines? Is it the shooting of Umtata schoolboys in pursuit of Apla?[12]

Such questioning of alleged common standards constitutes in one area what the country's power sharing arrangement faces in the entire public service. The military, as a microcosm, reveals starkly the likely future crisis of legitimacy that the ANC faces.

Similar rumblings of discontent occurred when 28 000 platinum miners in Rustenburg went on strike against court orders and National Union of Mineworkers (NUM) officials in July 1996. Unelected workers' committee members assaulted NUM members who favoured a return to work. All indicators point to a future trend where unions will join employers and government against workers and consumers outside the loop of labour relations. These unorganised segments will be repressed harshly if they threaten jobs and wage levels of the organised forces of a corporatist consensus.

A compliant ANC is almost set up for failure, but the implications for racial reconciliation of such a course are barely grasped now. In short, if the ANC loses its constituency, its rivals may triumph in the short run, but the consequences for the country's racial harmony appear disastrous in the long run. The Mandela "miracle" of racial reconciliation would finally unravel as a great delusionary mirage.

A possible worst-case scenario that would endanger nonracialism could unfold as follows: The ANC leadership proves unable to fulfil major expectations of its constituency. Just as MK leaders in government are already denounced by mutineering soldiers, so the government is perceived as a failure and is stuck with the label "sellout" on a gravy train. The National Party, together with other smaller opposition parties, now called the "Democratic Peoples' Union", reinforces the disarray in ANC ranks and presents itself as a more competent and reliable force for material betterment and the fight against crime. Since the 1999 election will have lost the aura of a liberation celebration and the charisma of Mandela has faded, or the unifying president no longer lives, the ANC faces the real prospect of losing some of its popular support. The new nonracial opposition Democratic Peoples' Union with some prominent blacks in the leadership and even some defectors from the ANC can make inroads into the black electorate, similar to the NP victory among coloureds and Indians in 1994.

The autocratic way in which the ANC leadership handled the expulsion of Bantu Holomisa and other dissidents or "redeployed" a popular premier (Terror Lekota) against the express wishes of a supportive constituency in the Free State encourages a backlash. A 1997 survey among African voters about preferred contenders for Mandela's succession revealed that Holomisa was more popular than Mandela's chosen successor, Thabo Mbeki, in the Eastern Cape (25 per cent versus 22 per cent) and the "exiled" Ramaphosa still commanded considerable support across all provinces, but particularly in Gauteng (25 per cent) and the Western Cape (37 per cent). The author, R.W. Johnson,[13] reports that 60 per cent of ANC voters "were uniquely willing to break the very strong ties of party discipline and loyalty to censure their party for the way it had behaved" in the Holomisa case. It must be remembered that the Holomisa expulsion was caused by allegations of corruption that allegedly brought the ANC into disrepute. With the party supporting a former prominent Western Cape ANC leader (Boesak) accused of fraud and misappropriation of foreign donor money, the perception is further reinforced that a seemingly insensitive and complacent leadership should be taught a lesson by disillusioned voters. With escalating crime at an all-time high, the scene is set for a post-Mandela political fragmentation in which none of the politicians is able to capture the imagination of voters across ethnic groups or even within their own traditional support base. Instead, everyone blames everyone else for the ills of a society that nobody can reform alone.

Riddled with faction fights and splits within its ranks, particularly from restless Cosatu militants, threatened by a revived PAC on the left and by a "nonracial" opposition party on the right, some ANC leaders may revert to racial populism. Radical nationalism and revival of memories of racial oppression give some ANC leaders instant popularity over more cosmopolitan rivals for leadership roles. Flogging the forgotten rewards of victory for "our people" provides the tempting formula that can stop the demise of the majority party. Black nationalism rather than inclusive nonracialism could assure the ANC a built-in numerical majority if only pride in being black can be mobilised. As the vast majority of coloureds, Indian and white minorities have been lost to rival parties anyway, it is quite conceivable that some ANC election strategists will forego "the promise of nonracialism" theme that made the party attractive to non-black minorities. Racial populism would pre-empt the dangerous black attacks on a "sellout ANC, dominated by alien Indians and lackeys of international capital". Allegations of sabotage by white civil servants explains the failure of delivery. The scapegoating of subversive Afrikaner bureaucrats further fuels racial perceptions.

This represents the unlikely worst-case scenario which needs to be contrasted with countervailing trends towards normal party political competition. To what extent the nonracial anti-apartheid history of the leading liberation movement can prevent a slide into counter-racism is open to conjecture. Reviving the ideology of the anti-apartheid struggle remains a double-edged sword: it could rally wavering troops with outdated slogans about a racial enemy, but it could also motivate a following to strive anew for the broad nonracial alliances of the past. How many ANC leaders under pressure of loss of power will be tempted by racial populism? As long as the SACP commands a decisive influence in the ideological discourse of the ruling party, such a shift towards racial confrontation is unlikely. It would be denounced as reactionary and alien to the socialist principles of internationalism. However, even a hegemonic SACP outlook may not be able to control a frustrated following that vents its increasing alienation in racial outbursts.

With Marxism-Leninism ever more discredited as a guiding ideology and its South African advocates themselves disoriented and drawn into bureaucratic comfort, an activist rump SACP will be more dependent on the ANC than vice versa. Despite an increasingly anti-labour government policy, the remaining communists are unlikely to break away as a "socialist" opposition. They will continue to argue that they are far more influential inside than outside the ANC where they form the party's working class conscience, guarding against a sellout. When Tony Holiday first publicly recommended a split, his SACP colleagues rejected it on the grounds of their historical role.[14] Holiday reasoned that the SACP "will be permanently condemned to live cheek-by-jowl with free-marketeers, social democrats, liberals and rank opportunists in the hybrid body which the ANC has become". It is precisely because of these trends, his opponents argued, that the SACP is needed in the ANC more than ever.

The SACP has always been presented as a strategic conspiracy to hijack the ANC. As the chief ideologues and think-tank within a non-class organisation, SACP tacticians were portrayed as the real class-conscious power behind the throne. In reality, however, the SACP has had to toe the ANC line, at least since Mandela assumed office. When the government first introduced its neo-liberal Growth Employment and Redistribution (GEAR) policy in mid-1996, surprisingly the SACP glowingly endorsed it. "When Cronin did get around to criticise GEAR," reports an observer (Hein Marais, *Mail & Guardian*, November 22-28, 1996), "he got an earful from Mandela and a visit from ANC top brass." Ever since, the SACP's orthodox "working-class perspective" has unconvincingly tried to locate the alliance's conservative economic policy "within a Marxist metaphysics". Behind the jargon hides a reality of ideological confusion and organisational weakness of a party (despite a 75 000 claimed active membership) that needs to piggyback on the ANC's legitimacy and patronage far more than the ANC in power needs to cultivate a left image.

On the other hand, as long as Communists are part of the ruling group, claims that a privileged elite neglects its poor constituency are deflected. In this sense, Communists serve as a useful alibi. Inasmuch as the SACP cannot afford to shed the spoils of power for ideological purity, so the ANC also benefits from its Marxist-Leninist ally, at least domestically. Even among global capitalists, Marxist-Leninists have long lost their once deterrent image and are sought out as reliable business partners from China to Cuba, their undemocratic systems and human rights violations notwithstanding.

The SACP allows the ANC to present itself as a people's party that also has the interests of the poor at heart. The more frustrations tend to boil over, the more the ANC needs the Communists. It is an open question how long unionists and Communists in power can contain mass anger before they too are openly rejected as part of a hated system that fails to deliver. In the short run, these cleavages can be manipulated; in the longer run, ANC unity and mass support is unlikely to be sustained.

In summary, the ANC itself embodies a heterogeneous coalition of divergent interests that constantly strain party cohesion. A party without the charisma of a unifying Mandela is likely to split between radical populists and pragmatic social democrats. With the ideological leadership of an increasingly divided SACP fading, the strategic guidance of a vanguard with its past discipline and heroic appeal among followers no longer ensures unquestioned unity, particularly among frustrated socialists, self-enriching bureaucrats and fledgling black capitalists. Splits are also encouraged and facilitated by a proportional voting system that guarantees defectors representation. In the winner-takes-all Westminster system of constituency representatives, they would disappear.

The inevitable failure to deliver on high expectations will disillusion followers. People cannot be pacified with symbolic gratification indefinitely. It is true, as Mattes, Gouws and Kotze observed that: "The intense experience of the liberation struggle is likely to have created a strong and enduring psychological bond that will endure a great deal of dashed hopes before it begins to erode."[15] But erode it will and the euphoria of a liberation election cannot be maintained endlessly. The intense partisan loyalty to the cause begins to weaken the more the cause itself has become institutionalised.

Although a major ANC split is unlikely to occur before the second election in 1999, the prospect of an unravelling dominant party thereafter remains greater than the prospect of unity. It is another question whether such a split is desirable for political stability and public order. From the perspective of democratic theory, however, smaller party blocs clustered around economic interests, loose ideological orientation and overlapping traditional racial divides would finally herald the advent of normal politics in the apartheid land. The rapid embourgeoisement of a black elite together with the diverging interests of short-changed masses would suggest such a development rather than the indefinite success of manipulation in the name of nonracial patience.

This optimistic scenario has not considered the prospect that a threatened multiracial elite reverts to multiracial domination by suspending the democratic rules altogether. Such a technocratic authoritarianism, however, is remotely conceivable only in a severe crisis bordering on anarchy and economic collapse. A technocratic dictatorship that ignores the carefully grafted constitutional compromises would face the same crisis of legitimacy as the previous minority regime, even if it were multiracial and superficially Africanised.

In an open letter to Mandela, Breyten Breytenbach has succinctly sketched the likely options: "If we were to go down the Algerian road of a liberation movement bringing to power a largely exiled leadership which then sets about looting the state in a prolonged orgy of corruption (and some of your ministers already have this sweet tooth), we shall surely reap the same whirlwind; in due time a generation of fundamentalists will rise up to vomit the very ideals transported by national liberation – namely tolerance and civilisation and emancipation, and learning for all and the separation of powers and national development. Except that our version will be of the racist as opposed to the religiously fanatic variety."[16] However, obstacles and countertrends to this dismal Algerian scenario must also be noted. The ANC's exiled leadership is matched by influential figures of internal resistance and political prisoners even more steeped in the culture of responsiveness and integrity. It would not be without an internal struggle for this tradition to be set aside. While many are tempted by the new opportunities for sudden enrichment in the civil service, a culture of transparency and accountability also prevails. In this respect, as a commentator noted, "the government is a victim of its own virtue".[17] While the old guard cynically exploited the state by concealing its patronage, the new rulers have to account for their expenses and salaries publicly. The heightened concern over corruption may well reflect these new practices and sensitivities rather than actually increasing incidents of graft.

In the authoritarian Arab states, Muslim fundamentalists generally represent the poor and forgotten. In the name of true Islam, they inveigh against Westernised elites who ignore the plight of the marginalised. Therefore, the rulers are considered infidels. Although the creeping embourgeoisement of the South African liberators engenders similar resentment, in the absence of religious commitment it is much more difficult to mobilise in the name of race when the ruling culprits are of the same race. A South Africa whose democracy has been deeply entrenched during an anti-racist liberation struggle differs from an authoritarian Algeria which had never experienced true democratic rule even after liberation in 1962.

As this analysis has stressed, South Africa as a complex industrialised society has long developed beyond the stage of dictatorships in the African continent. South Africa's evolving institutions of bargaining and democratic conflict resolution cannot be set aside by any government if its wishes to function effectively. That sobering legacy of the apartheid regime applies to its successor as well and provides the structural basis for an overall optimistic prognosis regardless of the intentions of incumbents in office.

Veteran historian Leonard Thompson ends the revised edition of his seminal *A History of South Africa* with the contingent verdict: "If, in the coming years, the democratic current controls the anarchic, reactionary ethnic, authoritarian, oligarchic and populist countercurrents, twenty-first century South Africa will indeed be a shining example to the quarrelsome and violent world beyond its borders."[18] This hope resembles the statement "If there were no sin, earth would be heaven!" It assumes a South African exceptionalism for which there is little evidence in the human nature of the country's people. However, because of the unique social conditions, interrelationships and institutions that apartheid history has forged, better than comparative prerequisites for democratisation persist alongside all the other counter-trends. In the dialectic

199

between mobilisable divisions and pragmatic unity, in an ongoing political contest about rationales for controversial decisions, South Africa's future unfolds open-endedly, accessible to prudent intervention as well as laissez-faire paralysis, like everywhere else in the political life of a state.

Chapter Eleven

Conclusion: The underclass versus the liberation aristocracy

The ANC Deputy Minister of Trade and Industry, Phumzile Mlambo-Nguka, stated that black businessmen should not be shy to say that they wanted to become "filthy rich". Such an attitude rings of crass materialism, implying the neglect of the poor majority in the drive to self-enrichment by an elite. Testing the reactions of fifty black students and aspiring business executives revealed four clusters of opinions. Endorsement of the controversial statement overshadowed all criticism.

The vulgarity of being "filthy rich" amidst a sea of shanty towns notwithstanding, the desire concurs perfectly well with the logic of capitalism. Why should blacks exempt themselves from behaviour that rewarded white beneficiaries so handsomely in the past? Criticism of black fat cats without including white fat cats smacks of racism indeed. Had an equal playing field been provided in the past, "black business people would probably have been stinking rich already". Not only is such a success story overdue, but rich blacks create jobs and enlarge the narrow white tax base. Lamenting the rise of a black bourgeoisie perpetuates the stereotype that it is "natural" for blacks to be poor and whites to be affluent. To step outside one's customary status is never unproblematical. The resentful surprise about black Africans in luxury cars and fancy houses, albeit a tiny group, mixes sneering envy with condescending admiration among many less fortunate whites. The old white capitalists on the other hand delight in parading their new-found allies in profiteering. The more black faces, the easier to reject charges of racial capitalism.

Yet legitimate concerns about "filthy rich" blacks persist. Those uneasy worries can be broken down into (1) moral; (2) egalitarian-socialist and (3) political objections.

Moral reservations focus on ostentatious consumption by a few while the many suffer in poverty. An African communitarian cultural tradition is said to impose obligations on the better-off to remember where they came from. Giving back to their fellows and "brothers" is seen as a moral duty. The wealth of their white counterparts was achieved partly through apartheid exploitation. By endorsing a similar black selfishness, a new elite merely continues what is seen as the same shameless greed by hook or by crook. Unlike socialism that aims at levelling all wealth, the moral criticism does not assail affluence per se, but focuses on *how* it has been acquired. The speed with which new black millionaires emerge makes it unlikely that they have earned their fortune by the sweat of their brows. Therefore, moral critics have a field day denouncing this enrichment as unethical behaviour. Yet even the politics of embarrassment prove ineffectual in a climate where "filthy richness" becomes an unabashed goal in itself.

Egalitarian-socialist objections point to similar concerns. Encouragement of the filthy rich occurs at the expense of the weak. While a minority of opportunists enrich themselves, the masses are sidelined and ignored. From this principled position, Mandela needs to be applauded for rejecting outright the black business (NAFCOC) request to have all outstanding taxes before 1994 relinquished. However, the refusal to entertain special tax exemptions for black business should not only have been justified with the confusion it would create in the tax collection system, but with the duty of the rich to finance the new order, regardless of past "taxation without representation". Yet such moralistic and egalitarian reasoning falls on deaf ears in a neo-liberal climate which celebrates individual success at all costs. Communal solidarity impedes the accumulation of individual fortunes. A global market celebrates rootless and ruthless profiteering, eschewing civic connectedness and national sacrifices as old-fashioned virtues.

Political reservations about filthy richness stand on the strongest ground. Not only is it unwise for an ANC cabinet minister to provoke her poor constituency with such inflammatory language, but the ANC encourages class warfare if it loses sight of a destabilising inequality. The ANC turns its back on a history of struggle that once had racial capitalism as its main target. In that distant past activists romanticised the simple, modest life with survival wages for unionists. Bourgeois lifestyles were denounced as those of the class enemy. At the most, Toyotas, not German luxury cars, were to be the signature of successful revolutionaries. Nowadays, according to an insider, some parliamentarians almost panic at the thought of being overlooked for directorships and other private sector appointments where the real power is seen to be located. When former activists become instant millionaires by what is called "overdue career changes" they not only bury their own history but confirm the triumph of nonracial capitalism. Therefore was the anti-apartheid struggle never more than getting a larger slice of the pie? Was it merely a materialist fight against racist exclusion from capitalist spoils rather than creating an alternative, more humane and equal social order?

Thabo Mbeki was asked what went through his mind when he flew over a squatter settlement. He answered: "I think there is an enormous amount of patience among the people in those shacks. I don't think there's any kind of explosive sentiment in reaction to the perceived lack of delivery of houses."[1] Yet Mbeki also realises that patience wears thin sooner or later. Mbeki of all ANC leaders has shown a keen awareness of the explosive political potential to be found in the growing gap between rich and poor among black South Africans. He is the main architect behind the GEAR macro-economic policy of the ANC, which shows clearly the battle between economic growth and development and the difficulties of trying to sacrifice the one for the other.

Economic growth and development seems to have emerged as a national policy, behind which all factions should unite. However, the strategy to achieve the elusive goal is intensely contested, as the debate about the macro-economic policy GEAR indicates. It is a conflict over growth at whose costs, and the noble goal proves more divisive than unifying.

Redistribution and transformation have been other initial core ideas, but they too have been diluted and modified. Redistribution would happen mainly at the expense of whites and is associated with discredited socialism. Redistribution through progressive taxes would create a hostile investment climate. South Africans already feel overtaxed. A one-time limited levy for equalisation along the lines of a German *Lastenausgleich* has been almost unanimously rejected by the old establishment. That leaves only transformation in the minds and attitudes of people where no costs are involved.

Reconciliation and nation-building operate only in the symbolic realm and fail to deliver material improvements.

The once uniquely inspiring vision of nonracialism has also faded away. Nonracialism has been undermined by racially based affirmative action, an economically inexpensive and politically wise corrective for the legacy of legalised racism from a business point of view. After decades of colour consciousness, colour-blindness can hardly be expected. Claims for entitlements and greater representativeness of the racially disadvantaged remain on the agenda of blacks and populists. Racial integration at the social level has so far been confined to a small elite. Even university students drift into the cultural comfort of their own groups, with only superficial interaction across racial boundaries.

So what is left to inspire the heterogeneous ideologies and interests of ANC members to be pursued in a single party? Black empowerment – a euphemism for more control by a small privileged elite? Will patronage and personal enrichment constitute the new glue for a fragmenting movement? Endorsing "filthy richness" seems the surest recipe for self-destruction in a party in need of a new mission.

Economic globalisation has bound South Africa inextricably into what has been called "the Washington consensus". Being part of a global order limits ANC policy options severely. It may also lead to the neglect of South Africa's biggest problem: finding imaginative solutions to bridging the growing inequality. Ironically, even the self-styled champions of the poor – socialist unions and a Communist Party in government – are increasingly drawn into a global corporate hegemony.

One of the wealthiest and most sophisticated corporate representatives, George Soros, warns on the other hand against the global laissez-faire ideology of the market as a new pseudo-perfectionist doctrine, akin to communism. "I can agree," he wrote in the US magazine *Atlantic Monthly*, "that attempts at redistribution interfere with the efficiency of the market, but it does not follow that no attempt should be made."[2] When the South African Finance Minister in an unguarded moment utters similar heresies about "amorphous markets", the Rand drops in free fall.

In a survey[3] among white and black business executives about the issues hurting economic growth in South Africa, it is not surprising that crime ranks top with 60 per cent, followed by the exchange rate (47 per cent) and trade union activity (31 per cent). However, while crime may deter super-anxious American tourists from visiting South Africa, few coolly calculating foreign investors shun a country because of its crime rate. Foreign money flows into Eastern Europe although the security situation in Moscow, Warsaw and Bucharest is worse than in Cape Town. The international car rental agencies, for example, do not allow West European rental cars to be driven into Eastern Europe but are quite happy to operate and expand in South Africa. In short, despite the justifiable anxieties about crime inside South Africa, the really destabilising issue for the country in the long run lies in the underlying cause of crime: the moral decay and growing impoverishment of an unrepresented and margin-alised underclass. While the country focuses on racism in rugby or side issues such as who will succeed De Klerk, the number one problem for long-term stability has faded into the background.

Comparative extreme inequality remains South Africa's ticking time bomb. The wealthiest 10 per cent of households receive fully 50 per cent of national income, while the bottom 20 per cent capture a mere 1,5 per cent, according to the report by the Labour Market Commission.[4] Moreover, this skewed income distribution overlaps with race, although the white-black income gap is narrowing. Still, 85 per cent of the poor are black and 65 per cent of blacks are poor. Only 0,7 per cent of whites are classified in this category. At the same time, the internal stratification among blacks is widening with the emergence of a new bureaucratic bourgeoisie far removed from the lifestyle of "the masses".

There is still a widespread belief that the ANC administration pursues the economic interests of the poorer half of South African society. In his reply to Mandela's opening speech of the 1997 Parliament, DP Leader Tony Leon accuses the ANC of "socialist schemes and revolutionary romanticism". Similarly, F.W. de Klerk insists that his National Party articulates "the true mainstream alternative to the ANC's inherently socialist direction".[5] Even Wilmot James writes, "Since 1994, South Africa's approach to economic growth and development has been mass-oriented, in the sense that it has always been tied to the interests and needs of the poor and previously disadvantaged."[6]

However, such an orientation has existed in rhetoric only. Taking the self-image for reality means believing in fairy tales. In reality, a liberation aristocracy has emerged. New office-holders allocate themselves disproportionate spoils while their constituency is ignored. The often cited masses merely serve as a legitimating backdrop for the necessary radical adjustment to the new world economic order.

The government's macro-economic blueprint, GEAR, represents the very opposite of a socialist vision or revolutionary romanticism. Guided by the World Bank and warmly embraced by South African business, the ANC is constantly exhorted to implement its neo-liberal GEAR. Cabinet Ministers have promised to deliver finally on privatisation, wage flexibility, deficit reduction and massive public service cutbacks. Finance Minister Trevor Manuel described this as "deep transformation" in his 1997 budget speech. It amounts to transformation indeed, but it means free-market transformation rather than the redistributive transformation that was associated with the concept of transformation popularised during the anti-apartheid struggle. There can be both left-wing and right-wing transformation. The popularity of transformation discourse in South Africa results from everybody being able to project contradictory visions onto the radical-sounding term.

A similar confusion is reflected in the large number of business people who consider "union activity" an obstacle to growth. In reality, a recalcitrant union leadership has been partly co-opted, cajoled or silenced for fear of being marginalised. Weakened by global corporate legitimacy and structural unemployment, socialist unionists will soon become an endangered species. Even with a history of politicised independence from the powers that be, the South African labour movement is toeing the line and not rocking the boat of export-driven growth. With the exception of public service unions, union membership is stagnating or declining worldwide. South Africa is no exception despite its different history of labour politicisation. How little influence trade unions now exercise on government policy can best be demonstrated by the catalogue of measures which COSATU's general secretary demanded from the 1997 budget: "If (Finance Minister) Trevor Manuel wants to reduce inequalities he must introduce a capital gains tax, set a tax rate of 55 percent on the superrich, tax luxury goods at a higher rate, have more zero VAT ratings on basic necessities – water, medicines and basic foodstuffs – increase levels of corporate taxation and close the loopholes used by the wealthy to reduce tax liabilities." Since these suggestions would send the wrong signal to the new investors on which GEAR depends, none of the union proposals has been included in the budget.

In the end, the rump of a bread-and-butter oriented labour movement will be dominated by a few powerful labour bosses who co-operate with the ruling political class as in the US, or more likely are part of the revolutionary establishment as in Mexico. There, power-less but militant "unofficial" unions have split from the mainstream official unions which still deliver most of the votes for the ruling party and are rewarded with patronage in return. Unlike the dependent unions in the former communist bloc that were mere transmission belts for the party in power, the new South African union leaders increasingly command their own economic empire. Already several former socialist union organisers in South Africa have joined the corporate system at the head of huge union investment funds. Making profits for provident funds is marketed as a legitimate union activity, although the private "fixing fees" which the comrades in business receive on the side are not publicised.

Joining the once much maligned capitalist system not only tests private gain versus collective benefits. Union democracy and grass-roots input are inevitably sacrificed when take-overs and financial transactions require secrecy. Hierarchical orders dominate in the corporate world, quite apart from the difficulties ordinary workers would encounter in making intelligent investment decisions. On the crucial decision as to whether unions should set up their own investment companies, the much celebrated internal COSATU democracy did not produce one discussion paper. It just happened. Nor is it much contested with whom the union billions should be invested, so that the funds often land up with union-hostile companies.

To top it all, even the South African Communist Party is considering establishing an investment arm among a number of options intended to make the party financially self-sufficient or "to trade its way out of the red", as the clever pun of a headline writer suggested.[7] Although the SACP general secretary hurries to assure a bewildered following that the party "would definitely not compromise our principled position and become a capitalist party", the reliance on capitalist principles for financial survival speaks louder. Will a "socialist" union mobilise a strike against a firm on which it depends for vital income? Will a Communist Party still want to replace a capitalist system in which its functionaries have vested interests? In reality the official Marxist-Leninist Party long ago adopted reformist social-democratic policies, although to be called a social democrat still amounts to a swear word for an orthodox socialist of the Leninist variety. Social democrats are accused of having accommodated themselves within the capitalist system, having sold out or having been co-opted into giving an exploitative order a humanitarian veneer, thereby strengthening capitalism rather than overthrowing it.

Such revolutionary fantasies may have had some hope of being realised as long as "really existing socialism" lasted in Moscow. With the disappearance of this last colonial empire, the Marxist vision of greater equality and non-alienated labour has changed into a pipe dream. Even the Chinese Communist Party exhorts the official slogan: "Enrich yourself". Globalised capitalism has indeed triumphed everywhere, starving North Korea or Cuba's bankrupt regime notwithstanding. However, the growing inequality and misery that Marx first addressed remains on the agenda, particularly in South Africa with its large section of outsiders.

Does the disappearance of official socialism mean that South Africa's 40 per cent outsiders are satisfied with the capitalist crumbs they may pick up? Who is representing the interests of the downtrodden in the political system or at Nedlac? While unions and the ANC claim to look after the poor, everyone knows that they champion their own middle class and employees' interests first. Will it be left to a populist yet to emerge or a revived PAC to mobilise the underclass? What will the ideological platform be if not a refurbished socialism under another name? It is a mistaken belief that the forgotten poor simply adopt a lethargic, apolitical apathy, incapable of organised opposition.

While the concept of the underclass has been hijacked by conservatives to project social anxieties onto the poor in what has been called "moral panic", underclass is used here in the Marxian sense of *Lumpenproletariat*. The shack dwellers in informal settlements are literally clad in *lumpen* (rags). However, as more recent arrivals from the countryside they frequently lack the nihilistic, anomic attitudes that Marx attributed to the "down and outs". The South African underclass is certainly not in its position by choice, nor does it constitute a proletariat, because most have never held a formal job, and structural unemployment makes it unlikely that they ever will. However, in contrast to the poor of Europe or the unemployed of the US during the great depression, the South African underclass has never experienced downward mobility but can only hope for gradual improvement. This expectation of upward mobility probably explains the extraordinary patience of the poor amidst extreme affluence. The South African underclass does not suffer from a sense of relative deprivation because rich whites are not necessarily a reference group, but wealthy blacks may well become one. While the underclass is generally not a political threat through organised political opposition, its size in South Africa hugely increases the cost of containing, policing and caring for the outsiders.

While everyone agrees that the prospects of addressing inequality depend on economic growth, business and government on the one hand and the union federations on the other pursue opposing paths to the elusive goals. Business stresses job creation, the unions emphasise inequality as the crucial starting point. However, labour flexibility as a magic means of job creation can hardly be the panacea since 80 per cent of employers already use casual, non-standard labour, as Frank Horwitz[8] has pointed out. Business and government build on external investment, the unions on internal demand, stimulated by public work programmes and the new purchasing power of the hitherto disadvantaged. Clearly, South Africa cannot afford a welfare state of the Western European or Canadian model at its present stage of semi-development.

A futile battle over slogans usually focuses on whether GEAR amounts to an extension or reversal of the RDP. The left argues that the RDP's "growth through development strategy" has been replaced by GEAR's "development through growth" policy. Union leaders rightly point out that the ANC is unlikely to win or lose elections over the issue of whether or not the government has reduced its debt, but they ignore the fact that debt control and fiscal discipline is now considered the most important indicator for investor confidence in a country. Providing for basic needs may indeed boost sustainable economic growth, as the RDP assumed, but the advocates of deficit financing close their eyes to the severe penalties of overspending in an economy that must be part of an international market.

Whether the country can finance greater equity with differential tax rates is open to legitimate debate. While half of the government revenue came from corporate taxes in the 1970s, corporate profits contribute only 14 per cent to government coffers now. VAT as a source of state income benefits the rich and disadvantages the poor, who spend almost all of their income on food and commodities. The poor pay 9,1 per cent of their income on VAT, the rich only 5,5 per cent. In short, the current tax system favours one class over another. If there is to be any redistribution at all, the most feasible way would be through a more equitable progressive tax system. Yet the affluent scream at the very suggestion that there should be a temporary levy or a higher tax rate of 55 per cent for the super-rich with annual incomes over R200 000. No wonder that chief executive officers and company directors disapprove of having their individual million rand remuneration packages revealed to shareholders, a practice prescribed by law in many Western jurisdictions. South Africa also lacks a capital gains tax on which many industrialised states rely; nor does South Africa tax land outside municipal boundaries, a practice unheard of elsewhere in the world.

Hermann Giliomee[9] has cautioned about the pace of the ANC leadership's understandable insistence that "blacks had to be empowered just like the National Party empowered Afrikaners" (Mathews Phosa). Giliomee emphasises the relatively slow progress Afrikaners made despite heavy state patronage ("... in terms of personal income Afrikaners only caught up with English-speakers by 1976"). However, all indicators point to a much faster black empowerment two decades later for several reasons. Business has long discovered the advantages of affirmative action, both for a progressive public relations image and the utilisation of an additional pool of talent, but above all for the advantages black management bestows in marketing to a fast growing black consumer market and establishing linkages with government for state contracts. Three years after the installation of the ANC government, black conglomerates already control 10 per cent of market capitalisation in the Johannesburg Stock Exchange. The voluntary unbundling of white-owned corporations looking for black partners is occurring at an accelerating pace. Even conservative firms appreciate having at least one black and female non-executive director on their board. This board tokenism still comprises a relatively small group of prominent figures who elevate their status and income by an average R25 000 or a regular retainer fee for merely lending their names or attending infrequent meetings. Even the Johannesburg Rand Club, former bastion of male colonialism, begs black businessmen to join, relaxing dress codes to admit traditional African garb and Nehru collars. Few Jews and women joined after they were admitted earlier but many prominent black tycoons responded to the late offer. Multiple directorships are as sought-after among the comrades in business as they are a status symbol among the old establishment. They reflect the extraordinarily high concentration of capital in a few conglomerates, a particular feature of South African capitalism. None of the black corporate comrades as yet is able to match the 25 directorships of some of their white counterparts. It should also be pointed out that 90 per cent of all boardrooms are still exclusively white and male, although black women are now heavily hunted trophies.

While the ascendancy of African women in the public realm has been dramatic since the ANC took over the government, the historical legacies persist in the private sector. McGregor's 1996 Director of Directorships, for example, shows that of 8 401 directorships, 7 920 are in the hands of white men. White women hold 92 such positions, while black women only occupy 32 board chairs, although both categories are now highly sought-after as appointees for a favourable affirmative action image.

When Afrikaners assumed power, English business not only despised apartheid politicians for historical and cultural reasons but found itself under little pressure to accommodate a minority. In contrast, a privileged white business sector of Afrikaner and English firms alike are keenly ingratiating themselves with a majority now. In the 1940s or 50s it was much easier to find state employment for a few hundred thousand poor whites, compared with the millions of permanent economic outsiders now. Their looming threat exercises additional pressure to cultivate a black bourgeoisie as co-defenders of affluence for the relatively few who ignore the growing poverty of the many.

In light of the globalised South African political economy in contrast to the much more isolated situation of a colonial outpost at the beginning of Afrikaner nationalism, the performance of new political and economic incumbents is also under much greater scrutiny. The high administrative competence now required comes in for much more criticism than bungling did in the past. Afrikaner nationalists had to acquire fewer administrative skills than the high qualifications demanded of black appointees now. Yet the accelerated drive to blacken the South African institutions at all costs frequently means the sidelining or retrenchment of experienced civil servants of the old order. Whether this has negatively affected performance levels is hotly contested and depends very much on the ideological outlook of the assessor. In a survey of indicators contributing to the levels of pessimism, "quality of government administration" and corruption ranks top. It is mentioned by 79 per cent in a sample of 245 white business executives, but it is also a prime complaint of African business, albeit at a lower level (54 per cent).[10] When despite higher levels of general confidence in government among African business many are disillusioned with the service they receive, a serious reconsideration of appointments criteria is in order. When representativeness is achieved at the expense of expertise, pessimism about declining standards cannot be dismissed as racist grumblings by privileged losers.

Hermann Giliomee has argued that crucial groups are excluded from the centres of decision making under ANC rule, just as other voices were absent in the days of NP rule. He identifies the excluded forces as "representatives of whites and working-class coloureds, of the great majority of businessmen, commercial farmers and of people who pay the most income and company tax, and most of the rates and service charges".[11] The complaint is based on the assumption of a deeply divided society in which the constitutive ethnic groups or respective political parties should be represented in a power-sharing government. In contrast, the ANC chose the liberal model of individual rights. Individual citizens from the different ethno-racial groups join or vote for nonracial parties on ideological grounds. Therefore, the question becomes: do the businessmen, farmers and people who pay most of the taxes – who also happen to be overwhelmingly white – prefer ethno-racial group rights or interest representation as individual citizens who can organise lobbies and political parties as they please? A second question follows: what influence do these minority interests have in a majoritarian system?

On the first question of the preferred form of minority representation, the minorities themselves are deeply split. The larger section prefers the liberal democracy of the new South African constitution. It was after all negotiated and approved by the National Party. A minority of the minority accuses the National Party and its leader of surrendering ethnic rights (single-medium language education in particular) unnecessarily, of not securing a stronger federalism and of giving in to ANC majoritarianism in general. This charge ignores the real danger of further racial polarisation and possible civil war, had the former regime refused to negotiate in good faith.

Indeed, the National Party could have hung on to power for some time; its state and security apparatus had not been split or defeated. Capitulation had not been imminent. However, stalling the transition carried a high economic and political price which increased the longer the hold-out. De Klerk has to be credited for understanding this dynamic: he could expect a better deal while still relatively strong. The ANC deserves credit for accommodating this pragmatism with temporary power sharing. The "miracle" also lies in the high degree of rationality on both sides. However, this subjective rational behaviour in encompassing the opponent's predicament flows ultimately from an objective reality of interdependence. Even if one side had acted irrationally, the power of circumstances exercised severe constraints.

The same situation continues to restrict majority rule now, regardless of whether or not there is power sharing at the political level in a government of national unity. The National Party has become dispensable in this situation because business can now deal directly with government. The ANC on the other hand has to take business representation much more seriously than an apartheid-tainted Afrikaner National Party. Therefore, real power sharing has in fact increased rather than decreased. As Alan Fine[12] wrote in a review of Patti Waldmeir's book: "There is still power-sharing due to 'SA realities'; but it is with other organised interests such as business, the security forces and other parts of the public service."

While business people grumble about the various administrative shortcomings of the new regime, from taxes which are too high to the quality of the civil service, a vast majority, particularly big business, feels comfortable and relieved. In this respect, the views of the doyen of South African big business are indicative, although the retired Harry Oppenheimer has often been more progressive and not necessarily representative of the attitudes of his associates. In an interview with Benjamin Pogrund[13] Oppenheimer expressed himself as "immensely pleased at what has taken place". He believes the government is "making a serious effort" and "is doing quite well" to build the economy – the answer to meeting the aspirations of the have-nots before their rage boils over. With the old economic order unaltered and with the ANC endorsing free-market neo-liberalism, profit-making in nonracial capitalism has acquired new legitimacy and new opportunities. Far from being at odds with the state, organised business is not only carefully listened to formally and informally, but also has the economic clout to make itself heard should the state contravene its vital interests. In fact, state and business interests coincide in the goal of a growing economy. The only major potential conflict lies in how the surplus of growth should be divided, because growth alone does not guarantee greater equality.

Therefore, it is doubtful whether South Africa's constitution "produces permanent winners and permanent losers" as Giliomee fears. This outcome, based on ethnic voting and a built-in ANC majority, applies only in the narrow electoral sense. It also assumes that the ANC can hold together. While the ANC may not be able to be defeated from without it may well destroy itself from within. Regardless of party-political manoeuvring, today's political losers still remain the economic winners and today's seeming winners remain mostly material losers, the emergence of a black bourgeoisie notwithstanding.

In a sociological sense, a minority is defined in terms of power, not in terms of numbers. A black bourgeoisie has been empowered materially and all the previously disenfranchised have been dignified legally. Most previous losers, however, still remain an underclass and the current numerical losers hold on to most of the economic power. That is their permanent win. Business, farmers and other taxpayers constitute a minority only in a numerical sense.

South African politics, like the politics of other Western democracies, is increasingly devoid of ideological divisions. The ideological thrusts of all parties broadly resemble each other. They all advocate market-oriented economies within a liberal human rights constitution. Differences emerge about implementation, style and effectiveness of generally agreed-upon policy goals. Cultural traditions and the ethno-racial make-up of political parties then substitute for the lack of ideological distinctiveness. In other words, the more the policy programmes are similar the more the ethnic differences and historical mythologies gain importance in shaping a distinct image of the contenders.

This dilemma besets the National Party's and Democratic Party's attempts to shed historical baggage and form a new opposition front against the ANC. Pre-empted on the left by COSATU's and the SACP's traditional claim to represent the interests of the disadvantaged and pre-empted on the right by the ANC's neo-liberal GEAR economic policy, the old National Party cannot make inroads into the all-important black African vote on ideological grounds. It can only claim greater competence and efficiency in implementing common goals like fighting crime or securing employment. Whatever truths such opposition claims may entail, they are overridden in the voter's perception by deep-seated distrust of ethnic outsiders and preference for ethnic insiders. Only if a new opposition were to be able to transform itself into a credible African party with authentic black leaders of historical integrity would it be likely to succeed in gaining new support. It is probably easier to reconcile whites with such a reinvented opposition front than to make blacks forget about the apartheid history of an Afrikaner/white party in African disguise. Unless administrative chaos and criminal disorder cause total havoc with the aspirations of the African majority, it will prevail with its traditional loyalty to the ANC, even if the electorate is increasingly disillusioned with ANC performance and delivery. At present all indicators point to disgruntled ANC voters abstaining rather than joining the opposition.

Therefore, the alienated underclass is unlikely to be mobilised by the traditional NP/DP opposition but rather by new populist or Africanist forces yet to be identified. The ruling ANC will need all its skills and savvy to prevent racial agitators on the left and right of its vulnerable flanks from exploiting the widening gap between liberation promises and a globalised reality. The more GEAR is seriously implemented, the more blood has to be spilt, particularly among a shrinking public service. Should the government indeed axe 100 000 superfluous civil servants from its current contingent of 1,2 million, they would have to come mostly from the under-qualified section of low-ranking former Bantustan officials. Not only will it create potential opposition support in this way, but by privatising more traditional state functions the government will de-prive itself of the most effective tool of the National Party in power to create support by putting voters on the payroll. The promise of public service rationalisation in the face of contrary political pres-sure and advantage amounts to a brave undertaking indeed.

Since no ideologically creditable alternatives to global economic imperatives exist, the danger lies in the racialisation of heightened competition. How long the ANC's professed nonracialism can con-tain and dilute the demands for racial empowerment by both the underclass and the newly emerging black bourgeoisie remains to be seen. While the self-enrichment of sections of a liberation aristo-cracy and its dubious allies in the empowerment lobby can be delegitimised more easily, the claims of the neglected underclass will carry far more weight, regardless of the form in which they are expressed.

The ANC is engaged in a delicate balancing act. It must adhere to the broad dictates of the market unless it risks being heavily penalised. On the other hand, it cannot afford to be perceived as having abandoned its concern for the masses and the unions. As an editorial in *Business Day*[14] commented, "The last thing that the ANC needs in this sensitive period is a perception of itself and business ganging up against COSATU." Yet adhering to the "Washington consensus" of the market means objectively sidelining the unions. The ANC resolves its dilemma by pursuing neo-conservative economic policies but obfuscating it with an occasional dose of so-cialist lip service to redistribution and the desires of the masses. To be sure, the party also genuinely prioritises the less privileged who are after all its main reservoir of voters. However, the ANC is so constrained by unfavourable repercussions both locally and inter-nationally that it cannot translate an ideological commitment into practical policy if it clashes with vital business interests. Wavering between pleasing free-market and privatisation lobbyists and alienating its left, the ANC is frequently paralysed. In this dilemma the leadership has concentrated on winning over COSATU leaders without incorporating the social agenda of labour in its economic policy.

The appeal of racial mobilisation of the underclass by populist forces in opposition to the ANC is both undermined and facilitated by the behaviour of a black bourgeoisie. The professed patriotism of the black business class could serve to unite and bridge class differences through community empowerment and national incorporation. All strong democratic nations thrive on an economically secure and politically involved bourgeoisie. On the other hand, the greed of a parasitic elite could further reinforce the alienation of the marginalised underclass.

Profiteering has united former ideological foes into a common search for new opportunities. "So strong has the lure of capitalism been," writes Thabo Leshilo[15], "that former political enemies from the African National Congress, Azanian People's Organisation, the Pan African Congress of Azania and the Inkatha Freedom Party have abandoned their ideological differences. Even former socialists and Communists have united under the new concept of the patriotic bourgeoisie!"

Patriotism legitimises the burgeoning black middle class with the ring of fulfilling a duty for the new nation. In its self-legitimisation the patriotic bourgeoisie is even engaged in sacrifices to uplift the black community just as socialists intended with their goal. Capitalism and socialism are blurred into "national socialism". One of its ideologues, Don Mkhwanazi, who launched the National Economic Trust with R300 million capital, explicitly asserts that there was little difference between the struggle of socialism and black business determination to work for the economic empowerment of its community. Mkhwanazi sees socialism saddled with the image of poverty. In contrast, he articulates the unadulterated American ideology that everyone who works hard enough can reach the top. "I want every black person to feel that he or she has the opportunity to become rich and only has himself to blame if he fails. The more black millionaires, the better for the country," says Mkhwanazi.

Above all, the patriotic bourgeoisie eyes the state assets yet to be privatised. Already 10 per cent of the parastatal Telkom has been earmarked for black empowerment groups. The lobby clamours for more preferential treatment, particularly in state tender procedures. While affirmative action for disadvantaged minorities is generally accepted worldwide, what is highly contested is the extent to which a state should favour one rich consortium over another unevenly on the basis of skin colour. Capitalising on past restrictions, the "patriotic bourgeoisie" plays on colour to reap advantage. Even Thabo Mbeki has warned the new black elite to avoid being perceived as a parasitic class that thrives only on pillaging state resources.

Black embourgeoisement could nonetheless be supported if it were to trickle down to the poor. However, most black empowerment deals are limited to existing economic activities and do not create new employment. A few black entrepreneurs enter the market through asset acquisition and financial engineering but neglect the training required to equip a functioning bourgeoisie. There is also the danger that some empowerment deals will go sour and then demand to be bailed out in the public interest. The 1996/7 buyouts take place at a time of inflated stock prices and unusually high real interest rates. Even if properly managed, performance above the debt load is not guaranteed and enthusiastic new companies could face financial difficulties later.

In the meantime, the new liberation millionaires earn huge salaries and options to purchase shares in the deals they fix on behalf of unions or black empowerment groups. Yet for a long time the underprivileged individuals of the formerly disadvantaged collectives will not enjoy significant returns as the empowerment companies struggle to reduce their debt, particularly if the market does not perform well. The liberation management has nailed the fortune of its constituency to a speculative market without its executives fully sharing the risks. The liberation managers will have become rich anyway from the lucrative deals on the basis of their representation, with the promised trade-offs for the represented looming in an uncertain and distant future. The comrades in business are innovative risk-takers rather than entrepreneurs who start from scratch to create new wealth. What advantages the liberation entrepreneurs is their empowerment or union credentials, a unique window of opportunity which many think may not last very long. The old establishment may foreclose further black empowerment deals once a certain ratio has been reached. The union constituency may rebel against its representatives using union money without immediate tangible benefits. Deanne Collins, editor of the *South African Labour*

Bulletin (February 1997), in an open letter questions two former COSATU MPs (Johnny Copelyn and Marcel Golding) about their exit from Parliament into the corporate world with trust funds from union surplus: "Does the speculative nature of such investment ventures not, in fact, put workers' money at risk? Is it possible to be both a business executive and represent the trade union interests?"

While such questions preoccupy the traditional left, the new South African elite banks on unlimited economic growth. While its infectious optimism may be unfounded, it is not out of line with world trends of expanding globalised growth. The former colonial outpost and relic of institutionalised racism has joined its competitors for its share of the market regardless of ideological hang-ups of the past. South Africa's international trade with some of the world's leading violators of human rights (Iran, Nigeria, Indonesia, China) is soaring. While this does not distinguish the country from its Western counterparts even they raise eyebrows when a senior official suggests that certain criminals resemble animals that should be locked up in disused mine shafts never to see daylight again. When South Africa is selling small arms to Rwanda, helicopters to Malaysia or considering supplying Syria with sophisticated tank technology, the country has become a "normal" national entity, deprived of its former moral glory. Once its idealised president has left the political stage, the country will further resemble its competitors. Whether the ANC has squandered a moral high ground by its own faults or whether the South African government merely complied with global imperatives will be debated endlessly. After all, who says that one can survive on a moral diet of liberation purity once the routine of political office in an interdependent world squeezes seeming options into one-way solutions?

How "normal" South Africa has become, how American habits and taste infuse previous ideological purity, how moral sensitivities have been dulled and commercial considerations have taken over, are epitomised in a much reported event on Robben Island.

Most nations cherish their sacred places: battlefields where the soil is soaked with the blood of unsung heroes who gave birth to the new imagined community; prisons and slave houses that bear witness to the suffering of untold victims of human cruelty: Auschwitz and Birkenau in Poland, Buchenwald and Dachau in Germany, the forgotten unmarked gulags in Siberia and the museum with the remains of Pol Pot's genocide in Cambodia stand out as reminders not to let it happen again.

Robben Island is South Africa's equivalent sacred soil. During more than a quarter of a century, the country's anti-apartheid leaders from all ideological factions trod across the bleak, flat landscape. Mandela's eyesight was permanently damaged from the glare of the sun in the white lime quarry. Already in 1658, a few years after the arrival of Van Riebeeck at the Cape, rebellious Khoi leaders were banished to the island followed by slaves and Xhosa chiefs. From 1846 to 1931 the island accommodated lepers, chronically ill paupers and people designated as lunatics. The lepers are said to have wept so fiercely upon arrival that their point of entry is known as the "gate of tears". A lepers' church and graveyard, a Muslim kramat, an Anglican church, a lighthouse and a dull prison tract with various administrative buildings and staff houses are scattered across the Cape Town side of the island. A few ostriches, bushbuck and penguins occupy the rest of the wild southern side.

In this place 11 km from Cape Town's harbour, a helicopter dropped first a luxury bus into the sea by accident and then delivered without a hitch US celebrities, South Africa's captains of industry and the liberation aristocracy for a fund-raising dinner with a R250 000 admission fee, hosted by Mandela on March 20, 1997. Hillary Clinton, Bill Cosby and UN general secretary Kofi Annan were the most prominent foreign guests, matched by South African cabinet ministers, provincial premiers and a broadly smiling Miss South Africa. All were issued with rainbow coloured, multi-flowered shirts, popularised by shrewd designers as "Madiba shirts". Local newspapers reported in great detail on the sumptuous menu and selected Cape wines, served in colonial style by waiters in white gloves.

The contrast with the simple porridge prison food which Mandela described to his guests could not have been more striking. It also highlighted the insidious moral decline in which the ANC is unconsciously sliding by associating itself with ostentatious consumption even if it does raise funds for a worthy cause.

Among those who contributed money were tycoons, some of whom are not known for having publicly opposed apartheid, and manufacturers, some of whom have shown little evidence that they respect their unions, as well as other opportunistic characters who gain status by ingratiating themselves with the new rulers. While the former prisoners and Mandela especially cannot be bribed, their indiscriminate association with corporate funding smacks of poor taste. Big money can buy big commodities, pleasure and influence. Beyond its reach is only legitimacy. In South Africa, as in the United States, money can now also purchase the moral blessing that Mandela bestows. In associating itself indiscriminately with the controllers of wealth, the ANC diminished its own moral standing. By granting the twenty corporations who bought the double tickets the right to advertise officially as "Corporate Friend of Robben Island", they symbolically sold a sacred memory to the highest bidders. Ordinary people are excluded when the company of martyrdom can only be purchased. The corporate sponsorship undermines the ownership of the island by all South Africa's people.

No Jewish organisation would ever consider holding an exclusive gala dinner at Auschwitz in support of Yad Vashem, as columnist Jon Qwelane has aptly pointed out. Even Americans pay respect to the slave house on Goree Island off the coast of Dakar, from where thousands were shipped to the New World. Yet Cosby clowns in Mandela's tiny prison cell holding the spoon and bowl Mandela used, and stages an escape to the laughter of his audience.

Most people fall silent when they enter a nation's cemetery. Words fail to articulate the unspeakable. Tears are held back. You swallow hard to contain your emotions. More sensitive visitors weep openly. Hillary Clinton together with South Africa's new elite laughs on Robben Island. The celebrating gala party sings "Happy Birthday" for Cosby's wife into the silent night.

It still remains to be explained why the island's political prisoners themselves return so frequently. Why do Mandela, Kathrada and Sexwale joke at their place of degradation? Survivors of Auschwitz would reassemble for a memorial service but hardly enjoy visiting their place of suffering and trivialise it as a photo opportunity for the international media.

Do the former prisoners perhaps exhibit the Stockholm syndrome, the subconscious identification with the powerful oppressor? After all, Mandela built his Transkei home according to the exact design of his last prison cottage. But Mandela would be the last person to be intimidated by Afrikaner might, past or present. While he respects Afrikaner power for its potential for destabilisation and shrewdly assuages the danger with gestures of reconciliation, a secure Mandela has never bowed to his opponents.

There remains the more banal and probably most persuasive explanation. In the scramble for funds, the island's history provides a valuable resource. Locals and tourists alike participate symbolically in the respectable anti-apartheid struggle, even if the voyeuristic latecomers hardly identified with it before. The old men who symbolised the struggle in the prison have learned to market their experience effectively and at the same time enjoy the nostalgic memory of equal prison comradeship that life in the real world of unequal comrades in power increasingly denies.

It is appropriate to conclude a work of this kind with a few final observations on the political phenomenon: Nelson Mandela. It is virtually impossible to calculate adequately his impact on South Africa's transition. He more than any other person has brought his comrades into the business of government and corporate elite. And yet, as we have shown, there were other forces and trends that helped to shape the dynamics of transition. To explain them all in terms of the "Mandela factor" is to become the devotee of a cult rather than an objective analyst.

Personalising South Africa's successful transition by attributing it mainly to the reconciling magic of Mandela has become global conventional wisdom. Mandela's charisma and astuteness notwithstanding, his glorification as the guarantor of success both insults and endangers the fledgling democracy. Emphasising the president's crucial role assumes that the majority of his followers resemble a flock of blind sheep that disperses in every direction once the shepherd ceases to lead.

Mandela is considered a rare exception in the history of African mismanagement. Unruly masses, so the adulation of Mandela implies, can only be held together by an autocratic strongman. The ANC's long tradition of collective decision making is denied and the ability of an equally pragmatic and competent ANC leadership questioned. Clamouring for a demi-god who ensures salvation indicates how immature an electorate is that does not trust its own political autonomy.

Mandela's paternal warmth sits well with the adoring crowds who long for a super-father. This is affirmed by his rhetorical largesse:

I love each and every one of you. I sincerely wish the pockets of my shirt were big enough to put all of you in. I want to be amongst our people 24 hours a day. I regard you as my children and grandchildren, every one of you.[16]

With such inclusive style, Mandela is adored by his most hardened former enemies. Eugene de Kock, the supreme killer-commander of an aberrant police force, praises Mandela as the "most important person after Jesus Christ". Even 93-year old Betsie Verwoerd and stubborn P.W. Botha confirmed the Afrikaner tradition of deference to authority after the new leader graciously dropped by for tea.

Mandela's lack of bitterness has symbolically exonerated whites from their apartheid sins. Handing over state power to such a magnanimous figure made the National Party defeat during the constitutional negotiations more tolerable.

The worldwide personality cult directly endangers South African stability, as the dramatic plunge of the currency on rumours of Mandela's health demonstrated. The reaction by international markets reveals an underestimation of the strong institutions and economic infrastructure in place, regardless of who is at their helm.

In any case, leadership choices are nowadays severely limited. South Africa is bound into a global economy which allows little scope for foolish decisions. While Mandela's exemplary role in marketing the historic compromise must be fully credited, it reveals the political illiteracy of trembling investors who think that the "miracle" could or would be undone after the source of divine inspiration has disappeared.

Critics fear that even Mandela cannot bring cohesion and direction into a fractious cabinet or ANC caucus. Perhaps the opposite fear of too autocratic a president is far more justified.

Without consulting any senior members of the ANC except Vice-President Thabo Mbeki, the President ousted former Minister of Posts and Telecommunications Pallo Jordan from his cabinet although the outspoken maverick was by Mandela's own admission "one of our most competent ministers".

The independent-minded Jordan had repeatedly stood up to Mandela and Mbeki on various policy issues but lacked an organised constituency, which made him expendable while keeping poor performers in office. Far from acting as a neutral "chairperson of the board", delegating maximally and staying out of minor controversies, the cherished patriarch interferes on many issues where it would be wiser to stay aloof.

He opines on whether the national rugby team should keep its contentious springbok emblem (yes) and whether Afrikaans should be dropped as the army language (no). He tells candidates for university vice-chancellorships to withdraw and others to make themselves available. He imposes his favourite person as election leader on the reluctant provincial ANC caucus, as happened in the disastrous Allan Boesak affair in the Western Cape.

Since Mandela's word carries so much weight, few dare to contradict him. For example, the way in which the parliamentary committee on health was whipped into line when it summoned Minister of Health Nkosazana Zuma to account for wasteful spending on the infamous AIDS play *Sarafina 2* reflects poorly on both the chief executive and the legislature.

Only in dictatorships does a parliamentary committee allow itself to be silenced because the president announces that he is "personally satisfied" with the explanation given to him.

Indeed, as long as such behaviour risks the penalty of expulsion or non-nomination under existing rules, autonomous behaviour of parliamentarians is not encouraged. The necessary critique of government is thus unfortunately transferred to outside Parliament. Why should there be a taboo on criticising a remarkable president who nonetheless remains fallible?

It is to his lasting credit that Mandela admits to his fallibility, unlike other African autocrats. Flattered and embarrassed alike, he ironically strengthens the personality cult by criticising it: it is not only the implied denigration of other leaders that goes with the global adulation but also an authoritarian deference that violates the very ethos of a democratic liberation movement.

Each time a fawning editorial, foreign visitor or party hack wallows in the mesmerising influence of the great leader, a healthy democratic tradition is undermined. It is a sad comment on African affairs that Mandela commands the respect of everybody because a non-corrupt magnanimous leader has become so rare on the continent.

Ironically, there exists no other ANC leader who dares to espouse a sensible reconciliation so effectively. While some ANC Jacobeans still talk about whites and blacks having to settle accounts about stolen wealth or squaring different moral histories before the Truth Commission, Mandela alone genuinely transcends race.

Even white racists love him because this proves that they cannot be called racists in similar ways as anti-Semites proclaim that "some of their best friends are Jews". Yet by recognising the destructive potential of these ethno-racial remnants and cultivating their acquiescence to the new order, Mandela single-handedly neutralises a serious threat. Who can assert, therefore, that Mandela does not deserve the praise heaped on him with such relief? So important has been his role that the post-Mandela era may very well require renewed analysis.

We have argued that after Mandela's exit what is to be feared is not the ANC's strength but its weakness. While a personality contest for presidential succession is part of democratic tradition, it is doubtful that the party can survive such a bruising drama without ugly repercussions for reconciliation and unity. If contenders for office are tempted to mobilise Africanist resentment for support or outbid each other in populist demagoguery, past achievements are easily undermined.

Of course, the Mandela heir, anointed from above, may not fit well with the expectations of grass-root democracy from below. Yet the still fragile peace and stability is best served with the continuity and certainty of Mandela's legacy, particularly when confirmed by strong internal endorsement. For the time being, robust adversarial politics internally as well as competitive, rotating governments externally may be too stark a rupture for a still fledgeling, immature democracy, yet to be consolidated. On the other hand, only through its robust practice does a democracy mature and becomes firmly anchored in the habits and values of critical citizens. Finding the delicate balance in this predicament challenges all South African political actors.

References

Introduction: Moral, political and comparative perspectives

1 Mark Gevisser, *Sunday Independent*, 2 February 1997.
2 In Zimbabwe, the atrocities committed during the pre-independence bush war before 1980 as well as the human rights violations committed by the North Korean-trained fifth brigade in Matabeleland villages before 1987 have not been subject to judicial enquiries or much public soul-searching. A study by a pro-government lawyer commissioned by Mugabe was suppressed for fear of damaging Mugabe's international image. A second 280-page 1997 report prepared by human rights lawyers and church people after months of confidential interviews with villagers was not released by the Roman Catholic bishops for similar reasons. Without such evidence relatives of victims cannot press their claims for compensation, repeatedly refused by Mugabe.
3 Mahmood Mamdani, "Reconciliation Without Justice," *Southern African Review of Books*, November/December 1995, 3-5.

1. Comparing ethno-nationalism: Identity, racism and multiculturalism in global context

1 Geoffrey York, *Globe & Mail*, 22 June 1996.
2 Naomi Zac, *Race and Mixed Race* (Philadelphia: Temple University Press, 1993), p. 167.
3 Joan Scott, "Multiculturalism and the Politics of Identity," in John Rachman, ed., *The Identity Question* (New York: Routledge, 1995), p. 96.
4 Robert Kaplan, "Cities of Despair," *Globe & Mail*, 2 June 1996.
5 A. Sparks, *The Mind of South Africa* (London: Heinemann, 1990).

6 Adedeji Adebayo, "An Alternative for Africa," *Journal of Democracy*, Vol. 5, No. 4, October 1994, p. 126.

7 Chris van Wyk, *Mail & Guardian*, May 31-June 6, 1996.

2. Anti-Semitism and anti-black racism: Nazi Germany and South Africa

1 M. Shain, *The Roots of Anti-Semitism in SA* (Charlottesville: University of Virginia Press, 1994).

2 Ibid., p. ix.

3 Ibid., p. 151.

4 Ibid., p. 152.

5 Ibid., p. 152. See also Immanuel Suttner, ed., *Cutting Through the Mountain. Interviews with South African Jewish Activists* (New York: Viking, 1997).

6 Kader Asmal, Louise Asmal and Ronald Suresh Roberts, *Reconciliation Through Truth. A Reckoning of Apartheid's Criminal Governance* (Cape Town: David Philip, 1996).

7 Ibid., p. 149.

8 Ibid., p. 148.

9 Ibid., p. 33.

10 Ibid., p. 83.

11 *Business Day*, November 11, 1996.

12 Kader Asmal et al., op. cit., p. 201.

13 See Leo Lowenthal and Norbert Guterman, *Prophets of Deceit* (Palo Alto: Pacific Books, 1949). As Ali Rattansi has pointed out in contemporary Britain, Asian women are perceived as backward, traditional, pliant models of family stability, defying feminist emancipation. At the same time, they are portrayed as seductive sex objects in airline advertisements.

14 As Sander Gilman has written: "The image of blackness projects much of the repressed anxiety surrounding the Jew's sexual identity in twentieth century Europe. The depth of the association of Jews with the black enabled non-Jewish Europeans during the nineteenth century to 'see' the Jew as black." See Sander Gilman, *Difference and Pathology: Stereotypes of Sexuality, Race and Madness* (Ithaca, NY: Cornell University Press, 1985), p. 34.

15 M. Shain, op. cit., p. 4; S. Gilman, op cit., p. 34.

16 See Heribert Adam and Kogila Moodley, *The Negotiated Revolution* (Johannesburg: Jonathan Ball, 1993).

17 Stuart Hall and Paul Gilroy have stressed that, contrary to deterministic and reductionist analyses, there are different histories of racism. Thus Floya Anthias and Nira Yuval-Davis point out that "racism cannot be limited to the experience of black people but had taken different forms in relation to the Irish, the Jews, the Gypsies and Third-World migrant workers, as well as other White minorities who may be migrant workers". See Floya Anthias and Nira Yuval-Davis, *Racialised Boundaries* (London: Routledge, 1992).

18 *Globe and Mail*, September 21, 1994, p. A9.

19 When former killer commander, Dirk Coetzee, was questioned by the Amnesty Committee of the Truth Commission as to why two of his victims had been poisoned and allowed to suffer the ill effects over days rather than being shot immediately, Coetzee replied that "it had been hard to look someone in the eye who was stone cold sober knowing one was about to kill them". The killers of the Nazi regime felt no such morbid scruples. In a similar South African police killing, the two victims were asked whether they had a last wish or wanted to say anything. One of them cried and pleaded for mercy and the perpetrators despised him. The other captive wished to sing the national anthem for the last time and was allowed to do so while his killers expressed admiration for such a brave stance.

20 Shmuel Ettinger points to a sacred duty of the church to define a separate legal status for Jews during the Middle Ages and the occasional wiping out of entire Jewish communities. "But even in those periods, never was the opinion sounded (as it is by modern anti-Semites) that the fate of nations – of the world, even – depends on their attitude to the Jews and on their definition of the Jews' status among them." See his "The Origins of Modern Anti-Semitism," in Yisrael Gutman and Livia Rothkirchen, eds., *The Catastrophe of European Jewry* (Jerusalem: Yad Vashem, 1976), pp. 3-39.

21 As Steven Katz demonstrates, each atrocity had distinct roots and resists simplistic generalisations. See his *The Holocaust in Historical Context* (London: Oxford University Press, 1994).

22 Eric J. Hobsbawn dates the racialisation of anti-Jewish sentiment to the late 19th century, after Darwinian evolutionism was supplemented with genetics that provided racism with its pseudoscientific gloss. "Anti-Semitism did not acquire a 'racial' (as

distinct from a religio-cultural) character until about 1880 . . ." See his *Nations and Nationalism since 1780* (Cambridge: Cambridge University Press, 1990), p. 108.

23 Shmuel Ettinger, op. cit., p. 8.

24 In this sense, because of the special circumstances of a wounded people or a nation of industrial latecomers, spurned by an irresistibly seductive leader, Nazi crimes do not qualify as an historical aberration. See Tony Kushner, *The Holocaust and the Liberal Imagination* (Oxford: Blackwell, 1994).

25 Milton Shain, op. cit., p. 145.

26 Michael Ignatieff, *Blood and Belonging. Journeys into the New Nationalism* (Toronto: Penguin Viking, 1993), pp. 185-86.

27 Ibid., p. 186.

28 This is how Michael Burleigh has characterised the dominant attitudes of the Austrio-German Jewry in a review of recent Holocaust literature. See his "Synonymous with Murder – Survivors' and Historians' Perspectives on the Holocaust," *Times Literary Supplement*, March 3, 1995.

3. How did South Africa talk itself through a revolution?

1 Patti Waldmeir, *The Anatomy of a Miracle* (New York: Viking, 1997), gives a vivid account of how De Klerk's 2 February 1990 speech was deliberately kept confidential by a selected few.

2 Dan O'Meara, *Volskapitalisme* (Johannesburg: Ravan Press, 1983) and *Forty Lost Years* (Randburg: Raven Press, 1996).

3 Will Kymlicka, ed., *The Right of Minority Cultures* (London: Oxford University Press, 1995).

4. The first elections in South Africa: What miracle?

1 S.S. van der Merwe, *International Roundtable on Democratic Constitutional Development*, Commonwealth Secretariat, 17-20 July 1993, pp. 17-21.

2 Mac Maharaj, ibid., pp. 14-16.

3 Tom Lodge, "The South African General Election April 1994: Results, Analyses and Implications," *African Affairs*, October 1995. "The most comprehensive election analysis," in R.W. Johnson & Lawrence Schlemmer, *Launching Democracy in South Africa* (New Haven: Yale University Press, 1996) comes to similar conclusions. For another useful account of the election campaign

see Andrew Reynolds, ed., *Elections '94* (Cape Town: David Philip, 1994).

4 R. Taylor, "The New South Africa: Consociational or Consensual Power Sharing," *The ASEN Bulletin*, No. 8, Winter 1994-95, p. 16.

5 Tom Lodge, op. cit.

6 Arend Liphart, *Democracy in Plural Societies* (New Haven: Yale University Press, 1997).

7 Robert Mattes, *The Election Book: Judgement and Choice in South Africa's 1994 Election* (Cape Town: IDASA, 1995), p. 35.

8 D. Horowitz, *A Democratic South Africa* (Berkeley: University of California Press, 1991). H. Giliomee, "Democratisation in South Africa," *Political Science Quarterly*, Spring 1995.

9 H. Giliomee, L. Schlemmer and S. Hauptfleisch, *The Bold Experiment* (Halfway House: Southern Book Publishers, 1994), p. 157.

10 R.B. Mattes, A. Gouws and H.I. Kotze, "The Emerging Party System in the New South Africa," *Party Politics*, Vol. 1, No. 3, 1995, pp. 381-395.

5. Is South Africa a liberal democracy?

1 Adam Pzreworski, "The Neo-Liberal Fallacy," *Journal of Democracy*, Vol. 3, No. 3, July 1993.

2 R.A. Dahl, *Democracy and its Critics* (New Haven: Yale University Press, 1989).

3 Phillipe Schmitter, "Dangers & Dilemmas of Democracy," *Journal of Democracy*, Vol. 5, No. 2, April 1994.

4 H. Kotze, ed., J.I.K. Gagiano & Pierre du Toit, *Consolidating Democracy in South Africa: The Role of Civil Society in SA*, Konrad Adenauer Stiftung, 1996.

5 D. Horowitz, *A Democratic South Africa?* (Berkeley: University of California Press, 1991).

6 R.W. Johnson, "Fear in the Miracle Nations," *London Review of Books*, 2 November 1995.

7 John Kane-Berman, *Freedom Today*, August 1995.

8 Pierre van den Berghe, ed., *State Violence and Ethnicity* (Niwot: University Press of Colorado, 1990).

6. Can a South African nation be built?

1 Kerniche Ohmae, *The End of the Nation State* (New York: Harper Collins, 1995).

2 A. Adedeji, "An Alternative for Africa," *Journal of Democracy*, Vol. 5, No. 4, October 1994, pp. 119-133.

3 U. Ra-Anan, "The Nation State Fallacy," J.V. Montville, ed., *Conflict and Peacemaking in Multi-Ethnic Societies* (Livingston Books, 1990), pp. 5-20.

4 Theo Hanf, *The Prospects of Accommodation in Communal Conflicts*, A. Dödrin et al., eds., "Bildung in sozio-ökonomischer Sicht," in *Festschrift für Hasso von Recum* (Freiburg: Böhlau Verlag, 1989).

5 M. Heisler, "Ethnicity and Ethnic Relations in the Modern West," J.V. Montville, op. cit., pp. 21-31.

6 T. Nairn, *The Break-Up of Britain* (London: New Left Books, 1977).

7 Floya Anthias and Nira Yuval-Davis, *Racialised Boundaries* (London: Routledge, 1992).

8 Claude Ake, "What is the Problem of Ethnicity in Africa?" *Transformation*, Vol. 22, 1993, pp. 1-14.

9 Rupert Taylor & Mark Orkin, *The Racialization of Social Scientific Research on South Africa*, Manuscript, 1993.

10 Claude Ake, op. cit., p. 13.

11 D. Horowitz, *Ethnic Groups in Conflict* (Berkeley: University of California Press, 1985).

12 Theo Hanf, op. cit., p. 101.

13 L. Greenfield, *Nationalism: Five Roads to Modernity* (Cambridge, Mass: Harvard University Press, 1992).

14 N. Alexander, *International Roundtable on Democratic Constitutional Development*, Commonwealth Secretariat, 19-20 July 1995, p. 173.

15 Afrikaner liberals such as Serfontein and Giliomee argue "that it is the right of individuals to send their children to schools where they are educated in their mother tongue and in their culture" (H. Giliomee, Letter to the editor, *Business Day*, February 20, 1997). Giliomee refers to similar constitutional rights in Western democracies, such as Canada. However, in Quebec immigrants are not allowed to send their children to the schools of their choice (English-medium), because this is considered a threat to the survival of French culture. In other words, the defence of a communal culture (French) – a goal most liberals would endorse – is also used to restrict parents' choice and individual rights. Giliomee's desire "to depoliticise and de-ethnicise the issue of education" may be wishful thinking because in a society with competing ethnic groups education will always be a political issue.

For a more philosophical debate on these issues see Amy Gutman, ed., *Multiculturalism* (Princeton: Princeton University Press, 1994), particularly the seminal essay "The Politics of Recognition" by Charles Taylor, who endorses restrictions of parent rights in Quebec. Another excellent source is Will Kymlicka, *Multicultural Citizenship* (Oxford University Press, 1995) and his edited volume *The Rights of Minority Cultures* (Oxford University Press, 1995).

16 H. Giliomee, "Liberal and Populist Democracy in South Africa: Challenges, New Threats to Liberalism," Presidential Address (Johannesburg: South African Institute of Race Relations, 1996) is the author's most sophisticated elaboration of this theme.

17 R.W. Johnson, *Focus Letter*, Helen Suzman Foundation, December 1996.

18 H. Giliomee, *Cape Times*, 21 March 1996.

19 P. van den Berghe, ed., *State Violence & Ethnicity* (Niwot: University Press of Colorado, 1990).

20 D. Horowitz, *A Democratic South Africa?* (Berkeley: University of California Press, 1991), p. 141.

21 Theo Hanf, op. cit., p. 100.

22 D. Horowitz, *A Democratic South Africa?*, p. 140.

23 Czeslaw Milosz, *New York Review of Books*, 11 May 1995, p. 15.

24 D. Horowitz, *A Democratic South Africa?*, p. 137.

25 Gordon Craig, "How Hell Worked," *New York Review of Books*, 18 April 1996.

26 Moeletsi Mbeki, *Development & Democracy*, 9 December 1994.

27 Charles van Onselen, *The Seed is Mine* (Cape Town: David Philip, 1996).

28 Eddie Webster & D. Ginsberg, *Taking Democracy Seriously* (Durban: University of Natal/Indicator Press, 1995), p. 55.

29 Allister Sparks, *Cape Times*, 5 February 1996.

30 Dennis Davis, Interview with André du Toit, *Die Suid-Afrikaan*, No. 55, December/January 1995/96. Like many other critical voices, this excellent journal has ceased publication due to lack of funding and interest in dissent after apartheid.

7. What about the Zulus?

1 Paul Pereira, *Fast Facts*, September 1995, p. 2.

2 Nadine Gordimer, "The Shell House Affair," *New Left Review*, 213, September/October 1995, pp. 125-129.

3 Penuel Maduna, *Sunday Times*, 23 April 1995.

4 James Fenton, "A Short History of Anti-Semitism," *New York Review of Books*, 15 February 1996.

5 Ken Owen, *Sunday Times*, 17 April 1994.

6 Simon Barber, *Business Day*, 29 March 1994.

7 R.W. Johnson & L. Schlemmer, *Launching Democracy in South Africa* (New Haven: Yale University Press, 1996). This is the definite scholarly account of South Africa's first nonracial election but should be read together with a somewhat differing interpretation by Robert Mattes, *The Election Book* (Cape Town: IDASA, 1995).

8 Ken Owen, *Sunday Times*, 5 October 1995.

9 Alexander Johnson, *Democracy in Action*, No. 9, 1 July 1994.

10 Roger Burrows of the DP, *Business Day*, 12 April 1996.

11 Johnson & Schlemmer, op. cit.

8. Corporatism: Business-union-state relations

1 The most comprehensive overview is still Gerhard Lehmbruch and Philippe C. Schmitter, eds., *Patterns of Corporatist Policy Making* (London: Sage, 1982).

2 Leif Lewin, "The Rise and Decline of Corporatism: The Case of Sweden," *European Journal of Political Research*, 26, 1994, pp. 59-79.

3 Kenneth D. McRae, "Comment: Federation, Consociation, Corporatism," *Canadian Journal of Political Science*, 12, 1979, p. 520.

4 Arend Lijphart and Markus M.L. Crepaz, "Corporatism and Consensus Democracy in Eighteen Countries: Conceptual and Empirical Linkages," *British Journal of Political Science*, 21, 2, 1991, pp. 235-256.

5 Ibid., p. 245.

6 "Corporatism, Pluralism and Political Learning," *Journal of Public Policy*, 12, 3, 1992, pp. 243-255.

7 For Austria, see Markus Crepaz, "From Semisovereignty to Sovereignty. The Decline of Corporatism and Rise of Parliament in Austria," *Comparative Politics*, 27, 1, October 1994, pp. 45-65. See also his general overview, "Corporatism in Decline?" *Comparative Political Studies*, 25, 2, July 1992, pp. 139-168. For Sweden, see Leif Lewis, "The Rise and Decline of Corporatism: The Case of Sweden," *European Journal of Political Research*, 26, 1994, pp. 59-79. For Japan, see Dennis McNamara, "Corporatism and Co-

operation among Japanese Labour," *Comparative Politics*, 28, 4, July 1996, pp. 379-397. For Switzerland, see Gerhard Lehmbruch, "Consociational Democracy and Corporatism in Switzerland," *Publius, The Journal of Federalism*, 23, Spring 1993, pp. 43-61.

8 Ralf Dahrendorf, "Terium non-datur," *Government and Opposition*, 24, 1989, pp. 131-141.

9 Peter J. Williamson, *Corporatism in Perspective: An Introductory Guide to Corporatist Theory* (London: Sage, 1989), p. 151.

10 For an overview of the debate among SA unions by a union organiser in favour of corporatism, see J. Baskin, *Corporatism: Some Obstacles Facing the South African Labour Movement*, Johannesburg: Centre for Policy Studies, 1993, *Research Report*, No. 30. For a comprehensive analytical review of corporatism, see: Louwrens Pretorius, "Relations between State, Capital and Labour in South Africa: Towards Corporatism?" *Journal of Theoretical Politics*, 8(2), 1996, pp. 255-281.

11 Arend Lijphart, "Prospects for Power-Sharing in the New South Africa," in Andrew Reynolds, ed., *Election 94 South Africa* (New York: St. Martins, 1994), p. 222, has described South Africa's interim order as a model of consociationalism.

12 Leo Panitch, "Cosatu and Corporatism," *Southern Africa Report*, April 1996, p. 6.

13 Robert Fine and Graham van Wyk, "South Africa: State, Labour and the Politics of Reconstruction," *Capital and Class*, Spring, 1996, pp. 19-31.

14 See the title of an article by Adrian Bird and Geoff Schreiner in *South African Labour Bulletin*, 16, 6, 1992.

15 World Bank, "Workers in an Integrated World," Washington DC: *World Development Report*, 1995.

16 John Kane-Berman, *Fast Facts*, February 1996, p. 5.

17 Eddie Webster, "Cosatu: Old Alliances, New Strategies," *Southern Africa Report*, April 1996, p. 4.

18 *The Industrial Democracy Review*, Oct/Nov 1995, p. 40.

19 Jayendra Naidoo, *Business Day*, 29 January 1996.

20 K. von Holdt, "LRA Negotiation," *SA Labour Bulletin*, 19, 1995, p. 3.

21 Cited in Trevor Bernhardt, "The Nurses' Strike: A Well-Organised Plea for Recognition," *Industrial Democracy Review*, 4, 5, December 1995-January 1996, pp. 11-20.

22 Bernhardt, op. cit., p. 13.

23 A representative of the Worker' Committee, quoted in *SA Labour Bulletin*, 20, 5, October 1996, p. 48. The same anonymous observer also reports that a witchdoctor moved in with the dismissed miners in the hills. The spirits and the medicines the workers were anointed with would not only protect their bodies from bullets, but also ensure that they would succeed in their demands. The Minister of Labour who negotiated in vain with the Committee over this wide gap between modernity and superstition blamed the apartheid system for not "empowering the workers". This leaves, of course, the reasons for the worker's alienation from union representation unaddressed.

24 Vincent Maphai, "A Season for Power-Sharing," *Journal of Democracy*, January 1996, pp. 67-81.

25 Blade Nzimande, "ANC cannot pander to privileged minorities," *Business Day*, 13 February 1996.

26 Jill Wentzel, *The Liberal Slideaway* (Johannesburg: SA Institute of Race Relations, 1995).

27 R.W. Johnson, "Fear in the Miracle Nation," *London Review of Books*, 2 November 1995.

28 Vincent Maphai, op. cit.

29 *The African Communist III*, 1995, p. 2.

30 Ibid.

31 Stanley Uys, "Pressing the ANC to take power," *The World Today*, May 1996.

32 Jeremy Cronin of the SACP rejected such accusations.

33 David Welsh, "Majority Rules, OK?" *Indicator SA*, 13, 3, Winter 1996, pp. 6-9.

9. Where is the struggle now?

1 Geoff Schreiner, *Monitor*, October 1993, p. 68.

2 *Sunday Times*, 13 October 1991.

3 *Financial Mail*, 18 October 1991.

4 *Sunday Times*, 20 October 1991.

5 *The Natal Mercury*, 4 February 1991.

6 *Cosmopolitan*, March 1994.

7 Rian Malan, "Going Fishing," *Fair Lady*, 6 April 1994.

8 Chris van Wyk, *Mail & Guardian*, 31 May-6 June 1996.

9 *Millenium*, 21 June-20 July 1996.

10 *Sunday Times*, 21 May 1995.

11 Anthony Sampson, *Black and Gold* (London: Hodder & Stoughton, 1987), p. 23.

12 *South African Labour Bulletin*, Vol. 20, 5, October 1996, p. 39.

13 This was vividly illustrated by a synthesis meeting in the summer of 1985 in Johannesburg during which the merits and risks of the planned first Lusaka meeting were discussed for a full day with leading participants, as well as the then head of the SADF General Jannie Geldenhuys and Gavin Relly. At lunch Geldenhuys and several others left the meeting in order to watch a more important rugby game! So much for the regime's alleged panic and eagerness to cut a deal in 1985. The suggestion that the contact be used to initiate some formal bargaining between Pretoria and the ANC fell on deaf ears.

14 A. Sampson, op. cit., p. 198.

15 Personal interview, April 1982.

16 Louwrens Pretorius, "Relations between State, Capital and Labour in SA: Towards Corporatism," *Journal of Theoretical Politics*, 8(2), 265, 1996.

17 Jack Kelly, *USA Today*, 20 June 1994.

18 Commentary, CSIS, *Sunday Times*, 1996, p. 8.

19 At the rhetorical level this impression is reinforced when ANC leaders assert that whites still want to see the ANC fail and in turn are warned not to play the race card.

20 Geoffrey Wheatcroft, *The Wall Street Journal*, 22 April 1994.

21 Tom Lodge, "A Year in the New SA," *Indicator SA*, Vol. 12, No. 2, Autumn 1995, pp. 7-10.

22 IDASA, "Parliamentary Ethics and Government Corruption: Playing with Public Trust," *Public Opinion Service Reports*, No. 3, February 1996.

23 IDASA, *Parliamentary Whip*, 13 September 1996.

24 *Sunday Times*, Editorial, 2 June 1996.

25 The increase takes MP's salaries to R142 750 (US$32 000) in addition to an annual R36 000 (US$7 900) tax-free amount for constituency work and other free travel perks like airline tickets. Some CEOs in public corporations earned considerably more, with the Transnet Chief Executive reportedly receiving a package of more than R800 000 in 1996. Advisers and consultants to departments earn up to R24 000 per month, with the Finance Department employing 304 consultants alone. According to Saki Macazoma

236

(*Mail & Guardian*, 19-26 July 1996) "the practice of hiring outsiders at the drop of a hat landed the Government with a R500 million bill last year". Another official (State Expenditure Deputy Director Tobie Verwey) spoke of the government employing 2 359 consultants at an annual cost of R1 billion (*Mail & Guardian*, 11-17 October 1996).

26 *Mail & Guardian*, 6-12 September 1996.
27 For example, see the front page of the *Cape Times* (November 3, 1996) where TRC commissioner Mary Burton is pictured driving her modest Toyota Conquest with the caption "No shiny Merc for Burton". She is quoted: "It has been my concern . . . that the salaries we're paid are very high. We discussed it but were told we couldn't do anything about it as the salaries were laid down."
28 R.W. Johnson & L. Schlemmer, *Launching Democracy in South Africa* (New Haven: Yale University Press, 1996).
29 *Sunday Times*, Editorial, 17 March 1996.
30 Ruben Mathe quoted in the *Weekend Argus*, 23 March 1996.
31 *Focus Letter*, Helen Suzman Foundation, February 1996.
32 Ibid.
33 *Frontiers of Freedom*, 2, 1996, p. 18.

10. Is the future what it used to be?

1 Barbara Geddes, "Challenging the Conventional Wisdom," *Journal of Democracy*, Vol. 5, No. 4, October 1994, pp. 104-118.
2 *Journal of Democracy*, Vol. 3, No. 3, July 1992.
3 *Journal of Democracy*, Vol. 3, No. 3, July 1992.
4 Peter Berger, "The Uncertain Triumph of Democratic Capitalism," *Journal of Democracy*, Vol. 3, No. 3, July 1992, pp. 7-16.
5 Kim Kyong-Won, "Marx, Schumpeter and the East African Experience," *Journal of Democracy*, Vol. 3, No. 3, July 1992, pp. 17-31.
6 Claude Ake, "Devaluing Democracy," *Journal of Democracy*, Vol. 3, No. 3, July 1992, pp. 32-36.
7 Ralph Milliband, "The Socialist Alternative," *Journal of Democracy*, Vol. 3, No. 3, July 1992, pp. 118-124.
8 R. Dahl, "Why Free Markets Are Not Enough," *Journal of Democracy*, Vol. 3, No. 3, July 1992, pp. 82-90.
9 A. Pzreworski, "The Neo-Liberal Fallacy," *Journal of Democracy*, Vol. 3, No. 3, July 1992, pp. 45- 57.
10 A. Pzreworski, *Sustainable Democracy*.

11 Union leaders are strongly opposed to the privatisation of State assets. See Sam Shilowa, *South Scan*, 16 December 1994.
12 Vyani Klass, *New Nation*, 14 October 1994, p. 8.
13 R.W. Johnson, *Focus Letter*, Helen Suzman Foundation, No. 6, February 1997.
14 Tony Holiday, *Cape Times*, 3 June 1996.
15 Robert Mattes, Amanda Gouws & Hennie Kotze, "The Emerging Party System in the New South Africa," *Party Politics*, Vol. 1, No. 3, 1995.
16 Breyten Breytenbach, *The Memory of Birds in Times of Revolution* (Cape Town: Human & Rousseau, 1996), p. 85.
17 *Sunday Times*, Editorial, 1 June 1996.
18 Leonard Thompson: *A History of South Africa* (New Haven: Yale University Press, 1995), p. 227.

11. Conclusion: The underclass versus the liberation aristocracy

1 Thabo Mbeki, Interview with the *Cape Times*, February 11, 1997. See also the ANC Discussion Document, *The State and Social Transformation* (November 1996), which advocates that "the democratic state must establish a dialectical relationship with private capital as a social partner" (5.16).
2 George Soros, *Atlantic Monthly*, February 1997.
3 *Fast Facts*, February 1997.
4 Report of the Presidential Commission to investigate Labour Market Policy, *Restructuring the SA Labour Market*, Pretoria, 1996, p. 5.
5 *Sunday Times*, March 2, 1997.
6 Wilmot James, "SA needs to value middle-class," *Cape Times*, February 10, 1997.
7 *Business Day*, February 18, 1997.
8 Frank Horwitz, Professor at the Graduate School of Business, University of Cape Town, February 26, 1997.
9 *Cape Times*, February 6, 1997.
10 L. Schlemmer and C. Levitz, "The Albatross of Pessimism," *Fast Facts*, February 1997, pp. 4-6.
11 *Cape Times*, March 6, 1997.
12 *Business Day*, 10 March 1997.
13 *Mail & Guardian*, March 7-13, 1997.
14 *Business Day*, March 25, 1997.

15 *Sunday Independent*, March 23, 1997.
16 *Weekend Argus*, April 23-24, 1997.

About the Authors

Heribert Adam was born in Germany and educated at the University of Frankfurt. Since 1968 he has been Professor of Sociology at Simon Fraser University in Vancouver, Canada. He is the past president of the International Sociological Association's Research Committee on Ethnic Minority and Race Relations.

Since 1986, he has also been a Visiting Professor at the University of Cape Town and serves as a political consultant. He has published extensively on South African socio-political developments and comparative ethnonationalism.

His books include: *South Africa: Sociological Perspectives*, 1971; *Modernizing Racial Domination*, 1971; *Ethnic Power Mobilized* (with Hermann Giliomee), 1979; *South Africa Without Apartheid* (with Kogila Moodley), 1987; and *The Opening of the Apartheid Mind* (with Kogila Moodley), 1993, published in South Africa as *The Negotiated Revolution*, 1993.

Frederik Van Zyl Slabbert was educated at the University of Stellenbosch and taught Sociology at various South African universities.

In 1974, he was elected as a member of parliament for the Progressive Party and in 1979 became the leader of the official opposition. In 1986, he resigned his seat in protest against the intransigence of the P.W. Botha regime and the constraints of ineffectual white politics – a decision that shocked his foes and supporters alike.

His subsequent involvement with extra-parliamentary politics led him to organise the historic 1987 Dakar meeting between the ANC leadership and Afrikaner opinion-makers that paved the way for the official negotiations.

Together with Alex Boraine, he founded the Institute for a Democratic Alternative for South Africa (IDASA).

He is the author of *South Africa's Options* (with David Welsh), 1979; *The Last White Parliament*, 1985; and *South Africa's Quest for Democracy*, 1992.

He serves on various boards and is chair-man of Khula Investments.

Kogila Moodley is Professor of Sociology in the Department of Educational Studies and holds the David Lam Chair at the University of British Columbia, Canada.

Born and raised in the Indian community in Durban, she graduated from the University of Natal, and later from Michigan State University and the University of British Columbia.

Among her academic awards were fellowships from the Deutscher Akademischer Austauschdienst (DAAD) and the Australian National University.

Apart from her co-authored books on South Africa, her publications include some fifty articles in books and scholarly journals, as well as *Race Relations and Multicultural Education*, 1984; and *Beyond Multicultural Education*, 1993.

She serves on the board of the International Sociological Association's Research Committee on Ethnic Minority and Race Relations, and the editorial board of Ethnic and Racial Studies (London).